David Boyle, a journalist, [...] London. He writes about n[...] and the environment, and a[...]

FUNNY MONEY

In Search of Alternative Cash

David Boyle

Flamingo
An Imprint of HarperCollins*Publishers*

Flamingo
An imprint of HarperCollins*Publishers*
77–85 Fulham Palace Road,
Hammersmith, London W6 8JB

www.**fire**and**water**.com

Published by Flamingo 2000
9 8 7 6 5 4 3 2 1

First published in Great Britain by
HarperCollins*Publishers* 1999

ISBN 0 00 653067 2

Set in Meridien

Printed and bound in Great Britain by
Caledonian International Book Manufacturing Ltd, Glasgow

For my parents

Acknowledgements

Three books have been particularly useful to me when writing this book: Richard Douthwaite's *Short Circuit*, James Buchan's *Frozen Desire* and Kevin Jackson's *Faber Book of Money*, from which a number of the literary quotations are taken. Other useful books, publications and organizations are listed at the end.

It is one of the great luxuries of writing to have an agent and an editor, and without my agent Julian Alexander and my editor Lucinda McNeile, this book would never have seen the light of day – and I am enormously grateful to them. There are five other people also who particularly made the book possible: Ed Mayo, who read the whole text through and gave invaluable advice; Stuart Proffitt, who suggested I put pen to paper; Edgar Cahn, who inspired me on his two gruelling trips to the UK; Andrew Simms, who came up with the 'new alchemists' tag; and Betsy Niklas, who advised me and encouraged me when this was all just a series of disconnected interviews and fragmented ideas.

Nor would I have been able to undertake the research without a life-enhancing fellowship from the Winston Churchill Memorial Trust, and I am very grateful to them and their director Sir Henry Beverley for their help and for the great contribution they make so unobtrusively to British life.

There are too many others to thank them all by name – including all those I interviewed for this book – but I must particularly mention the following for their advice, inspiration, encouragement and sometimes all three: Janet Bell, Mark Campanale, Pat Conaty, Carol Cornish, Ellen Deacon, Judith Hodge, Joel Hodroff, Amanda Horton-Mastin, Ed Lambert, Kirsty Milne, Toby Mundy, Gill Paul, Sian Radinger, James Robertson, Kirsten Romano, Liz Shepherd, Marian Storkey, Tina Thonnings and everyone at the New Economics foundation. The mistakes are, of course, all mine.

Contents

Introduction

In search of the new alchemists

'Like a lot of mothers, Zabau Shepard has some charge cards, but she can't use them. It's not that her credit has gone to the dogs; it's that she *is* a dog.'
The Daily Progress, **Charlottesville, Virginia, 1990, quoted in James Grant's *Money of the Mind*.**

I

Picture the scene. Millions of people gathered on a rocky island off the northern coast of Europe, and getting hungrier. They only have two fivers and a couple of crumpled dollars between them.

'What do we do?' Gordon Brown asks Kenneth Clarke.

'Make them sit down,' he says. Then he converts the money into small change and, when he has given thanks, begins to distribute it among the crowd. And by the end the whole crowd was satisfied and there was enough left over to fill twelve large unit trusts.

The cabinet, commentators and economists, needless to say, were astonished. After all, it was quite a different method of creating money from the usual one, which involves taxing the small amount at 25 per cent, carefully allocating the proceeds, together with some words of wisdom about working harder, and carrying on doing so until it all runs out.

Money just isn't like that, is it. The one thing we learn about money is that it isn't infinite, and it certainly doesn't behave like the Feeding of the Five Thousand. Short of winning the Lottery, we are dependent on eking out our small incomes to fit our expanding bills.

But something peculiar is happening to money. There was a time when we knew where we were with it: good solid coins which burned a hole in the pocket just by jiggling up and down, notes which said the Chief Cashier promised 'to pay the bearer on demand'. You'd earn it, put it in the bank, count it, spend it, then it was gone, and you'd have to earn some more. It was simple and straightforward.

The Prime Minister Sir Alec Douglas-Home was even said to balance the budget using matchsticks. It was an endearing picture of a more innocent age: you could imagine Britain's First Lord of the Treasury wrapping hot towels round his head and putting off the dire moment when he would have to sit down and work it all out, complaining that he hadn't been any good at sums at Eton.

Nowadays things seem very different. The number of professionals involved in different aspects of looking after money, the futures dealers, the traders and arbitragers, reads almost like a cast list from *The Canterbury Tales*, with all its priests, pardoners and summoners. Finance has become a strange complicated global system fuelled by inter-linked computers and burgeoning information. A large institution like Citibank collects all the money in all its branches around the world electronically overnight and invests it until the morning. Tiny slivers of percentages of transactions are bundled together in deals to pay the traders. Nothing is wasted in the financial markets.

It is a peculiar shadowy world, where rumour and mood can shift billions of pounds in a few minutes. And where Chancellor Norman Lamont, looking at the fragments of his European exchange-rate policy after Black Wednesday, could describe himself as being 'overwhelmed by a whirlwind'. This view was echoed by former Citibank chairman John Reed, who famously described the financial markets as 'a little like the physicist who created the bomb'.

'We see about 400 billion dollars every day of foreign exchange transactions going through the system,' he said, and that was a good decade ago. By the end of the 1980s, $800 billion a day in electronic payments were going from bank to bank through the Clearinghouse Interbank Payments System in the USA, known as CHIPS – in Britain, we have a similar overheating system called CHAPS – and that figure rises every year. The daily flows in the currency exchanges are now running at an estimated $1,300 billion, and the World Bank reckons that 95 per cent of them are speculative, which means that only 5 per cent is actually related to the real trade which keeps our economies moving along. The rest is froth, but froth with terrifying power over ordinary lives.

If you knock politely at your bank manager's office door and ask actually to see your money, it's not going to be there. It will appear on your bank statements, of course, with bizarre fractions charged in interest and service. But you know it will probably be off travelling the globe, investing in massive dam projects, or dabbling in the Tokyo Futures Markets while you're asleep.

Actually, your money doesn't exist at all. Money is now blips on computer screens; its value can disappear overnight, it pops up unexpectedly in the form of credit or pseudo-money like air miles or supermarket loyalty cards. Its total demise is widely reported. 'Cash is dirty, cash is heavy, cash is quaint, cash is expensive, cash is dying,' said the *New York Times* magazine recently on its front cover, hailing the advent of sophisticated computer debit cards.

While some people seem to be able to surf this new world of money easily, others don't. When he fell off his yacht into the Atlantic, Robert Maxwell owed twice as much as Zimbabwe. The rest of us are stuck with the old idea. We believe there is a finite amount of money, which comes to us from employers and occasionally from the government, and we spend it just a little faster than we should. Why aren't our coins and notes as flexible as they are for what Tom Wolfe called the 'Masters of the Universe' in the City of London or Wall Street?

For most of us, money stays irritatingly concrete. It runs out, and we all feel increasingly fearful about it. In the world of glass towers, on the other hand, it is much more flexible: if you don't have it, you borrow it, discount it, arbitrage it, trade it, ride the market with it, knowing that money increasingly gets its changing value from the psychology of the international market: our hopes, fears, weather patterns, mood swings all effect the value of their money.

Money has become a psychological construct. So why can't we find psychological ways of getting more of it? Maybe we can put aside the narrow world of chancellors, bank managers and balance sheets, and work out ways to tap into this infinity of wealth for ourselves – as our prehistoric ancestors did when they wandered along beaches picking up shells to use as currency. Maybe we can take Monopoly money and somehow make it real: like the economics editor of *The Independent* Diane Coyle, who in her book *The Weightless World* describes using 'pretend money' from an old board game to pay her neighbours in her local baby-sitting circle.

Is DIY money possible? It is an idyllic dream by any stretch of the imagination, but it's what this book is all about. It is a journey to discover people who claim to have founds ways of conjuring money out of nothing, the so-called 'new alchemists' who can take the modern equivalent of base metal and turn it into gold – and with it turn all our ideas about money upside-down.

II

Why America? Partly because of Zabau Shepard.

Zabau Shepard was a dog from Virginia, who in 1990 suddenly started receiving free credit cards through the post. Her two-pronged name, in a nation where many people choose the most peculiar names, probably confused the computers. She was used as a symbol of the American financial malaise in a fascinating book by the financial journalist James Allen called *Money of the Mind*. If credit is endlessly available, he said, then there is nothing real about money. It means that anyone can buy almost anything.

Sometimes they do; sometimes they nearly do. The Cincinnati investment advisor Paul Herrlinger claimed to be bidding for the Minneapolis store chain Dayton-Hudson for $6.8 billion in 1987 – about $6.7 billion more than the assets of his company. In those heady days, when anyone could borrow anything, he was widely believed on Wall Street and Dayton-Hudson shares climbed $10. After his lawyer tried to head off disaster by explaining that his client was ill, Herrlinger was asked by TV interviewers on his lawn whether the bid was a hoax. 'I don't know,' he said. 'It's no more a hoax than anything else.'

But then the American attitude to money is more relaxed than ours. You only have to live in the United States for a few months before you get a direct mail cheque for $5,000 made out to you, sent by an obliging credit-card company touting for business. All you have to do is pay it into your account and the card and statements start arriving, with interest at anything up to 26 per cent. The credit-card companies have calculated that they gain more in extra custom than they lose in bad debts. 'It's like giving lettuce to hungry rabbits,' according to one observer. Perhaps that is why, leaving mortgages aside, the average American household is now $8,570 in personal debt, with three or four credit cards and five or six affinity cards. The figure in the UK is not as high, but since 1990 even British households have been spending more servicing their personal debt than they do on food.

All this is the culmination of a 3,000-year history of money, the origin of which is lost in the mists of time. Some experts explain the word in terms of the Latin for 'memory' and 'warning'; others say it comes from the Roman goddess Juno Moneta, Jupiter's matronly wife, who had the mint next-door to her temple in ancient Rome. Perhaps memory and warning are appropriate ways of describing the money system, because the invention of compound interest – which has solved the problem of penniless old age and driven away the workhouses – has also plunged the world into debt. Some prophets of doom will tell you that a penny invested at average interest rates at the time of Christ would now be worth in gold more than the entire mass of the earth. What they don't tell you is that the same would be true the other way round if you had borrowed the penny.

Before money, in the *Iliad*, values were measured in terms of cattle: the Latin word *pecunia* (money) comes from *pecus* (cattle). Money probably emerged, not to make shopping easier, but to mark celebrations or marriages, alliances or sacrifices to the gods – to build social relationships. The human race was able to do without money for trade until the Lydians – living in what is now western Turkey – first started stamping their metal tokens with official marks, thus inventing the first coins in the West. 'They were the first retailers,' said the ancient historian Herodotus, describing a society which sounds obsessed with its new invention. 'The customs of the Lydians differ little from those of the Grecians, except that they prostitute their females.' It is strange to think that the inventors of money as we know it now were also the first pimps.

Before money, people who wanted to pop down to the shops had to rely on bartering – but even then they would have to be able to agree on the value of the goods they were exchanging. That was why money evolved as locally agreed counters, some of them predictable, some of them most peculiar: like bronze tools (China), gold rings (Egypt), tobacco (Virginia) or twelve-foot stones (the Caroline Islands in the Pacific). The stones must have been pretty useless, but at least they were difficult to pinch out of handbags.

These developments moved slowly at first, possibly because money innovators were not as numerous as they are these days. Some came to sticky ends, like Johan Palmstruch of Stockholm, condemned to death for causing inflation by printing too many official banknotes. Others changed money in order to achieve something completely different – like William III, who began the National Debt in 1693 to fund another war with France.

The Dutch led the way for a while, then the French. But the innovators who have succeeded since then tend to be either Scots or American. Maybe it was a national fascination for money which meant that the Scots brought the world the pioneer economist Adam Smith, and John Law, whose paper currency and limitless credit became so unpopular in France that, in 1720, he had to escape with his life from Paris.

But it is not surprising that the Americans have produced so many money innovators. From next to nothing except their threadbare clothes and a couple of chickens, the passengers on the *Mayflower* and their descendants had to conjure up the enormous wealth to develop a whole continent. They had to trade their way into wealth, until their children and grandchildren could set up banks which made money widely available, and by doing so they built the place we see now, with its gleaming skyscrapers, penitentiaries and McDonald's. The cost, every generation or so, has been a tradition of regular bank crashes. The opposite of money innovation is money disaster. But without money innovators, the Wild West would never have been won, and the enormous investments they eventually attracted from Victorian England would never have been available.

Nor would the American Revolution have been paid for. It was financed by the new idea of printing more money which, as we now know, causes inflation: it loses its value. 'The Currency as we manage it is a wonderful machine,' said Benjamin Franklin, who printed many of the notes himself. 'It performs in office when we issue it; it pays and clothes Troops, and provides Victuals and Ammunition; and when we are obliged to issue a Quantity excessive, it pays itself off by Depreciation.'

While we Europeans agonize about launching a single currency, suddenly everybody in the United States is issuing money. There are phone units, subway tokens, affinity cards, cyber-currencies, time dollars, hours, Valley Dollars, Frequent Flyer Miles. Americans don't wait for the government to do it: they just get on and conjure the money for themselves. We have similar ideas on this side of the Atlantic, of course, but we also have a traditional disapproval of the elasticity and sheer availability of American money: Victorian moralists thought it led to the debauchment of youth. Our own venerable currency seemed sturdier and imperturbable somehow. 'When I listen to the anti-European rhetoric of some politicians,' wrote the psychologist Dorothy Rowe, 'I get the impression that they believe that, back in the mists of time when this most noble race first set foot on this sceptred isle, God gave the British the pound for their own special use.'

Britain is not a nation of great financial innovators. We invented the Bank of England, and sat back contented for a couple of centuries, assuming that our new race of bank managers were taking over the world – only to find that they hadn't, and the international markets were increasingly outside our control. British politicians hate this failure: they occasionally lash out, like

Harold Wilson, at the 'Gnomes of Zurich', but usually they prefer not to think about it. No wonder the arrival of the single currency keeps British politicians awake at night.

Does our lack of power over money matter? For anyone who gets a sinking feeling from reading their credit-card statements, this probably doesn't need spelling out, but there are wider implications. A Wall Street collapse today, says the historian Jean Gimpel, would probably mark the end of our civilization. As I write, commentators are peering at the plummeting markets of the Far East, wondering whether they will bring down our economies with them. But even if the system totters along, as it probably will, the international money system is certainly successful at some things – building motorways and superstores for example. It doesn't work very well in other areas.

After 200 years or so of economic growth, the planet is showing distinct signs of age, many people are still just as poor, and the ones that are richer are not obviously happier. For all the accepted cures peddled by politicians and experts, the system neither works as it should, nor is under their control, and still less is it under the control of ordinary people like you and me.

The problem is that money is partially blind. It draws a circle around the financial economy, and just can't screw its eyes up enough to see anything else – myopically peering at the instruments which register 'success', and failing to see beyond its own narrow interpretation of what wealth is. Economics is full of hidden costs, trading the health of communities and the environment for motorways and the promise of better times around the corner. Economic growth began by devastating the British cities in the nineteenth century, then started on the rest of the world. Forests have now disappeared, many people live with air which is barely breathable, dams have devastated thousands of square miles, chemicals have destroyed livelihoods and now many of us doubt whether the earth can sustain life for another century or so. Americans now spend over $400 million a year breaking into malfunctioning automatic car door locks: economists call this 'growth'.

Tropical rainforest, on which we all depend, continues to disappear at the rate of over 30,000 square miles a year, because money provides incentives for its removal. As a result, the deserts grow by six million hectares a year. All this is driven by money. In the long run, a blind economic system which takes no account of raw materials or waste disposal or happiness must go head-to-head with the systems that sustain life on earth. 'Man talks of a battle with nature,' said the pioneering economist E. F.

Schumacher in *Small is Beautiful*, 'forgetting that if he won the battle, he would find himself on the losing side.'

The amount of money in the world is now staggering, but it is very badly distributed. Donald Trump and his casinos have far too much, while someone like me – to take a random example – doesn't have nearly enough. And even with my letters from the bank and rickety car, I am considerably better off than the 60,000 British pensioners who die from cold-related illness every winter because they can't afford the heating.

Peasants in 1495 had to work about fifteen weeks a year to earn the money they needed to survive. By 1564 it was forty weeks, and soon they were having to move to uncertain futures in factories just to get by. Now those of us who can find work never seem to stop working. The majority of us in the West now have luxuries unimagined by our grandparents, but despite astonishing economic growth between the year I was born, 1958, and 1980, Americans reported feeling 'significantly less well-off' by the end of it.

I don't want to be dishonest about this. I want to be richer as much as anybody, but the money system is not serving us all very well at the moment, especially if you are excluded by it – or lie awake worrying that you might be. 'It is in the brain and soul that lack of money damages you,' wrote George Orwell in *Keep the Aspidistra Flying*. 'Mental deadness, spiritual squalor – they seem to descend upon you inescapably when your income drops below a certain point. Faith, hope, money – only a saint could have the first two without having the third.'

III

I claim to be an alternative economist. As such, I am interested in searching for ways of making money more available to everyone and to help them avoid Orwell's 'spiritual squalor'. Alternative economists have their own institutions. One of them, TOES (The Other Economic Summit), met for the first time when the G7 leaders of the seven richest nations held their summit in London in 1984. The thought of all those conventional economists getting together in limousines to ruin the planet so annoyed the alternatives that they held their own show. TOES 1984 was an enormous success, attracting a strange mixture of futurists, greens, renegade economists, new age businessmen, hippies, social critics and complete crazies. The media took no notice at all, but some of the ideas which emerged – green taxation, new ways of measuring success – are now on every politician's agenda, whether they like it or not.

Economists, with some notable exceptions, regard us alternatives with suspicion. Radicals get irritated because we don't think the world's problems are absolutely hopeless, and it spoils their pessimism. What Keynes called 'plain men' regard our ideas as bizarre perversions of the natural order of things. Alternative economists say the current world of money is quite bizarre enough already: the idea of fractional reserve banking, for example, means that banks create most of the money we use simply by lending it – anything up to ten times the deposits which they hold as backing. This is the real 'funny money'. 'The process by which banks create money is so simple,' said John Kenneth Galbraith, 'that the mind is repelled.'

There is a traditional critique of the money system, with a pedigree that goes back via Major C. H. Douglas – the inventor of 'social credit' – to Abraham Lincoln, Robert Owen and William Cobbett, and it now seems to have almost completely disappeared underground, though it pops up every so often on the right and left of politics, in US militia groups, or in strange men with carrier bags who shout 'Fraudsters!' from the back of the hall during political meetings.

This tradition is enraged by the way banks are allowed to create money, loading us all up with unrepayable debt. They argue that only governments should be allowed to do so, and they should do it interest-free and debt-free. Both Britain and America have experimented with ideas like this to stave off a banking crash: Lincoln by printing 'greenbacks' during the American Civil War and Lloyd George with 'Bradburys' during the First World War. Both were rapidly wound up under pressure from the banks, who were afraid they would create inflation.

But there needs to be money in circulation for the wheels of the economy to keep turning, and these arguments raged on both sides of the Atlantic until a century ago. In the USA this led to the great battle between gold and silver – between reliable money backed by gold, and available money backed by the much more plentiful silver. Now these ancestral battles are all but forgotten, ridiculed out of existence by the coruscating wit of George Bernard Shaw, and shunned because so many of the people who believed in an international bankers' conspiracy also believed it was Jewish. The changes they called for are now extremely unlikely to take place.

The issues remain, but this book is not about them – there are other people far better qualified to write about them than I am.

But I do want to write about creating money, because if its creation is so simple that banks and governments can do it, we may now be entering a world where we can all do the same thing for ourselves – which is the idea behind Local Exchange and Trading Systems.

LETS is a whole new kind of money altogether. What do you do, asked the people who came up with the idea, when you are in a community which is rapidly running out of cash? You have the people with skills and the time on their hands, and you have the jobs that urgently need doing – but no money to bring the two together.

The traditional definitions of money – a medium of exchange, a store of value and a unit of account – all apply equally well to LETS. Accepting money instead of a direct swap is a kind of agreement to accept something which is not useful in itself, but which you know can be exchanged later for something which is. It's the same with LETS, but with LETS you simply imagine a new kind of money and start trading in it. You go into debt to your neighbour, and denominate that debt not in pounds or dollars, but a whole new currency of your choice which you agree about. The first LETS currencies were called 'green dollars', but you can probably do better than that. And hey presto! The money exists, the job gets done, and somebody has to pay off the debt by doing something else in exchange for the same currency. No pounds or dollars are involved, no bank accounts reached into, but it is money nonetheless. LETS currencies are a magnificent burst of independence from governments, bank managers and bureaucrats: they allow people to create the money themselves. The idea emerged in British Columbia in the late 1970s, the brainchild of an academic called David Weston, and was given its present form in the early 1980s by Scots-Canadian Michael Linton, whose inspiration has taken LETS all over the world.

The biggest systems, like the Blue Mountain LETS in Australia, involve over 2,000 people. I ran across the idea in New Zealand, at the Auckland Green Dollar Exchange – a regular meeting of enthusiastic traders, surrounded by assorted knitted hats, jams, cakes, beer, eggs, leaflets and some bilious green armchairs. I watched astonished as one woman sold her genealogical skills for green dollars to a woman trading mittens. This was 1991, and already 0.1 per cent of New Zealand's population were dealing in green dollars. If you signed on the dole, the social security officials would give you a leaflet about it. It all seemed a long way from the UK.

Michael Linton brought LETS to Britain at the TOES meeting in 1985, and in 1992 – encouraged by the recession – it suddenly took off. By Christmas there were forty trading systems up and running, and the currencies had strange names which caught the imagination of journalists. The new currency for Stroud was called 'strouds', in Manchester 'bobbins', in Bath 'olivers'; 'groats' in Stirling, 'tales' in Canterbury. And in Brixton they were called 'bricks'; in Donegal, they fell back on 'sods', which must have been confusing. It was almost like a secret code – Salisbury has its own special money for kids, called 'kebbles'. Their parents trade in 'ebbles'. The turnover in local money was by then the equivalent of £100,000 a year.

The expansion has continued since. There are now over 450 local currency systems in the country. Some involve just a few neighbours. Some, like the local money in Kingston upon Thames, allow you to buy organic vegetables. Some, like the system in Manchester, allow you to pay part of your rent. The European Commission gave a grant to Bradford City Council to set up its own currency, and researchers think the equivalent of £2 million is traded in LETS currencies in the UK every year. The idea links people across class, age and income, and it allows them to think more widely about the kinds of things they can do – be it making cakes, T-shirts, sewing, baby-sitting, accountancy, law, building or drawing astrological charts. People report feeling liberated using these whimsical new currencies, and it builds communities. And not a penny comes from the banks.

'It attracts more open-minded people,' one member of a Northern Ireland LETS money system told Jonathan Croall for his report *LETS Act Locally*. 'And that helps to bridge the gap between the two communities. That's important to me, after my narrow upbringing. I have dreamt that LETS will eventually grow big enough in Northern Ireland to make a real difference.' LETS is now an increasingly familiar idea in Britain, though it is too early to tell whether it is going to stay in a marginal niche or break out into the mainstream. The real innovations are happening in the USA.

IV

So I went there to find today's new alchemists, to the land of the Treasury bill and Wall Street and the dustbowl and the Great Crash and Michael Milken, rumoured to be earning $1.5 million a day before his fall from grace. I went there because I wanted to write about the American attitude to money, because I thought it might be an antidote to our own rather puritanically English attitudes, and because there is another money revolution going on there. I wanted to find people who were looking for practical ways of producing the money we need ourselves, but I had another motive as well. I wanted to see someone I had known in London and who I missed when she had gone home to the USA to work for a big bank in Princeton.

You may think love is irrelevant to a discussion about money, but actually it goes to the heart of the debate. Money is supposed to be a measure of wealth – economists will tell you that is what it is. But actually if you look at the aspects of life that make you wealthy, they go way beyond money. Hot chocolate and relaxing over a video are wealth. Hot baths are wealth. Love and friendship and children are wealth: everybody apart from the most narrow-minded of economists knows that. Maybe you can't measure such things in the nation's accounts, but even so, I was wealthier for knowing my friend in Princeton and I wanted to know her some more.

I remembered as soon as I arrived how different American attitudes to money are. They have a self-confidence about it which we lack. They walk differently: if they need money they usually know they will be able to get a job and earn it. If they have a money-making idea, they tend to have supreme confidence that they will be able to make it work – should they want to. You don't see those hunched, mournful types you run across every day on the London Underground, which is probably why there are now over 128 billionaires in the USA – 127 more than there were twenty years ago.

'Our people spend their whole time being told they can't do things, believing they can't do things,' said the British business guru Sir John Harvey-Jones – and he's right. Money is more available to Americans, somehow. They don't count it up and eke it out.

It is different there, and on one level we have always known it. For over a century, we have blamed American money culture for debasing our European standards, perverting our youth, causing crime, stultifying our men, luring away our women with expensive silk stockings. It's not that there isn't poverty in the USA – there is a terrible, powerless kind of poverty – but their attitude to the whole money business is different from ours. Americans don't seem to have the same awe, respect or care about money, just as they don't about land. They seem able to waste the former on glitz more than we can in Europe, just as they seem happy to waste the latter on mile upon mile of hideous ribbon development.

It is almost *de rigueur* for the British to be cynical about the USA, to deride its traditions and sneer at its judicial system, gun culture and bizarre romanticism, but I don't share that sense of superiority. There is a welcoming generosity there, combined with energy and imagination, which I find inspiring. Americans also seem to touch the source of money more closely than we do, and amid their undoubted difficulties, it seems to give them a sense of liberation – however tough the business of earning money may be to them at the time.

So by visiting the sources of money in the USA, and tracking down the people who are reinventing those sources and bringing them closer to home, I wanted to write about that liberation – maybe get some of it to rub off on to my life too – and enter that peculiar alchemical world where money gets conjured apparently out of nothing.

Because for someone brought up with the picture of sober-suited City gents, serious bank managers and careful budgeting, the US money system is enjoyably non-rational. Vast sums slosh across their computer screens, yet the pockets of poverty are even denser than they are in London or Liverpool or Glasgow. This is, after all, both the richest and the most indebted nation on earth, where astrologers earn a great deal of money predicting financial patterns to Wall Street analysts, and where dogs get sent credit cards even without applying for them.

But then Zabau Shepard wasn't able to actually use them: she found it hard to sign her name. It's good to know there are some safeguards.

Chapter 1

Washington: money as time

'Put not your trust in money. Put your money in trust.'
Oliver Wendell Holmes, *The Autocrat of the Breakfast Table*.

I

'Remember,' said Benjamin Franklin in one of his irritating homilies to tradespeople. 'Time is money.' He meant, of course, that sitting around chatting or watching *The X-Files* tends to waste time which could have been used earning. But imagine for a second that he meant it literally – that time really is a kind of currency.

If that were true, we would all be born with a regular basic income of twenty-four hours a day, eight of which we have to spend asleep – a kind of tax which keeps us relatively fresh and healthy the next day. Nobody would have any more than twenty-four hours a day, and every morning we wake up with twenty-four more. Everybody would earn the same, and it would give a whole new meaning to the phrase 'spend a few hours down the pub'. But maybe this is a theoretical universe we can learn something from, because anyone without pounds or dollars does at least have time – too much of it. If you *are* earning, and you do have access to money, the chances are that you are pretty poverty-stricken as far as time is concerned.

It may have been no coincidence that the time dollar idea should emerge in one of the world's most problematic, budget-stretched and exhausted cities – Washington DC – because Washington is going through both the best of times and the worst of times. It is the capital of the richest nation on earth at the height of its powers. It is the bankrupt, poverty-stricken city, crumbling like a small town in eastern Europe, administered by a mayor straight out of prison for drug offences. It used to be a relatively healthy-sized city of 700,000 people just twenty years ago, about the size of Sheffield. Now it has just 550,000 and the number is falling fast. The moment people can afford to move out, they go – and they take their taxes with them.

Add to this heady mix all of the following: a public-works budget that has been slashed by more than half in the past few years, leaving streets overgrown and bridges collapsing. A murder rate growing at anything up to 25 per cent a year. A third of the city's fire engines are kept out of service every day to save money. Officials have been pumping extra chlorine into the drinking water to counteract the bacteria from corroding pipes. AIDS clinics have to shut down periodically because they run out of drugs. It is terrifying, and the city is still running out of money. 'Everything has broken,' the city's chief financial officer, Anthony A. Williams, told the *Washington Post*. 'This isn't just a car which has run out of gas. There is something fundamentally wrong with the car. The gas pedal doesn't work and neither do the brakes.'

Over this huge disaster strides the figure of Mayor Marion S. Barry Jr, large, mustachioed and mayor for fourteen of the past eighteen years. Barry's term of office was interrupted briefly by a six-month spell inside for drug possession, after he was video-taped in a downtown hotel smoking crack. His re-election was one of the most astonishing political comebacks of all time. 'Mr Barry is a tremendous politician,' said the fearless Mr Williams. 'But he's a lot like nuclear power. On a good day, he can light up the city. On a bad day, he can blow it up.'

When I took the Amtrak train south to Washington it was swelteringly hot, as only Washington can be with its humidity and bogland – one of its metro stations is even called Foggy Bottom. I was visiting the Washington law professor Edgar Cahn, author of the book *Time Dollars*, which had such a long sub-title that I barely needed to read it: *The New Currency That Enables Americans to Turn Their Hidden Resource – Time – into Personal Security and Community Renewal*.

His book – co-written with Jonathan Rowe from the *Christian Science Monitor* – is a little hazy about where the idea came from. The authors imply it was the brainchild of the first person mentioned in the book – a disabled lady called Dolores Galloway, living alone in the notorious Washington district of Anacostia and running a time dollar bank in her apartment complex. 'We don't want charity,' she is quoted as saying. 'It's one hand washing the other. I wash your clothing. Maybe you can wash my dishes.'

But actually if you probe a little bit further into the history of time dollars, it emerges that the idea for a new kind of money came from Professor Cahn himself, lying flat on his back after a serious heart attack at the early age of forty-four. 'It became an obsession of mine,' he told me later, his eyes lighting up with excitement. 'I was lying in hospital, being waited on hand and foot by the equivalent of a retine of servants which, in normal circumstances, I could never afford. And I was wondering why I didn't like it. I realized I didn't like being useless. It was a very personal thing, and – this was 1980 – I also realized society was busy labelling all sorts of other people as useless too.'

During a visit to London, he had been haunted by the un-American words used by the BBC to describe the unemployed: 'redundant'. It scared him. Margaret Thatcher was then doing her bit to encourage more of this kind of redundancy and Ronald Reagan was doing something similar. 'So I started struggling with the question of how to put people to work and fulfil all those growing needs when society has no money to pay for them,' said Cahn. 'And I thought: why not create another kind of money?'

Cahn was also struggling in his mind with the problem of demographic change. By 2040, one in five Americans will be retired. Many of these will be the sprightly kind of elderly Americans we see on tourist buses all over the world, but many will be increasingly old and infirm – needing a range of services, from medical care through to simple companionship, which the present economic system doesn't seem able to afford. His money was not intended to work like ordinary money. It was supposed to fund the way families and communities used to behave: to be paid to people for helping each other out, minding each other's children, running errands, or just phoning each other up for a chat. It was supposed to encourage people to be good neighbours in a way that ordinary money doesn't any more – a way of paying for what you need using time. Cahn called it time dollars.

You go along to your local time dollars project, and tell them what kind of work you are prepared to do – anything from roofing to giving people lifts – and the things you need doing in return. All these details are entered into the computer. Then one of your elderly neighbours suddenly needs a lift to the doctor at a time when you are free – or maybe they just need driving to the shops. They phone the office, who call you up. The final judgement about whether the two of you are suited is made by the time dollar organizer, who phones up first to see if you are available and willing. Result: you spend an hour helping your neighbour and you earn one time dollar. You get a statement showing your earnings at the end of the month, and you feel good about yourself.

What can you do with your new-found wealth? Well, that

depends on the scheme. You could spend it on services from other people in the system. Or you could give it to an elderly relative who might need it more. Or you could keep it for a rainy day. Or you can just forget all about it: only about 15 per cent of time dollar earnings are ever actually spent.

When Edgar Cahn came up with the idea, he and his wife Jean were already well-known and successful radical lawyers. A *Washington Post Magazine* feature about them carried the cover headline: 'The brilliant angry careers of Jean and Edgar Cahn'. Jean was black; Edgar was Jewish – they were the perfect 'liberal' couple. Edgar had worked with Bobby Kennedy, writing his speeches when he was US Attorney-General in the early 1960s, and went on to advise Lyndon Johnson when he was president. He and Jean together had founded the Antioch School of Law, now the District of Columbia Law School, where Washingtonians can get legal qualifications without having to pay vast sums of money, and where students are sent out to learn on the job by taking on cases for people who can't normally afford lawyers. Both also set up the national legal advice service for people on low incomes. His sudden foray into alternative economics was characteristic, but a little confusing for the economists.

As Mrs Thatcher gathered the reins of the UK, he took up the offer of a spell at the London School of Economics, honing the idea against the cynicism of British academia. The trouble is that once academics get hold of an idea, they can worry it to death. The evaluations of his ideas at the time were full of fearsome possibilities. Would time dollars discourage governments from spending money? Would there be so many old people one day that the whole thing might break down? We need to be a little bit cautious here, academics say.

Back in the USA it was also difficult getting organizations to find out whether the idea would work, but by 1985 a number of pilot projects were running – all of them linked to caring for old people. The Miami project ran into immediate trouble with local bureaucrats in the divided and highly-charged world of Florida politics. Florida's officials finally emerged with a damning indictment of the whole idea in 1987: 'Volunteers are least suited to the types of services required for time dollar programmes, specifically personal care, homemaker, health support, and in-house services in general,' they wrote.

This followed a concerted campaign by officials at the Florida Office on Aging to stymie time dollars. First they came up with an estimate of the cost to set up a mammoth computer network across the state. It was $250,000. Then there were the bureaucratic requirements. Everyone taking part would have to undergo a full criminal reference check. Everyone who wanted a lift to the doctor's would have to fill in a ten-page form and read over thirty pages of detailed instructions. 'Had the department been assigned to invent the family, the procedures would have exceeded the entire Code of Federal Regulations,' wrote Cahn and Rowe bitterly. 'With further studies pending.'

But there were reasonable worries for the politicians. What would happen, for instance, if there was a run on the time dollar bank? If every time dollar earned is a potential demand on a hospital or government department, does that mean the state would be legally liable? The questions hung in the air. Then there was the problem of volunteers, the people earning the time dollars – or 'service credits' to use the official term – by helping old people. Should they be trained? What happens if they get sued? Or worse, what happens if they abuse or defraud the system? There were some organizations that were implacably opposed to the whole concept. 'We feel that one of the basic tenets of volunteer service is NOT receiving a quid pro quo,' the American Red Cross told congressional hearings on the subject.

But as Carolee DeVito from the University of Miami School of Medicine said: 'Service credits legitimize the worth of time.' And it was because of this that the Miami project was rescued suddenly by Florida's Senator Carrie Meek. She was enraged by the cuts to black elderly programmes in Miami being sponsored by the Florida Office on Aging. 'We missed out on urban renewal. We missed out on the War on Poverty. We missed out on the money to rebuild Liberty City after the riots. And we are NOT going to miss out on this opportunity.'

Senator Meek's 'volunteers' managed to attract old-fashioned dollars from the Robert Wood Johnson Foundation, the biggest health trust in the USA, which was just then looking for pilot time dollar projects. They arranged for twelve government-sponsored volunteers from the massive VISTA programme, and they divided the whole project equally between the blacks, the Hispanics, the Jewish community and the blue-collar Anglos.

Two years later, it was Miami's time dollar project which received the first nationwide TV coverage. The report covered a low-income block of housing for old people, 85 per cent black and 10 per cent Hispanic. They filmed one resident, a grandmother called Daisy with an artificial leg, tutoring in the local primary school in return for time dollars – and spending them on lifts from the store from Pepe. Pepe spoke almost no English, but somehow the two of them managed to get along on their weekly shopping trips. 'I don't know what I would do without Pepe,' she told the cameras.

Nearly a decade later, the Miami project was administering more than 8,000 hours of time dollar earnings every month, across thirty-two offices in the city. It had long since burst out of just helping old people, and the system had been taken over by the community as a whole. You could spend time dollars there on anything from plumbers to baby-sitting.

Miami was lucky. Just when they needed heavyweight backing, the Robert Wood Johnson Foundation was looking for them. Miami, Boston, New York City, Washington DC, St Louis and San Francisco were given enough money to fund time dollar banks for three years, paying wages to organizers, setting up computer systems, renting offices, and funding all those other mundane things you need in offices, like paper clips, plastic cups and lavatory paper.

The St Louis project also attracted media attention. They were based at Grace Hill, an energetic programme to help old people carry on living at home, backed by generous federal grants – which suddenly disappeared with a wave from a magic wand by the Reagan administration. Organizers were left with 750 frail old people on their books, 500 of whom would have to go into nursing homes if they received no support. What could be done? Board members locked themselves away for a day with a management consultant to come up with a solution. 'We told them we had to find a way to make less more,' said Grace Marver, later director of the local time dollar programme.

And that's just what they did. MORE – the Member Organized Resource Exchange – used time dollars to fund the services they needed. Now up to 10,000 volunteers help 1,500 old people stay out of old people's homes. Only a third of the volunteers told researchers that they had been motivated by earning time dollars, but then a third of them had never volunteered for anything before.

By 1990, three years later, the six projects in the six cities were already organizing more than 143,000 hours of time dollars every year and had attracted 4,500 participants to earn them. Edgar Cahn's idea was beginning to work, and some solutions to the potential pitfalls were also beginning to emerge.

The state of Missouri decided it would underwrite the value of time dollars themselves, like central bankers. They had been the first state to pass time dollars legislation, and had the good sense to realize that bureaucracy would kill the idea stone dead. They even managed to resist the temptation to draft regulations until a whole year after time dollars began there. Missouri still backs people's time dollar earnings: if the system collapses, the state will provide the services which honour the earnings. They 'promise to pay the bearer on demand'.

Most of the big time dollar banks decided to solve the 'volunteer problem' by taking out volunteer insurance. Most check out the people when they join. Many will refuse to fix young people up with tasks which would take them into old people's homes. 'It's not that I was afraid for the seniors,' said one organizer I met later. 'I was worried about the safety of the young people.'

In fact, according to Cahn and Rowe, in all the millions of time dollar transactions around the USA in over a decade, nobody has ever sued. 'People don't mess with their local support systems,' he said. No volunteer has ever been sued in writ-happy America, which is why you can still get a million dollars' worth of volunteer insurance for $3.

Then there was the big daddy of problems: were time dollars taxable? It would be a terrible waste if all those frail elderly people had earned their time dollar hoards by looking after their neighbours' children or by finger-aching achievements in crochet, only to face an IRS swoop for tax evasion. Worse, the IRS would obviously expect them to pay tax in old-fashioned dollars. The same problem was faced by the local money pioneers in the UK: 'I don't think the Chancellor of the Exchequer really wants his lawn mowed,' said one Inland Revenue official.

But Edgar Cahn was a law professor and this made all the difference. Time dollars can't be taxable, he said, because they are not real money: they are just records of services. 'In the old days, did you tax people when they looked after their neighbours' kids? Did people get taxed on the sugar they lent?'

The IRS agreed. Service credits are not taxable, they ruled, and so it remains. But they do have to be reminded every so often. 'When President Clinton summoned us to a "season of service",' said Cahn in a letter to the *New York Times*, 'I do not think he meant services to the IRS.'

'Time dollars represent a psychological and monetary reward for rebuilding the non-market economy,' says Cahn. It is a kind of social money, and it can be given extra value if it is backed by government departments or underpinned by businesses. And it seems to work. After over a decade of time dollars, the idea is now firmly entrenched, firmly researched and funnelling a new kind of money – mainly, but not exclusively, among older people. There are now nearly 200 time dollar banks operating across the USA, from the Community Carers Service Bank in Berkeley,

California to the Ohana Kokua Program in Hawaii; from the Give
and Take Service Bank in Ohio to the B E S T Time Bank in Laredo,
Texas. There are even a few experiments in Japan.

'When people came from Germany and Japan and Sweden
and said we need to do this too, I realized this was not a Ronald
Reagan problem,' said Cahn. 'Something was going on in every
industrial society that I didn't understand.'

What was going on? 'Gridlock: moral, political, fiscal,' said
Ralph Nader in the introduction to Edgar Cahn's book. Then
along comes the time dollar, 'an organized, inflation-proof currency that can provide as constant, as powerful, as reliable a
reward for decency as the market does for selfishness.' If you
believe that money began as a way of building relationships,
rather than as an essential aid to shopaholism, then time dollars
look as though they are going back to the roots of the whole
idea.

II

Having walked half a mile in the tropical heat, I arrived sweating
inside Edgar Cahn's home in Thirty-ninth Street, with its white
columns and its fantastically high street numbers. The air conditioning was battling away inside, but there was also another
kind of frenetic bustling heat. A large woman was leaving the
house, carrying on a forceful last-minute conversation about
youth activities in the summer holidays. A black man with a
beard like Abraham Lincoln's was gesticulating into the telephone. Someone was carrying a large pile of papers in a cardboard
box marked Pampers Stretch, and someone else was heaving the
intestines of a computer in the other direction. Three more were
typing away in the office to the side. Somebody was arriving with
bagels in a brown paper bag.

In the middle of all was a calm, donnish figure with wrinkled
eyes, thinning grey hair and a slight beard. He was dressed
immaculately, as you would expect of a professor of law, with a
white polo-necked shirt as you would expect from someone who
wants to change the world. This was Dr Edgar Cahn.

His wife had died four years before, his children had long since
grown up, and the whole time dollars venture seemed to have
slowly taken over the house. On the ground floor, a portrait hung
over the fireplace, and you could imagine it doing so over the
domestic dinner parties of Washington lawyers. But now there
were computers, canisters of bottled water, photocopiers, piles of

press releases and legal agreements, lines of videos of Cahn's various chat show appearances, rows of copies of his book and a big award certificate from the National Council on Aging. And somewhere amongst all that were the 5,000 requests for more information about time dollars which had completely over-whelmed the office after an article in *Parade* magazine.

His own space in his own home had been reduced to the base-ment, but when I went down there later – with its dramatic line drawings on the whitewashed brick walls – it was also piled high with paper, broken desks and computers in an early state of repair. Sharing a home with time dollars was clearly like sharing a bed with a buffalo. Edgar Cahn's own space seemed to have been shifted even further to a large mattress in the corner.

I was worried that nobody would remember that I was coming. Everybody was so frenetic and nobody seemed prepared even to look me in the eye, as if I would somehow involve them in more work. I sat quietly at a large oak table and felt inconspicuous. Cahn seemed to be vaguely making his way over to talk to me, but every couple of feet someone would dash towards the large white front door and engage him in conversation, or hand him a piece of paper. And he would take off his glasses and peer at it closely, like Dr Johnson examining his dictionary.

'David,' he said, at long last sitting down at the end of the table. I was expected after all. 'What I thought was that you could listen in to what we were doing. But if you don't understand something, maybe you could ask me about it later rather than now.'

Or in plain English, 'I haven't got much time'. Another thirty seconds, and he was giving calm, measured advice to someone whose elderly father-in-law was being given a tough time by the welfare authorities in some distant southern state. 'This is what I feel we should do,' he was saying. 'We'll talk to Amy. She has access to the welfare records on computer, and she's a nice lady.'

He had an air of quiet authority, and I found I was slightly in awe of him. So I was taken aback to hear him introduce me to other people in the room as 'an oddball'. Was it the English grey socks I was wearing with my shorts? Or because my face was bright red from my walk in the heat?

'You can't describe everyone as an oddball who shows up here, Edgar,' said Tina, who was down from Cleveland preparing to set up a project on a housing estate there. Clearly 'oddball' was a term of some approval.

I was introduced to the others in the office. Clarence, with the Abe Lincoln beard, was still waving his arms warmly into the telephone. There was Lisa, who had just put herself through law school while working as an air stewardess. 'And this is the Reverend Williams,' said Edgar. I shook hands with a genial man in a green T-shirt and shorts, carrying the remains of yet another computer.

'How long have you been involved with this kind of thing?' I asked Clarence.

'Right back to 1969,' he said, followed by a series of loud ironic guffaws about the state of American cities. 'And I haven't found the silver bullet yet.'

'And it's been getting worse,' said Lisa. They both laughed, embarrassed – as if it was somehow their fault that society seemed to be unvravelling itself, as if the sense of urgency in the office was to make sure it went on not a moment longer than it should. Most of the people dashing through the building turned out to have been involved with time dollars for only a few months. But all of them – Clarence from housing rights, 'Reverend Williams' from computer activism – felt that this new kind of money provided them with a lever which could make their other work more effective. It was like being in the centre of a whirlwind, which swirled around the calm figure of Edgar Cahn.

Clarence was working on a three-way link-up between time dollars, a new food bank and a vast sprawling inner city estate in the city's notorious south-eastern corner. If it worked, people would be able to buy food with the time dollars they earned. The computers were on their way to a time dollar base in Chicago, where they would be upgraded by unemployed youngsters, earning – naturally – time dollars. The software was going to Washington children for review, in return for time dollars.

'When did we have this idea?' asked Edgar.

'Just now,' said somebody. It was that kind of day.

Tina was there to discuss using time dollars to pay for security patrols in crime-ridden downtown estates. 'Maybe we should have fines in time dollars,' said Edgar, thinking aloud. 'Maybe we need childcare for the people involved in the patrols, which we can power with time dollars.'

'We've never done this before,' Edgar told me. 'You are watching a body of received wisdom emerge before your eyes.' They were all ambitious ideas, and seemed to have been dreamed up only a couple of days before. No wonder there seemed to be such manic activity. Why did it all have to be done so fast when the time dollar idea had been around for well over a decade, I asked?

A small flash of disapproval crossed Edgar Cahn's face. 'All these projects are based on relationships which have taken years to build up,' he said defensively. 'And anyway, time dollars are very much more than just bartering. The real issue is how you build a community,' he told me. 'We need to rebuild the "social capital" that we have all been living off – call it trust, reciprocity or just engagement if you like – and we need to find a beachhead wherever we can. Ultimately it is that social capital which is in severest need of repair.

'As I see it, this is the real function of time dollars. It is to provide value in a world where the market economy defines the work which the majority of people do – looking after old people, bringing up children – as useless. All those tasks are work which will never be adequately valued in a market system which must devalue what is common or universal. To give adequate value you just have to step outside the system.'

That is the issue which time dollars have been struggling with: how do we give value to all those aspects of life which old-fashioned dollars or pounds don't care about – love, neighbourliness, community, altruism, charity? 'Dollars value what is scarce,' he said. 'I hope these things are never in such short supply that they become valuable in the market economy.' And he's right. Time dollars are giving a value to our wealth, but it is the kind of wealth we forget about when we talk about money.

Upstairs, the campaign to change money-as-we-know-it had taken root in what must have once been bedrooms and walk-in wardrobes. In one small wood-panelled room, the cupboard was still full of the kind of detritus you expect in a family home – games and black plastic bags of old clothes. Copies of *The Legal Position of Native Americans* rubbed covers with broken and faded editions of Volume One of the collected poems of Robert Browning. One of the computers included a demonstration of the Timedollar programme which allows anybody to set up a time dollar bank. Written by a computer enthusiast in Maine, it very cleverly matches people's needs with what people have to offer. It then has a built-in fraudbuster. You can't delete or transfer anybody's savings from one person to another. If you cock it up, you have to leave the error there and label it 'mistake'.

Tina input my details, with my address in Crystal Palace, my almost non-existent availability, and my offer to do what the computer called 'advocacy work' – which sounded important and congenial. I also expressed the need for hot meals. I could also have opted for any of the following services: telephone assurance, yardwork – American for 'gardening' – companionship and religion. 'Religion' turned out to mean preaching. Somehow I don't think the machine will be able to match me, and nobody has yet appeared in London with a hot meal. Still, I live in hope of spending my first time dollar.

III

It was time to seek out my lodgings in a bed and breakfast in Dupont Circle, a bright area of bars, minor embassies and inquisitive dogs on very long leads. Walking from the Dupont Circle metro station, past the usual array of Scientologists and bizarre newspapers, the first thing you notice is the vast potholes in the streets – almost enough to engulf a British Mini. Then there are the real estate notices outside the houses for sale, many with photos of the smiling estate agent you would be dealing with. Could these people really believe their hairstyles would help sell houses? It hardly seemed possible. Dupont Circle is also a city centre outpost of Irish bars – 'give us your thirsty, your famished . . .' says one of them; a neighbourhood of ice cream vendors in shiny basements and strangely unkempt photocopy centres.

Every Washingtonian has a detailed inventory of exactly how safe each street can be. The subject seems to obsess them. Dupont Circle was described to me as 'pretty safe'. But since it is near the more dangerously cosmopolitan district of Adams-Morgan, I was urged to be careful. Yet when I arrived at my bed and breakfast lodging to find everybody out, there was an envelope addressed to me sticking out of the letter box. Inside was the front door key and a note. 'Hi,' it said. 'Welcome. The round key opens the front door, but please lock it when you get inside. Thanks. Irene.'

I struggled with the door once I had got through it, trying to work out how to lock it again. I thought it was worth following the instructions. Up the stairways, there was an unexpected clutter of statuettes, Indian wall-hangings with fake precious stones, sentimental pictures of *fin de siècle* actresses, heroic pictures of elephants. It was a bed and breakfast *tour de force*, all gathered around a worn red stair carpet and a large number of tiny faded handwritten notes of instructions for the guests. 'Please use the shower for no more than three minutes to conserve water. Thanks. Irene', said one. 'Please turn off the light in the bathroom. Thanks. Irene', said another.

When I made it to my bedroom on the top floor, there was a similar East-meets-West collection in there, setting off the white iron bedstead to advantage, cooled by the breeze from two fans.

I stared out of the window watching people in the surrounding apartments relaxing in front of the television or pottering around the kitchen. This was rather nosy of me, I admit, but Washingtonians don't seem to favour curtains, and it was purely in the interests of research.

My eye was drawn away by the sight of a most unusual bearded Buddha figure on the top shelf of the rattling white bookshelf in the corner. There was a note on it, and fascinated, I climbed gingerly on to a stool to find out what it was. I had hoped it would explain what was clearly an object of great antiquity, but the note said: 'Please don't put wet clothes over the furniture. Thanks. Irene'.

I met Irene the following morning, as she made me breakfast. She was an ebullient character, with a mound of carefully crafted dyed black hair and an encyclopaedic knowledge of English stately homes, which she expected me to reciprocate. She was not very interested in my quest, or about new kinds of money. She urged me instead to go and see a number of local galleries, and in particular, Dumbarton Oaks, where the original agreement to set up the United Nations had been signed half a century before. And I'm afraid I never did.

I even told her about Edgar Cahn. 'He sounds like a commie, pinko socialist,' she said, with a little laugh to show she was only half-serious.

IV

I wanted to see a time dollar bank in action, and set out after breakfast to look at one of the biggest, the Co-operative Caring Network – run by an enormous charitable monster called the United Seniors Health Co-operative (USHC).

After a little while in the USA, you realize that politically correct language has developed in a different way from its British equivalent. In the UK, it keeps changing as the shadowy people who decide these things hit on different ways of 'telling the truth', but has generally settled down to words which are unambiguous. British campaigners for the rights of elderly people have now hit on the idea of calling them 'older', which has the benefit of being manifestly true. Not so in the USA, where the word 'die' is shunned, as you might expect in a delicately polite spa town like Leamington. Americans say 'passed away' or even 'passed', which conjures up lavatories. They also avoid the term 'old': they call old people 'seniors'. The most evocative title of an organization for 'seniors' I found was the American Association for Advanced Living. Or as Roger Daltrey might have said: 'I hope I die before I get advanced'.

There is a tremendous and attractive American urge to look on the bright side, which seems to be particularly apparent in Washington. As I sauntered up to the palatial tower block which housed the USHC, I passed an old lady with three large sacks containing what I assumed were her worldly possessions. She was singing 'Give my Regards to Broadway'.

The Co-operative Caring Network (CNN) was an enormously ambitious project set up in 1993, aiming to involve 15,000 people, fifty different member organizations and shelling out time dollars to pay for up to 700,000 hours of work a year. They even had plans to record people's transactions by voicemail: all you would have to do was phone them up and tell them. IBM had donated six computers, the telephone giant Bell Atlantic had volunteered some of its staff, and each participant was going to pay $15 in dollars for the privilege of taking part. You didn't have to be Einstein to realize that, however much they may have been earning in time dollars, they would also be raking in up to $225,000 a year.

As I was to discover, the Network never quite worked out as planned, but they are still one of the biggest time dollar banks in the USA. And to prove it, I had been given a pile of leaflets explaining the whole idea. 'Co-operative Caring Network gives "credit" for the volunteer work you do,' said their introductory leaflet. 'For each hour you spend providing a volunteer service, CCN will give you a care credit.' There were piles of other leaflets in different colours and languages, all with the same cartoon of a bald man with a moustache looking deeply perplexed. *'Xe toi can sua chua,'* he was saying. *'Vay, bang cach noa me toi co the gen van phong bac-si duoc?'*

I was also given a list of happy success stories, couched in rather strange formal language. 'Estell Barrios earns Care Credits by providing clerical support to CCN staff,' said one of them. 'Ms Barrios cashed her credits in for handy man services. We assigned Mr Eduard Walker to help Ms Barrios out with a few odds and ends around her home.'

Others read more like Dateline: 'Maria Massey is a visually impaired senior, residing in Arlington, Virginia. Ms Massey requested a person to accompany her for walks. We found Mr Clark Egbert who is also an Arlington resident to walk with Ms Massey. Mr Egbert also has volunteered to pay Ms Massey friendly visits and take her for drives to the park for their walk. They are happy with the match.'

The CNN offices were unexpectedly expensive, in a large gleaming grey office block on Fifteenth Street, in Washington's commercial district. I took the lift to the fourth floor to meet Farrell Didio, the manager. She explained that the network linked thirty-three organizations in the Washington area, from Virginia in the south to Maryland in the north – covering flats, libraries, parks, old people, anything in fact which needed volunteer support. There are now 1,600 of them, which is not quite the planned 15,000, but impressive nonetheless.

Six federal 'volunteers' help Farrell and her assistant to administer the system, helping each network out if they find they can't service a request. Most of them are concerned with helping old people stay healthy and active and in their homes – not for the kind of things the health or social services should be paying for, but for everything else.

'We had a lady call, she's in a wheelchair,' said Farrell. 'She said "I do OK getting to the grocery store, but once I get there and buy my groceries, I have a hard time". Through the computer, we were able to find someone who can help her get her groceries home. Then there was a lady who was very visually impaired: we sent someone to the grocery store with her every two weeks so that she could read the labels on the cans. Life-threatening, no. But services that people find add to the quality of their life – you bet!'

Farrell Didio was getting into her proselytizing stride. 'I even had a gentleman who said, "You know, I just want to help people move their furniture round". That's not life-threatening either, but if you'd had that couch on that wall for twenty years – well, there's a lot of value in these things.'

There were a number of features which particularly interested me. For one thing, only people over fifty-five were allowed to save time dollars for themselves – the rest had to give them away, preferably to elderly relatives who might need to pay for services. Some high schools required pupils to earn credits before they could graduate.

Second, they still help people with no time dollars. 'It would be tacky not to,' said Farrell, and I agreed.

Third, they don't call them time dollars at all, for fear that the IRS will hear the word 'dollars' and prick up their ears. They simply call them 'credits'.

And fourth, the time dollar economy turns out to be excitingly different from the 'real' economy. This is a revolutionary world where everybody's time is worth the same. If you are an expensive lawyer, your time is worth exactly the same as if you are an elderly housebound widow making supportive calls. 'Some people say it sounds too good to be true,' said Farrell. 'They say: "You mean I'm going to get free trips to my doctor's office and in exchange I can make friendly phone calls to ask people how they are?" And I say: "Yeah, that's exactly it – that's the way it works". Then they say: "Are you sure?", and I say: "Trust me, I'm sure".'

So what went wrong? Well, to start with, the member organizations wanted to cling tightly to their hard-won lists of volunteers. That did for the idea of charging them $15 each. Then there were the potential volunteers who were afraid their names would end up on a computer list, and people would ring them demanding lifts to doctors far into the night.

I was getting to the end of my plastic cup of tea, but there were two other issues I wanted to discuss. What if you moved to another part of the USA: could you take your time dollars with you?

'Somebody was moving to Oregon and asked me that, and I said "It's OK. It's just paperwork". I think as people, we have got to make whatever allowances we can make to get folks served.'

'But won't there be a problem if you allow time dollars to move around the country?' I asked. 'Then they would all eventually flood to the rich areas and you'll have exactly the same situation that you get with dollars and pounds – some areas have lots and some have almost none? Doesn't it have to be local?'

'I think that's probably true,' she said, shifting her position slightly. 'But I have no problem with saying: "Gee, Mrs Smith's daughter lives here, so we can work something". I may not want to do it for 5,000 people, but I can do it for one or two.'

That's the joy of time dollars somehow. It's effective, but it isn't quite real. You don't have to account for absolutely everything. You can give a little bit here and there. You don't have to be a bank manager. But in spite of all that, these computer blips of what Edgar Cahn called 'funny money' do seem to drive a new kind of economy. They do pay for services which 'real' money can't. They do give a kind of value to what volunteers do, and anybody involved in their local community, and they do give dignity to the old people who get the services. This isn't charity: they pay for them.

But I had one final, crucial question: what does the Co-operative Caring Network cost to run? 'Do you know,' said Farrell

Didio with a knowing smile, 'I don't think I'm going to talk about budgets.'

V

How do you judge danger in places you have never been before? It's difficult: in practically every city from Aberdeen to Auckland, people say similar things about local crime. They make the kind of noises garage repairmen make when you bring your car in for a service and explain that it's getting worse and worse. They tell you confidentially that there are some places where you should take the advice in *Carousel* and never walk alone. Or in the case of Washington, never walk at all.

Of all the cities you might visit in the United States, Washington must be the most fearful about crime. And not surprisingly, because this is one of the cities vying for the title of 'murder capital of the world'. When I reached the city in June 1996, 183 people had already been murdered in the year, compared to 161 for the same period the year before. Arrests had been made in only about a third of the incidents – what the *Washington Post* described excitedly as 'slayings'. Police stations in the poverty-stricken neighbourhood of Anacostia are often lucky to get their patrol cars out on the road. One station visited by the *New York Times* had only one typewriter – a manual. 'If you want to type your reports, you have to bring your own ribbon,' said one police officer.

Washingtonians may leave their front door keys in envelopes sticking out of letter boxes, but they are terrified of murder. Different cities, I find, worry about different types of crime. In London we are obsessed with burglary or having our cars stolen. In Washington, which is on the face of it a far more dangerous place, these things don't seem to worry them – they even leave their cars unlocked. What worries the people of Washington isn't that they will lose their cars while they are parked, but having them stolen at gunpoint while they are waiting at traffic lights. Next time you're on an American plane, take a look at the executive toys for sale in the magazine. Some of them sell a blow-up 'fella', looking tough and determined, which you can put in your passenger seat. This isn't to enhance your sex appeal, or even to prevent lonely feelings at night: it's to discourage car-jackers.

I wondered idly whether car-jacking was Washington's alternative to public transport. The buses are scarce, and taxi drivers are liable to pick up other passengers while you're hurrying along in their cab. They also tend to start the ride with the words: 'And how are you today?' – as if you have accidentally flagged down a psychologist.

Parts of the city clearly are extremely dangerous, but even so the fear seems almost unnatural in its intensity – whole sections of the metro map are treated almost as no-go areas by the 'respectable' half of the city. The Yellow and Green lines seem to a visitor to be a transport version of *Nightmare on Elm Street*. Take many Washingtonians to areas in the east of the city and they will be entirely unfamiliar with the road layout.

The only Washington person I met who seemed entirely unconcerned about these things was Edgar Cahn. He wanders around south-eastern Washington – the kind of place which gives Washington matrons nightmares by its mere existence – and comes to no harm, he told me. And he's always done so. 'I'm quite safe,' he said, in a wonderful statement of American liberalism, reminiscent of what Arthur Miller says about his own behaviour in New York. 'Because these people *smell respect*.'

'Where are you going tomorrow?' asked Irene the evening before, as I passed her sitting room. Emma Thompson was speaking in the background from a costume drama video of *Carrington*.

'Oh,' I said, trying to sound nonchalant. 'Somewhere in the north-east, near Shaw-Howard.'

'Well,' said Irene severely. 'That doesn't sound like a good idea at all. Last year there was this British guy and his father came out of the back door of the National Gallery by mistake and walked just a couple of blocks, and he got jumped for his camera. Killed. So I always like to ask my guests where they are going.'

I gulped. Shaw-Howard was more than a few blocks past the National Gallery. 'It's only a hundred yards or so from the metro. I'm sure I'll be fine,' I said. She pursed her lips disapprovingly. Later that evening, a British friend of mine – living in the much more salubrious district of Georgetown, with its restaurants and dinky fashion shops – said I was crazy to go by myself. 'It's not brave or anything,' she said. 'It's just stupid.'

So by the time I passed Gallery Place on the metro, I had begun to worry whether this trip had been entirely sensible. I changed on to the Green line, and wondered a little about my shorts, grey socks and black briefcase. Graffiti, torn posters, bits of old automobile bother me at the best of times, and especially when I looked like a refugee from the set of *Jeeves and Wooster*. I did feel a little silly, but if our forefathers had worried about wearing silly clothes, the empire would never have been won.

Shaw-Howard metro station was almost empty. Even the

advertising billboards in the station looked a little half-hearted – one of them was for Valujet, owners of the downmarket holiday plane which had just crashed into the Florida swamps. The first estate I walked into, with its sand-coloured bricks and desert appearance, was clearly the wrong one. A few men stared at me absent-mindedly. I wished I hadn't brought my briefcase. 'Where can I find Lincoln-Westmoreland?' I asked one.

'Huh?' he said. It is a strange phenomenon that many Americans have not the slightest idea what Brits are trying to say. I moved hastily across the tree-lined street, hoping I looked like I knew where I was going, and there it was. I don't know what I expected from a block of flats named after America's second-greatest president and a Vietnam War general, but it was leafy with the faint whiff of oasis about it. The flats were beautifully kept and landscaped. Compared to the burnt-out shacks down the road, it was a model of imagination and pride. But there was no doubt that the neighbourhood was poor.

But then Edgewood Management Corporation, which manages low-rent flats in twelve states, is known for its enlightened approach to housing. Lincoln-Westmoreland has 223 apartments in three blocks and one high-rise tower, and thanks to the Corporation, a concerted attempt is made to organize activities for the people who live in them. Since the average size of family is only three – there are only a handful of two-parent families, and the vast majority of offspring are looked after by single mothers or grandmothers – the focus is on activities for children.

The 'power house' for these activities is in the tiny community centre, which I had been searching for. It looked like a doctor's waiting room inside, with toys packed away – as if the patients would keep spreading them out over the floor – and a range of uplifting leaflets about body problems. One notice was headed 'Caring and Sharing'. 'As one of our great African-American leaders has said,' it went on, 'you don't have to know Einstein's theory to serve ... you only need a heart full of grace.' 'No fighting or using profanity', said another.

And, at last, evidence that we were in the presence of a new kind of money; one notice was advertising a trip to Barnum and Bailey's Circus which could be paid for in time dollars.

Organizing the few children in the room was Tomeka Smith, a former biologist and nurse – 'Hoping to start a family one day,' she told me, and in the meantime looking after an alternative family: there were never fewer than twenty children in her office during the summer afternoons.

She had worked for almost a year to get the time bank up and running, squaring the management and the residents' council. The system had begun a year before I arrived, but after three months the project began to unravel. The volunteers floated away and the time dollars went unspent. So Tomeka stopped and thought it through again. When they re-launched it, six months later, she knew that every time a volunteer arrived, they had to find something for them to do quickly before they lost interest.

Tomeka pump-primes the value of time dollars by donating places on their children's six-week summer camp. Residents could buy places there with time dollars earned in about three months of regular work. 'They couldn't afford to pay the price of the camp,' Tomeka told me, sitting with her back to the gigantic toy cupboard. 'And it was a time when we were very short-staffed in the office and we needed volunteers.'

Here was an example of the way the real and time dollar economies interact. If Tomeka had failed to attract people to help her, she would have had to pay old-fashioned money for the extra help. As it was, by increasing the value of time dollars, she was able to attract people to help her in return. How do you increase the value of time dollars? You provide something out of your own margins – in this case, places on the summer camp. The real dollars not earned on the summer camp were offset against the money saved on administration in the office: what was a time dollar transaction was in some ways also a book-keeping shift.

And it all seemed to be working very well. Tomeka now had more than thirty members of her time bank. The youngest were two eight-year-olds, who cleaned the office and used their time dollars to pay for tickets to the circus. After five years' work building the community centre, Tomeka seemed to be getting things to run smoothly. 'Any bright light, any beam of light – that's my job. We are getting more members every day,' Tomeka told me as she very kindly escorted me the few yards to the metro station.

'They see what their neighbours are doing and want to do something themselves. They're not even interested in what they can get now, they're interested in what they can give. I've been amazed at some of the people who come in, people who have always been looking to see what they can get – but I can see the effect it's having on them. They are realizing they can do something. Some of them have low self-esteem and don't believe they have any worth or anything to give back to society, and they are really learning now that they have some skills.'

VI

The battle over money has made politics pretty boring – an endless succession on the *Today* programme of small politicians demanding money from big politicians the world over. But maybe, just maybe, time dollars could provide a way out of our worldwide budget squeeze. We may have to carry on squeezing the budgets and resign ourselves to the fact that people suffer, but in the case of old people that would often mean they have to leave their own houses to be looked after in miserable old folks' homes – at far greater expense to the public purse. One alternative might be accessing the wealth in people's time and use this new 'time money' to pay for what they need.

One objection is that this lets the government off the hook, which really bothers earnest academics – some of whom would no doubt prefer to keep the suffering just to maintain the pressure; another is that these kinds of jobs should really be carried out by people with degrees, diplomas and years of training. Edgar Cahn answers this with a strange little essay about cleaning your teeth. The market economy works by specialization, he says. We buy the specialized services we used to provide ourselves, except – he says – for teeth-cleaning. 'If we tried to do so, we couldn't just ask anybody: we would have to pay an oral hygienist and the price would include taxes, malpractice insurance, administrative costs, certification, worker's compensation licensing and overheads.

'We can't afford even the simplest tasks done for us at market prices,' he writes. 'Yet that's our approach to most of society's needs: we try to buy back piecemeal, at market prices, the things we used to do for ourselves and for each other.' And then, of course, the professionals say they can't do it without our help. The schools need the involvement of parents and the police need Neighbourhood Watch. 'It looks like we're going to have to keep brushing our teeth.'

When academics study these ideas in practice, things become strangely clouded. Even the people who have studied for a decade to find out whether time dollars work have come to no clear conclusion. 'I'm not sure we've proved it yet,' said Kathleen Treat from the University of Maryland's Center on Aging, with satisfaction. I suppose proving it would bring the research programme to an abrupt end.

'Oh,' I said, rather nonplussed. They had been studying it for nine years, after all.

'Well, in some places it has been fairly active and successful. In other places the programme has stayed small, and in some places the projects have not been able to sustain themselves and have gone out of business. We will admit to you that there are a number of these programmes which have folded – though it's hard to get that out of Edgar Cahn. As for the volunteers, if you ask them, they say: "Oh no, the credits don't mean a thing to me". But that is not necessarily the right answer: the volunteers will say in the same breath: "Hey, there's a mistake in my statement!"'

This was as close to a definitive answer as I was going to get. Their department had been working away at this since 1987, in a grey windowless bunker, with a basketball court above it – which meant its rooms echoed to the constant bangs and crashes of trainers, bodies and basketballs against the floor. Their reports have helped give an academic legitimacy to the time dollars idea, and have shown how time dollars can attract people into 'volunteering' who would never usually do any such thing, and keep them – the Miami project had a drop-out rate of just 5 per cent a year – and that old people earning time dollars stay healthier longer. I was also able to ask them how much it costs to set up a time dollar bank. This usually means a computer, an office, somebody on the end of a phone, postage, heating, administration, posters, office parties at Christmas, morning coffee, envelopes and – most of all – old-fashioned, common-or-garden money.

You can pay for the administration in time dollars to some extent, like they did in Lincoln-Westmoreland, and if you do that too much, the credibility of the system begins to teeter. You are, after all, doing the equivalent of what bad governments do in bad times – printing money and causing inflation. Or, in other words, lowering the value of the time dollars.

It costs at least $50,000, they said. You could beg, borrow and use donated space but 'you really have to be a true believer to make that work'. Their most frequent calls these days are from established time dollar banks wondering where their next grant is going to come from. It's a paradox, isn't it. But as the problems increase, so does the advice. The Center on Aging now publishes a newsletter called *To Your Credit*, with help on where to get funding, how to deal with volunteers who want to give up – and a smattering of sentimental advice. 'Everyone has a talent someone else needs,' said the copy they gave me. I wasn't sure this applied to journalists or alternative economists.

'Do you get along with Edgar Cahn?' I asked.

There were peals of laughter and then a slightly awkward silence. 'Our relationship is very cordial,' they said once they had recovered themselves. I wasn't altogether sure I believed them, because there even seemed to be different philosophies behind the various different 'service credit' softwares.

'Either you design it so that every service is paid for and accounted for, or in Edgar's vision, which quite frankly I'm not sure I understand, it is completely open-ended and there's no accounting of credits. I'm not sure, without that, they have any value,' they said.

And in that apparently small difference, there is actually all the difference in the world. Are time banks like ordinary banks, where everything has to add up in the end? Or are they just a way of funnelling goodwill? Edgar Cahn describes his creation as 'funny money', and he means it. 'Sometimes it doesn't add up,' he said to me, 'and I don't give a damn.'

Take Miami, for example, because this was one of the jewels of Edgar Cahn's time dollar crown. And not surprisingly: Florida now has so many old people that by the year 2000 they will require $400 million a year in Medicaid funds. 'By carefully watching what is happening now in Florida, we stand to learn a wealth of information about the problems and opportunities the whole nation will face in the future,' says the futurist John Naisbitt.

The time bank there has been built up from nothing by a former international banker called Anna Miyares. She took a big pay-cut to set up in Little Havana because her daughter was at university near there. But in spite of her banking background, Anna Miyares has backed away from the whole idea of banks. 'I used to be a happy person, but as a banker I became a different person,' she said. 'So basically I'm doing this because it gave me the opportunity to be myself, to do what I always wanted to do ... Now I have more friends than ever before. I used to wonder if people were friends just because they wanted me to arrange a loan. To me this is not working: this is my extended family.'

You don't get bankers talking like that, but then you don't usually get bankers like Anna Miyares. She used to make people sign slips agreeing that their volunteers had worked the hours they claimed to earn their time dollars. Now, in an effort to cut bureaucracy, she just takes them at their word.

Time dollars made me look afresh at the whole idea of banks – and of money too. When I put my earnings into the bank, or my £1 coin into my pocket, where does it come from? Well, the Royal Mint, of course. But where does the actual 'money' come from in the first place? The answer is that it is produced by banks, who go into debt to create true money to lend to businesses, who use it to pay their suppliers, who sometimes even use it to pay me: the banks conjure the money into existence. It is different with time dollars, because you do the conjuring yourself. Old Mrs Plummet needs to be given a lift to the doctor, and she goes into debt in the system to organize one. By doing so, she conjures wealth into existence which can be used to power other services for old and young people alike.

The value of pounds is backed by our belief in the banks and the continuing value of what Harold Wilson used to call the pound in your pocket. The value of time dollars is backed by our belief in the system and the willingness of the local community to do the work. Or belief in each other, in other words.

Generally speaking, I prefer the idea of Mrs Plummet creating wealth which will eventually trickle up to me than NatWest creating wealth which may trickle down – but which certainly won't trickle as far as housebound, dependent Mrs Plummet. Of course we don't have to have one or the other, but I am thrilled by the thought that Mrs Plummet's various needs can make us all richer.

Chapter 2

Still Washington: money as moral energy

'Actually, money does grow on trees.'
Kate Frederiksen, wealth therapist, Colorado.

I

I took the Washington metro back into town wondering what had been missing from the academic study I had just witnessed, and slipped into my guesthouse in Dupont Circle. Irene was watching an ancient episode of *Are You Being Served?*. 'We're watching one of your TV shows,' she said, falling about laughing as I passed the door. 'Do you want to join us?'

'It's very old,' I said, trying to wriggle out of responsibility for it. I needed time to make sense of what I was learning; after a few days of watching the controlled creative chaos at what Edgar called Time Dollars Ground Zero, I realized he was being much more ambitious than I had expected. He was attempting more than just providing services for old people, and much more even than creating a new kind of money. He was trying to redress the balance of the modern world from selfishness to unselfishness – encouraging people to be nice to each other. Even if you believe, as Washington 'liberals' tend to, that deep down people are pretty nice really, this was an enormous task. 'You're trying to do more than invent a new currency, aren't you?' I had asked him. 'You're trying to create a whole new economy.'

He laughed. 'Or maybe we're trying to create one which used to exist but doesn't any longer.' And this seemed to be what had been missing from the cold academic discussion earlier in the day: a sense of the powerful brand of nostalgia wielded by Farrell Didio, Tomeka Smith and Edgar Cahn as they popularize the idea – not just as a new kind of money, but as a very old kind of wealth. As his book points out, three out of four Americans don't know their next-door neighbours. Once upon a time, there was a kind of wealth in the way people looked after each other; grandparents had a vital role bringing up grandchildren, and so on. And somehow, it doesn't really matter whether this is true or not – it has enormous power to sway audiences.

We have got economics wrong, says Edgar. Money isn't like water. You don't pour it in the top and watch it filter down: hardly anybody believes that any more. It moves around a community, invigorating it like electricity. Without being plugged into the energy source, everything just goes limp.

There are anyway two economies in the economic gospel according to Cahn. One has supermarkets, bagel shops and factories, the networks which make us rich and bring us the material things we need. The other drives families, neighbourhoods and communities, the networks which educate, bring up and nurture. One is formal and the other informal. Economists study the first and only partly believe in the existence of the second, but the second needs to be energetic for the first to thrive.

'We used to have a second economy which was invisible,' he said. 'And it's the economy we don't talk about, which used to be called community. And if we're honest, this economy ran on the subjugation of women and slave labour. Now we live in a different world, but the community has disappeared.'

How do we get it back without the subjugation? Edgar's first battle has been to prove the existence of this other economy to doubting economists who believe that everything has to have a price. 'I do not know any family where someone holds up the wishbone and says "What am I bid for this tonight?" ' he says aggressively. 'Or where the market value of walking the dog versus putting out the trash is the key factor in a household decision.'

The second stage is to show that time dollars reward and reinforce those very things that money generally doesn't: caring for family, neighbours and friends. 'To use the economists' phrase, this new currency appears to increase the "competitive value" of relationships of trust, in relation to monetary gain,' he told me. No wonder the only definition of time dollars by an economist I have come across is 'an inferior semi-money'. Well maybe it is, but as long as it works, perhaps that doesn't matter. And it is a semi-money which drives the kind of neighbourhood life we all depend on, like steam drives a machine.

II

So the scene was set for stage three. Edgar was preparing himself for a new phase in his economy-building. The problem of services for old people was dealt with; time dollars were well-established for that, but maybe they could do other things as well. In Chicago schools, for example, where time dollars are being paid to children to tutor fellow-pupils two years below. They find that both tutors and tutored improve their grades. They even stop bullying each other: you don't beat up your pupil after all, and you don't let anybody else do so either.

'These are kids who have already been told by the school system that they are "dumb",' said Edgar. 'But they know the alphabet and they know that one plus two equals three, so if they're dumb it is inconceivable that these younger kids won't learn it. They don't do the kids' homework for them because they know the kids can do it, because *they* understand the problem – and all of a sudden they are starting to get As and Bs for the first time.'

But for all these things to be achieved, time dollars need to be under-pinned, and this is beginning to happen. In El Paso, you can now buy children's clothes with time dollars. In Pittsburgh, a shop run by Aid to Families with Dependent Children provides toys, nappies and secondhand clothes in return for time dollars. An organization in New England provides a $40 bag of groceries for $14 plus two hours of time dollars. The point about pump-priming this social economy with children's clothes or food is that you can get hold of surplus or waste – things that were actually going for nothing – and then make them available for time dollars.

Habitat for Humanity, the US low-cost homes charity, already lets people make their mortgage down-payment in 500 hours of time dollar work building homes for other people. By charging for their expertise in time dollars, or by letting people into their health centre for time dollars, lawyers and local councils can create this time dollar debt – a debt which has to be paid off by people improving their neighbourhood. If you charge in pounds or dollars, neighbourhoods would not be able to afford it, but by charging for services in time dollars, you can involve neighbourhoods in their own salvation.

Edgar Cahn calls this 'co-production': 'Without co-production, nothing that professionals, organizations or programmes do can succeed,' he says. 'With co-production, the impossible comes within reach. As a lawyer, I get to make sure someone isn't evicted from their home, but I can't make that home somewhere I would want to live. For that I need that person's involvement.' Because the economy is half-blind, it takes no notice of these assets – people's time, skills, energy and willingness to give back. It leaves them lying around while we all believe we are running out of money. Time dollars are a way of recycling the assets and getting them to work.

GMB general secretary John Edmonds – one of Britain's top trade unionists – tells a story of the secretary of a big social club in north-west England who is actually employed by a big chemical company, 'As the club secretary, he demonstrates considerable skills as a communicator, organizer and manager; the chemical company employs him as a semi-skilled packer,' he said in a speech to the Royal Society of Arts. He went on: 'The extent of John's talent came to the attention of management when the company carried out a staff aptitude and experience survey. Showing me the results, the managing director delivered a bleak verdict: "We are wasting the ability of about half the people who work here".'

Multiply this by every office, neighbourhood and street and you realize just how much hidden skill and human energy there is in society. And we thought we were running out of resources.

But there is something rather old-fashioned and moralistic about the time dollars idea, which I wasn't sure would go down very well in cynical old Britain, where the slightest whiff of the 'deserving poor' gets a broadside from the people who watch out for these things. On the other hand, Edgar does some of this asset-recycling himself. He charges for his work in the legal advice centre in time dollars. He linked the major law firm Holland & Knight with a community group which wanted to clear out the drug-dealers and corrupt policemen from their neighbourhood in Washington and lobby to release funds for local improvement – in return for a retainer paid in time dollars. In 1996, the firm billed the equivalent of $234,979 to the community in time dollars, paid back in clearing up rubbish, planting flowers, school tutoring or taking down the car numbers of local drug-dealers.

Of course you can give this kind of stuff out for free, but shouldn't it be paid for somehow? And if you are a law firm with the expertise and the local community has the energy, you need some kind of money system to bring the two together. 'Lawyers have a lot of guilt,' Edgar said later. 'They know that the time they give is unleashing community development, but only if they charge in time dollars.'

Meanwhile, Edgar Cahn's imagination was doing overtime. How about paying tax in time dollars? What about parking? What if city-centre parking spaces were reserved for people with time dollars? Imagine what an injection of credibility that would give to the idea of helping out in your neighbourhood. How about student loan payments in time dollars? 'That's next,' he said as he took me to the front door the following evening, a little glint in his eye.

We were distributing ourselves into various cars, me with a video screen and a presentation stand on my lap. It was time for the time dollars bandwagon to descend on one of Washington's more notorious estates. We were going to a housing block called Arthur M. Capper to discuss setting up a food bank with the residents. US cities are dotted with subsidized food banks, providing surplus food and groceries to poorer people at extremely low prices. Anyone with backing from a reputable organization can use these centres to supply their own local food banks.

Our job was to persuade the people who lived there to link this new food bank to time dollars, and use it to fuel a new kind of self-help. It was tricky: the residents had asked the Time Dollar Institute to be their official sponsors for the food bank. They might not take kindly to the morality bank which they were going to get. We drove past the Capitol, a kind of mental boundary between Washington's safe and dangerous states of mind, past the trendy Irish pubs, underneath the urban motorways and down towards Anacostia. I hoped some of Edgar's 'smell of respect' might rub off on me.

If you use the phrase 'housing estate' to Americans, they look at you blankly. To them, an estate is somewhere you grow cotton in the deep South. 'Housing complex' is equally bewildering: something your analyst might diagnose. Nor can you say 'public housing', because many of the apartment blocks where Washington's poor live are actually private, though funded by subsidies from the city or one of the federal agencies.

The Arthur M. Capper block was one of these – a vast red-brick monstrosity, without character or redeeming features. Hundreds of dour little windows looked down on to a grassless, pitted, littered open space, wired off recreation areas and hundreds of bits of old cars. It was one of those strange modern wastelands whose appearance had been twisted somehow by the availability of grants. Clearly a great deal of money had been available at some point for floodlighting the recreation areas; obviously none had been forthcoming for landscaping. Poor old Arthur M. Capper, to have his name remembered in this way.

But there was no sense of menace or threat, and we were clearly expected. I heaved the screen through the front door, past the painted breeze-block walls and into what was evidently the 'community room'. It was the kind of green-painted, fluorescent-lighted, orange-curtained, lino-covered hole you would expect in a block like this, with piles of elderly plastic chairs covered with specks of whitewash, some folded tables and a small framed copy of Leonardo's *Last Supper* which looked as though it had come out of an old calendar. A notice informed us that 'hand-washing prevents infection' and a small digital clock told us that the time was 3.52 – which it wasn't.

Fourteen or so black women meandered into the room, with children attached and a faint air of having better things to do. Apart from the time dollar promoters and what seemed liked a whole coachload of housing rights activists, there was only one man. It wasn't quite clear why he was there: he was in his seventies and evidently had not lived in Arthur M. Capper for some years.

'Where's the free food?' said one child near me. His mother in an elderly T-shirt flapped a hand at him, but began looking quietly round the room herself.

'It's not actually free. Nothing in this life is free,' said one of the housing activists glumly. 'We know that.'

By the time Clarence rose to speak, explaining that time dollars were a 'mechanism that brings people together', the room was extremely noisy. Babies were banging the table, mothers were disciplining their charges, and the air of a 5 p.m. maths lesson pervaded the room. 'You folks are in a state of dependency, dependent on the government to provide food stamps and shelter,' he said. 'But we don't want to be in this business any more. We are trying to figure out how to get a little piece of money that you can save.'

As a method of introducing new kinds of money, it was curiously crablike. The mothers were shifting in their seats, eyeing the door for signs of the free supper. As one of only three whites in the room, I took on a studied air of absence. The meeting clearly wasn't going terribly well. Then it was Edgar's turn. I wondered how a white Jewish law professor would go down in a place like south-east Washington, especially in his habitual white polo-necked shirt. But I need not have worried. He spoke calmly and very simply, and he worked his audience like an old-fashioned politician.

'My message is simply that we all need each other,' he said. The women stilled for a second. His directness seemed to carry a little weight. 'Everybody in this room knows what it's like having to be in at least two places at one time. If you only had somebody you could turn to, it would be better – but you don't want to ask for charity and you don't want to be indebted.' People had stopped shifting in their seats. Edgar's approach was having some effect.

'Some years ago I began to think: why can't we create our own kind of money – a kind of money just between ourselves? A little bit like a blood bank. Why can't we create some kind of time bank?'

And then a risk, but a calculated political one. 'I was married to a black woman, and when we were first married, I knew what it meant for neighbours to help out neighbours. This is what neighbours have *always* done for neighbours. And you never had to declare that to the authorities. We can rebuild that sense of community we used to have.'

It was quietly spoken, mild and modest – but a bravura piece of politics for all that.

'It is a kind of bank where you deposit care and giving,' said Edgar, quoting Ralph Nader. 'When you need care and giving you can withdraw it. In thirty-eight states where people have been doing this, nobody has been ripped off and nobody has been mugged. I can't tell you that they are all angels, but I can tell you that people don't mess with the people they have to live with.'

I wasn't so sure about this, but the women carried on listening. Their range of dangling green, pink, blue and yellow earrings were uncharacteristically still. Even the children were a little quieter.

'Nowadays all the rewards are for doing bad, and there are very few rewards for just being a decent neighbour,' he said. 'I know they say you can go to heaven, but I want you to get those rewards before that.'

It was convincing, inspiring even, but also perhaps a little confusing out of context.

'What's this got to do with setting up our food bank?' asked one of the audience. Edgar had reckoned without 'Miss Mary', the tough-minded residents' council chair, who had her own very clear political sense. She knew what she could sell, and she didn't think she could sell her committee the idea of their new food bank being conditional on earning time dollars.

'We wanted to be able to give the food away free,' she said. Other voices followed, as they began to see the snag.

'What happens if some people are dishonest?' asked one.

'Some of us got our food stamps five days late this month, and we need to be able to use the food bank.'

'Yeah, I ain't got mine yet!' As in all public meetings about new ideas, all the questions were directly relevant, but jumbled up. So were the answers.

Clarence weighed in: 'This time bank idea is something where people can begin to do things for each other in a very positive way. There are different activities which need doing which we can help do for each other – or get our friends to do it.'

'I don't have no friends,' said one of the more obstreperous women. 'I don't need no friends.'

This was the signal for an enormous argument about something completely different. The woman with no friends stormed that her mother was in hospital and was losing her flat and nobody was helping. The rest of the audience ignored her. It was impossible to follow exactly what was happening. Mary braved her denunciations and said she would help tomorrow. The woman with no friends stalked out of the room in tears, knocking over a few of the plastic chairs as she went.

There was silence for a moment, but it was clear the meeting was over. Large boxes of chicken and coleslaw from the Roy Rogers chain had arrived and the children were queuing up. Here was the free food. Then in the corner of the room, as everybody else began to clear away, the real negotiations were beginning. Edgar, Clarence, Tina from Ohio and Mary huddled together looking serious. Mary's big bunch of keys jangled at her wrist, while her small son Michael wandered about in an Old Navy T-shirt at her feet.

'The question is, can people with time dollars get anything extra from the food bank in return for being good neighbours?' said Edgar, setting out his case.

'No,' said Mary. It just wouldn't work. It would be favouritism. She wouldn't dare.

'What do you think about the idea?' said Tina sensibly, and immediately the atmosphere lightened.

'I love it, but –' said Mary. 'But I wouldn't dare.'

There was going to be no movement. Edgar signed the papers anyway, so that the Time Dollar Network would sponsor the food bank at Arthur M. Capper. He would return to the issue later.

III

There is a problem about all this, isn't there? Old people may want lifts to the doctor or supportive phone calls. Parents may want nappies or groceries. But the last thing you want as a six-teen-year-old is children's clothes or a lift to the local super-market. If Edgar Cahn suddenly wanted to pioneer the idea of providing time dollars to America's disaffected youth, in return for so-called altruistic behaviour, he needed to pump-prime his new economy with something different. Somehow the sixteen-year-olds would have to be persuaded that this was new money worth having.

The answer came to him in the shape of former teacher and computer activist Ken Komowski, though I wasn't aware of this until I arrived at Edgar's home and office at 10 a.m. the next day – only to be told I had been expected to meet Ken a good hour before. The Time Dollars office was that kind of place.

By the time I had dived down into Edgar's basement-cum-bedroom, Ken was preparing to catch the train back home to Long Island. He looked carefully-turned out, fiftyish, with a dapper moustache and a great untidy, labyrinthine mission: as he puts it, to 'eliminate the virtual ghetto'. By which he means: give power to the American underclass by making them computer-literate.

Ken was one of the pioneers of computers in education, but found himself increasingly irritated by the pattern of educational change. He could have been one of those disaffected British teachers you meet in pubs, complaining about what Ken called 'constant innovation but no change'. In 1994 he wrote an article in the US magazine *Education Week* entitled 'The 81 per cent Solution', urging that we restructure our schools and communities for life-long learning, instead of the brief intense period of inattention we know as 'school'. The title came from the idea that children spend only 19 per cent of their time in class. What about the other 81 per cent?

'You *are* what you learn,' Ken told me, warming to his subject and checking his watch. 'What you take into your mind is as important as what you take into your body. In the larger media ecology, children are an environment which is in many ways more toxic than their physical environment – in terms of the consumer mess on television, the sex and violence and the drug culture which they talk through on their way back from schools. That toxicity needs to be countered with a message that engages them.'

What is the message he wants? Well, one of them is that children can learn and earn money at their own home computer.

How could somebody like Edgar Cahn resist a challenge like that? Here was a whole new aspect of the social economy waiting to be built. The result was that Ken and Edgar set up the LINCT Coalition – or Learning and Information Networks for Community Telecomputing: Americans love these endless acronyms – so that the whole process could be driven by time dollars. Ken had already spun out his organization, a kind of *Which* for schools called the Educational Products Information Exchange, and was busy campaigning for people with computers to feel responsible for people who don't. He was one of those who calculated that American business and government departments throw out an average of fifteen million perfectly good but slightly old computers every year. That's one computer for every poor household in America.

The concept has reached as far as the White House, from where President Clinton has signed an executive order to make it easier for government departments to help. But it isn't as simple as that, says Ken. You could just give each of the fifteen million households a computer, but he and Edgar don't want to do it that way. 'We don't believe in that,' Ken told me. 'Computers have value and should be earned.'

Earned with time dollars, of course. And how do you earn the time dollars? In the usual way, or by what he calls 'electronic sweat equity'. For you and me, that means you can earn them by teaching yourself to *use* computers. In Suffolk County, Long Island, where Ken comes from, people on Workfare can meet their twenty hours a week requirement by learning computer skills at home, rather than picking up rubbish.

'Not that garbage doesn't need to be picked up,' said Ken. 'But that's not a highly marketable skill. When you burn the grey cells learning how to operate the sucker, you are helping yourself earn a computer and modem. And you can own this after paying for your training which is provided by "computer-haves" in the community, who are of course paid for their time in time dollars.'

Neat, isn't it? And there's more.

'All of the earning of time dollars is recorded,' he told me. 'Not just on the time dollars software, but under a grant we got from the legislature in New York state recently, we are currently programming a cyber-banking system for time dollars – so we can extend the time dollar record-keeping software into interactive electronic banking. So when you earn your time dollars, you can go online and see your bank account.'

If people regularly earned time dollars for their voluntary activities, you could provide a snapshot of 'economic' activity to rival the GNP. In the UK, for example, twenty-three million people are involved in the voluntary sector and only twenty-two million are in paid employment. But the Treasury only notices the second category, because it involves 'money'. Or as Edgar Cahn puts it: 'Every time we put a grandmother in a nursing home, that is a contribution to GNP. Every time we enable her to continue to live at home, it's not.'

This is all part of the notorious blindness of economics. 'There are a million non-profit organizations in the US,' Ken told me, with one foot out of the car. '750,000 of them have an annual operating budget of under $25,000 – yet those organizations, because they are run by volunteers, have no way of documenting how much they contribute to society. Edgar and I believe that the cyber-banking system I've been talking about can begin to document that. Hopefully one day you can have the whole country using this alternative non-market economy to shore up the social needs of the community, and we could create a social GNP – a true balance sheet for the country.'

And he was gone, preceded by his moustache and followed closely by his bag. A time dollar GNP is revolutionary stuff, because John Kenneth Galbraith said once: 'If you don't measure it, you can't change it.' If we think the things people do for time dollars are important, we have to measure them or nobody will take a blind bit of notice.

So how to you pump-prime the time dollar economy with refurbished computers? Edgar had decided to set up a string of computer refurbishment centres, staffed by young people without jobs who are paid in time dollars. There remained the small difficulty of getting hold of the old computers. Anybody who has given the problem thirty seconds' thought will know that there are piles of forgotten computers in nearly every cupboard in every office in the land. But somebody has to ask for them and go and pick them up.

Which is how I made the acquaintance of Rev. Fred Williams, a former USAF policeman with a disturbing resemblance to Lenny Henry. He had been a constant brisk presence in the Time Dollar HQ since I had arrived, hurrying up and down stairs with computer components, greeting me genially and offering me the chance of some heavy lifting. I had managed to avoid this until now.

Fred was part pastor, part computer consultant. He was one of those frighteningly competent men who know how to load a removal van and tie down the furniture to stop it leaping around in the back. He and I followed the van in his big grey car, with a broken radiator, with his white sun hat sitting neatly on the back seat. All cars in Washington are really just vast air conditioning systems on wheels.

And we certainly needed air conditioning. The merest thought of getting out of the car to heave computers around made me feel exhausted. 'Even if we get a hundred computers, that'll be good,' he said. Fred had his feet on the ground, but was clearly one of those people who looked on the bright side.

First there was a pile of computers from the campus of the American University. Then on to the National Trust. This name conjures a calm sense of summer days, polite elderly ladies in stately homes, chandeliers and cream teas. But in Washington it means the National Trust for the Development of the African-American Man. There we found piles of prehistoric computers waiting for us at the top of the four flights of stairs. The lift was broken. It was hotter than ever.

'Happy Wednesday,' said Tina to everyone we passed sweating on the stairs. Looking on the bright side is a major business for time dollars people.

Well over one hundred computers later, after a short mind-numbed rest in the back of the van, I was back in the car. 'When I was last in England, I watched a prostitute on breakfast TV and then ran into her at Heathrow Airport,' Fred was saying.

'Really?' I said, perking up a little in the air conditioning. 'What did you say?'

'I said she should accept Jesus Christ as her Lord and Saviour,' he said with a slightly self-deprecating laugh. 'She didn't.'

IV

'You're failing,' Professor Cahn claims he told Washington's top judge as they discussed youth crime. 'Why don't you enlist kids to help you? You may wear a black robe and bang a gavel, but the kids learned how to tune that out years ago.' Edgar has all the trappings of the establishment: he's been to Yale and Cambridge and writes articles for the *Yale Law Journal* – and he uses this to be able to say this kind of thing to top judges.

Probably he wasn't quite as blunt as he said he was, but there is no doubt that the system is now so overloaded that first, second and even sometimes third offences tend to be ignored. The unintended message to the young offenders is that you get three freebies before you are taken seriously.

And so it was that time dollars were used for their most ambitious test yet, to revitalize the District of Columbia's exhausted youth courts. Washington's courts are, of course, a small part of an exhausted urban system in the USA. By the end of the Reagan years, nearly 1.2 million Americans were in prison, and the figure was rising so fast that – if you believe these kinds of trends – half the population was due to be inside by the year 2053. The prison population was increasing at the rate of 2,000 a week, at the cost of another $100,000 a week. 'In five years, the corrections obligation could easily double the current national debt,' said the Governor of Maryland's report in 1992.

In the face of all this, Washington's youth courts can barely keep the lid on an explosive situation. The time dollars proposal to take over some of the youth courts and bring in teenage jurors paid in time dollars was agreed at the start of the year. It went ahead officially from April 23 – Shakespeare's birthday, I was pleased to note – with a budget of just $200,000 over two years. By the time I arrived three months later, 600 young people had already gone through training as jurors, ready to try non-violent first-time offences like shoplifting, what we Brits would call 'taking and driving away', criminal damage, drug possession, truancy.

There were already some success stories, such as the boy who had initially refused to speak because he had seen his brother killed, and trusted no one. And another, accused of slashing his teacher's tyres because she made him stay after school. What the youth jury discovered was that he had also promised his parents to escort his younger brother and sister home that evening, through the unpleasant gangland which lay along their route. His teacher had refused to listen. Even so the jury was tough with him: they made him pay for the damage, write an apology to the teacher and to his brother and sister – because he had shown them the wrong example.

The court itself was quite unlike anything I expected. There were no police, no warders, no social workers, no officials, no pomp or circumstance. It was hard to quite fit into the category of court at all – yet that is what it was, under licence from the District of Columbia. I walked up with Edgar, into the monstrous concrete of the DC Law School, past the signs which said 'Kiss and Ride' – where people could drop their husbands and wives off at the metro – and up to the third floor, past a sign scribbled in red felt pen: 'Teen Court Room 4800'.

Room 4800 turned out to be a large open-plan office of the kind where people hold Christmas parties and stamp cigarettes and Twiglets into the carpet. The floor was a limp purple, and the metal chairs an unpleasant shade of lime green. One of the Venetian blinds was broken. Gathered around two round tables in the middle of the room were eight young black girls and boys, in a generally upbeat mood. Every one of them was impeccably turned out – though clearly not for the benefit of the court – with sunglasses perched on their heads and beautifully coiffured hair. One of the only two boys had a shiny waistcoat, white shoes and a frighteningly wide mouth like a crocodile. He stayed almost completely silent.

These were the jurors – all of them earning three time dollars for three hours' jury service that evening. A TV crew from Denmark were fussing around with microphones. Debbie from the Time Dollars office was laughing with the jurors. Youth court organizers were whispering seriously. The defendant – we'll call him Jimmy, because I had to take the same oath of confidentiality as everyone else – sat at the end of the table. The 'teen court' model in the US has been known to cut re-offending to as little as 5 per cent: at first sight, Jimmy did not look a likely candidate for success.

He was between his 'buddy', a juror in a Harley-Davidson T-shirt assigned to speak on his behalf, and his mother in sunglasses, big gold earrings and a fearsome purple outfit with more airholes than dress. She was absent-mindedly sipping at a can of Coke. All we needed was the judge. 'It won't start without Dr Cahn,' I had been told. 'Nothing starts without Dr Cahn.'

'You'll all have to look like serious jurors now,' said the law student observer next to me, hardly older than they were.

Edgar had arrived and finished arranging his papers. Apart from me and the Danish TV crew, he was the only white face in the room – and it was by now a magisterial one. 'I want to welcome you to the Time Dollars Youth Court,' he said. Everyone's eyes turned to him. 'I am here to help the jury work on a resolution to this case. We are here to try to help young people who get into any kind of trouble.'

And then, an implied warning to Jimmy the defendant to be open: 'We can only assist if you feel comfortable sharing the issues that you have. The jury has the authority given by the courts of the District of Columbia to choose between a number of consequences they can impose.'

There was no oath to be honest, no truth, whole truth and nothing but the truth, so help me God. But then this was also a court without any of the other usual trappings – flags, microphones, gowns, ushers, silence. Edgar ran instead through the list of possible sentences the court could impose – though sentence is not a word you would hear uttered in this radical court experiment. Jimmy could 'make amends', pay back damages, get counselling, be given up to ninety hours' community service – or be sentenced to sit on a youth court jury. Not what you would call throwing away the key, but it all had to be completed within ninety days.

At the end of the table, Jimmy looked blank and rather dismissive, unsure quite how to sit, barely articulate when he first spoke. He was charged with possession of cannabis, 'with intent to distribute' – which meant he was caught with a large quantity of it. This might not be the most serious charge in the world, but Jimmy had already been arraigned in the big court and advised of his rights by a lawyer, before somebody suggested he should be sent here instead.

Inez, the sixteen-year-old jury foreman with carefully moulded hair, read a prepared statement rather stiltedly, asking Jimmy about 'your goals, your dreams, your hopes'. She clearly didn't write it herself. The atmosphere was suddenly awkward.

It was Jimmy's turn to speak, and he barely seemed to be able to say the words. You could see the contempt and the shyness in his eyes that he was even being asked to do so. 'The police just jumped out at me,' he said. He denied buying enough cannabis to sell.

But asked about his ambitions, he seemed able to string the words together a little better. He wanted to go to a school of electrical engineering: 'My goal is to be a success, to make something of myself, to be somebody – not just a statistic aged eighteen,' he said mechanically. He was in fact eighteen already and had dropped out of school. It was hard to know whether this was articulate or just a cliché he had picked up somewhere.

Now it was his mother's turn, and – clearly unused to talking to young people – she adopted a haughty tone, blaming Jimmy's father and anybody else she could think of. She had sent Jimmy to live with his father before the incident, and his father no longer wanted him there, she said: 'He came between his father and the other two women in his life. Jimmy doesn't really have a male role model in his life.' This turned out not to be entirely true. But as we listened to his mother, and her various conflicting explanations about why she sent Jimmy away, a sad picture of him hawked from home to home began to emerge.

'It's not true that we smoked marijuana in my house,' she whined, explaining that she needed financial help from Jimmy's father to bring him up. 'And I can't really speak for Mr T.' Somehow the phrase conjured up an unpleasant mental picture of Jimmy's father, like something out of *The A-Team*. Then, preening herself slightly: 'I think Jimmy's father wanted me back, but I didn't come with the package.'

And a further complication – Jimmy's sister had been gang-raped two months before. His mother began to break down. In its British equivalent, this would be a cause of consternation and embarrassment, but instead the sudden movement in the Youth Court was a sign that even the spectators were searching their bags for paper hankies.

Next Jimmy was questioned by the jury. How long had he smoked hash?

'One year.'

'Do you smoke a lot?'

'No.'

'How much?'

'Er . . . every weekend.'

'Do you have control over your smoking habit?' The jurors were feeling uncomfortable in their role.

'Oh yes.'

'Would you say you smoke to forget things?'

'My problems?' said Jimmy, seizing the opportunity. 'Yeah. If I don't deal with it that way, I'd have to deal with it a different way.'

'What was the result of your drugs test?' Now Jimmy's mother was looking uncomfortable.

'NEGATIVE!' she shouted, drowning out what her son was saying and banging down her can of Coke. The judge spoke at last. 'When the police arrested you, you had thirteen ounces on you.'

'No. I don't know how I could have got thirteen ounces out of one dime.' A dime in this context means a small unit of cannabis.

There was silence in court as the jurors racked their brains to think of something else to ask. Police sirens wailed in the street outside.

However cynical I felt as an outsider, Jimmy had faced real tragedies. Apart from his sister and the constant re-packaging of his home, a close friend of his was killed just before Christmas. His jacket had caught on the bumper of a passing car. 'I was out with some friends I grew up with, some ni–' he broke off, embarrassed. The jurors sniggered. The word 'nigger' – which can get you shot if you use it in Washington as a white person – is used in a self-deprecating way by black youngsters to refer to each other.

Nor was this the only tragedy. An older man he had been close to almost throughout his life had been shot. 'I was in his house one day and heard somebody had got shot,' said Jimmy dismissively. 'It was in the neighbourhood where my grandmother lived and I figured it would be somebody who was close to me – but I never expected it to be somebody like that. I went to his funeral, and I started smoking then.'

I looked at Jimmy and his monstrous mother with new eyes. Of course this was a skilful play for sympathy, and his story isn't particularly unusual for the part of Washington he came from, but he was nonetheless a more sympathetic figure – hard almost to grow up in parts of Washington and *not* get shot. The fact that he was up before the youth court on such a minor charge seemed almost a success.

Edgar Cahn was questioning him about the kinds of things he wanted to do. Had he ever done anything around computers? Somehow this seemed unlikely. 'I just like fixing stuff,' said Jimmy, pushing up the sleeves of his sweatshirt. 'And messing around with wires.' This seemed much more believable, and it was a glimmer of hope for the court. They did not, after all, have a long list of punishments they could hand down: perhaps it was a good thing they didn't have something really serious before them.

The hearing was coming to an end. Inez the chairman was fiddling with her hair, and Jimmy's mother was making a last-minute plea for her son.

'I think this is a pretty good programme,' she said patronizingly, but the jury seemed to take her tone as an understandable reaction to their unusual authority. They probably felt something similar themselves. 'As far as Jimmy is concerned, it would be good if he could get into computers and stop smoking marijuana. As I told him – nobody's gonna help him but himself. He's a good son and I thank God for him, but he's such a lot to deal with. My brother is dead too,' she added irrelevantly. 'He was close to Jimmy.'

The moment the defendant and the judge left court, the jury relaxed and started laughing among themselves. The dark glasses pushed up on the heads of the girls glinted in the lights as they shifted around. The court director, whose job it was to manage the proceedings, took the chair – and asked them to come to a meeting to discuss how the hearing went, and what other questions they could have asked.

'I want you to think very carefully how you managed this one. OK?' he said. He had clearly not been impressed.

But the jurors were already getting an animated and confused discussion under way. The juror with the crocodile mouth stayed silent, occasionally smiling with his long lips, but the girls became excited. 'He's not hurt anybody else, so there's no need to feel remorseful,' said an attractive juror with white-framed sunglasses. I had expected one of them to say this: I felt the same myself. It wasn't as if he was Jack the Ripper, after all.

'But he wasn't telling the truth about everything,' said Inez, searching for her questionnaire.

'How do you know?'

The questionnaire was to help the jurors make a decision, but the first two questions are both confusing. 'Did the respondent recognize the inappropriateness of the behaviour?' 'Were there mitigating circumstances?'

'I don't understand that word,' said White Glasses.

There was heavy coughing from somewhere else on the table: 'I need a drink.'

'Somebody give her a time dollar!' Everybody giggled.

At long last the crocodile spoke: 'I think he was set up.' Most of the table agreed, and the argument slipped back and forth. It turned out that one of the other jurors had been muddling the meaning of the word 'negative' with 'positive' – an easy mistake to make: I do it myself sometimes. Another one was listing some of the things they should not say to the judge: 'Dr Cahn is a Catholic or something – he's some kind of weird religion.'

Another was getting at the crocodile: 'I don't know why you bothered to come,' she said with adolescent dismissiveness. He finished his can and made moves to disappear.

The court director, meanwhile, suggested some possible directions for 'sentence'. They were all taken on board. Rather unexpectedly, the jurors had a sense of their position, and were irritated that Jimmy had been 'economical with the truth' over his charge. They had taken against him because of this.

'How many hours can we make him do?' asked White Glasses. 'He gets the maximum.' Jimmy's buddy came back in – he was supposed to be outside – and endorsed the plea for a harsh decision. 'I'm all for it,' he said. 'I think he needs a big brother. Get him to work in the computer workshop.'

But a sudden doubt crept into the mind of White Glasses. 'Wait!' she said quickly. 'Those are our computers he's working on. I don't want him messing about with them.'

At long last, a decision. Two jurors rushed out of the room to bring back the defendant, ragging each other as they went. Jimmy was wearing a new sweatshirt and a relaxed grin. So was Dr Cahn.

'Here comes the judge . . .' rapped one juror. Edgar smiled at her.

He read out the sentence: Jimmy was being sent to a substance abuse programme at a centre where they can also give him experience with computers. It would take him a total of seventy-five hours – plus nine hours serving on a youth court jury. For this work and the work with computers, Cahn explained that he would earn time dollars which would eventually pay for a computer of his own. Jimmy looked completely blank: was he feeling he had escaped or that nearly ninety hours is harsh? It was impossible to tell.

And there was no time to decide, because the judge was getting suddenly lyrical: 'We wish you and your mother all kinds of luck,' he said. The jurors looked solemn. 'The future will take all kinds of strength, but you are not alone any more and there are people here who believe in you.'

This was rather an exaggeration, but the jury obviously felt pleased with themselves. And as an outsider it was impossible to tell whether this was a travesty, or whether something exciting had been happening. The jurors clearly felt a sense of responsibility, and they may even have succeeded in helping Jimmy. As his mother said, it was up to him.

I asked Jimmy what he thought afterwards, and he gave me the acceptable answer: 'It has given me a chance to change my life,' he said, but then maybe it was true.

Inez agreed, and perhaps she should know. She was practically a jury-addict, having come along every time since the programme began its trial phase six months before. She had also been studying what she called Street Law in high school.

She skipped out of the room, and I witnessed a brief exchange which made me feel differently. As she passed Jimmy by the door, he said, 'Thanks'. It was a bit like the man on the rack thanking the Spanish Inquisition for making him taller.

'Why are you thanking me?' said Inez, embarrassed at her role as sixteen-year-old inquisitor.

'Oh, because you didn't sentence me to death or anything,' he said.

Why did that cheer me up? Perhaps because it crystallized my feeling that the process had made sense to Jimmy – even if from my position on the hideous green chairs it had seemed bizarre and confused. 'Like you said,' said Edgar, as we collected our papers. 'It isn't just about barter.' I wasn't sure I *had* said that, but it was certainly true, because Edgar Cahn is one of those old-fashioned specimens: a real radical. He sees his youth court as a way of undoing some of the damage caused by the 'proper' courts – for all their pompous attorneys, tough sentencing and white-faced social workers.

'It is clear that the message given by the legal system has reduced the issue of norms of acceptable behaviour to a question of risk aversion – about what the percentages are of getting caught, and what the consequences are of getting caught. The legal system is in fact sabotaging its own attempt to shape and affect people's behaviour.'

In other words, the criminal justice system was turning into a kind of money. Theft costs three years, murder costs fifteen, and the free market in its amoral way decides what you should and shouldn't do.

Once again we came back to the old-fashioned morality at the heart of time dollars. Time dollars are all about right and wrong, but they are also about inventing a kind of money which can make sure wasted resources – people's undervalued time and skills – get used more efficiently. And some of the biggest waste in Washington seems to be wasted youth.

'The Youth Court came about because it seemed a natural application of the principle of co-production,' Edgar told me later, during a brief attempt to interview him on tape. 'That means that those who are designated as problems are in fact assets. But for them to be re-classified as assets, they need to go through a process it was clear the legal system was not capable of generating. We need to redefine people as productive. We professionals keep defining other people by their defects, their needs, their liabilities and their problems. What time dollars are about is allowing people to redefine themselves as contributors.'

And so it was that one youngster a week – and later to be four a week – came before a jury of their peers and ended up drawn into a new kind of money. It's a strange idea, but it might be better than prison.

V

'It is physically impossible for a well-educated, intellectual, or brave man to make money the chief object of his thoughts,' wrote the great social and art critic John Ruskin in 1866. 'Just as it is for him to make his dinner the chief object of them. All healthy people like their dinners, but their dinner is not the main object of their lives. So all healthily-minded people like making money – ought to like it, and to enjoy the sensation of winning it: but the main object of their life is not money. It is something more than money.'

It is a neat way of describing a very traditional thought – that money and wealth are different things. What I so enjoyed about time dollars was the way they turn this whole argument on its head. Edgar Cahn calls for added emphasis on the non-monetary values of America – the love, compassion and neighbourliness which link people together, but then he invents a whole new kind of money to encourage them. And then he twists things even further by making the stuff of old money – clothes, food, computers – available for the new.

Amazing, when you think of it. But then, time dollars turn everything upside down. In the time dollar world, everybody is paid the same – corporate executives and great-grandmothers. Love and compassion suddenly become valuable commodities to be hunted down by Wall Street arbitragers. From that point of view, the 'real' world looks pretty crazy. You look at the great products of the dollar economy, and wonder why? Why, for example, Dunkin Donuts? Why Alton Towers or *Baywatch* or Quaver crisps or any of those other aspects of modern life whose purpose is unclear, but which the economy nonetheless strives to create?

These kinds of questions make Professor Cahn a deeply dangerous man. But he has an old-fashioned moral sense, and the system badly needs him. He may be wrong, but then nobody else has the slightest idea how to rescue Chicago's inner city schools or Washington's system of youth justice – let alone how to inject any kind of energy into them.

Of course there are great mountain ranges to climb yet for time dollars. They are well-established as a way of providing services to old people, but there may be difficulties if we extend them to other sectors of forgotten society. Will the tax authorities continue to zero-rate time dollars for tax if you can buy computers with them? Will they become so successful that pump-priming with computers isn't enough? Will handing them out to young people lower their value for everybody else? Or will time dollars act differently to other kinds of money? And where do they come from anyway? But behind all the sense of disbelief about the current money system, Edgar Cahn really wants to make people nicer. Time dollars are supposed to transform people, as they told me they did at Lincoln-Westmoreland.

'I don't really understand how they do, though,' I said to Edgar as we drove through Dupont Circle on my way back to Irene's lodgings. 'Why do they?'

'I don't know,' he said. 'I guess people want to be valued.'

Chapter 3

Philadelphia: money as burden

'Every day, I dance a fine line between my two identities: as the dedicated college chaplain working for modest wages and as the husband of a multi-millionaire . . .'
The Rev. Steve Keller, quoted in *More Than Money*.

I

The body of thirteen-year-old Shaline Seguinot was found, half-eaten by rats, on a piece of waste ground near her grandmother's house in Camden, New Jersey. It was 1995, and the tragic discovery launched one of New Jersey's occasional periods of breast-beating about a city where rats seem considerably more numerous than people. But then rats are almost the only inhabitants of Camden who are not afraid to come out at night. They probably peep across the Delaware river, rather as I did, and glimpse Philadelphia glittering in the sunlight on the other side. Like Liverpool and Birkenhead, Camden and Philadelphia are divided by a river, but they are linked by a busy bridge – named after Philadelphia's most famous inhabitant, the philosopher, printer, politician and money pioneer Benjamin Franklin. The two sides regard each other suspiciously from opposite banks.

Philadelphia is also divided in its perceptions. On the one hand it is William Penn's City of Brotherly Love. On the other, it is the place W. C. Fields mentioned on his deathbed: his famous last words were that 'on the whole' he would rather be in Philadelphia. I approached from the W. C. Fields aspect, via Camden, because I wanted to track down a successful time dollar bank there. I was set to be disappointed: they had abandoned the idea, but the reasons why it had failed were a surprise. It was as if Camden had decayed just too far.

Shaline Seguinot was Camden's thirty-sixth murder victim of the year in a city where getting on for one in a thousand of its 87,000 inhabitants end up murdered every year. There is an added reason for that. Until 1994, Camden played host to an unpleasant drugs cartel called the Sons of Malcolm X, who profited by buying up cocaine and heroin in New York and bringing them down to sell in Camden. Not to the locals, because they could barely afford it, but to wealthy New Jersey weekenders who would pop in and out in their shiny jeeps. It was a modern example of the well-known money maxim known as Gresham's Law: that bad money drives out good. It certainly does in Camden – and more widely: nearly every dollar bill in circulation now shows microscopic traces of cocaine.

But what was particularly unpleasant about this cartel was their initiation ceremony. New initiates had to carry out a killing: it didn't matter who – the first person you come across would do fine. On some nights the body count was as high as three, and others presumably accounted for a good number of Camden's frightening backlog of unsolved murders. The leaders of the Sons of Malcolm X are now inside, but their followers are still trading and their graffiti codewords are still splattered in paint on the walls. 'Life is so cheap here,' assistant district prosecutor Gregory Smith told *New Jersey Monthly* just before I arrived. 'They think other lives are cheap too.'

The current money system does not put a high value on Camden people, which is why it is one of the four poorest urban centres in the USA – maybe even *the* poorest. It is not just a city without money; it also lacks a rush hour. It has almost no energy. There is a shortage of almost everything except rats and wasteland. The remaining top-class supermarkets, restaurants and cinemas disappeared in a night of Hallowe'en arson a few years ago. About 60 per cent of the dwindling population are on welfare. For anybody like me who constantly fears they are about to descend into poverty and helplessness – the unspoken fear of all alternative economists – Camden provides a nasty little shiver. Because it wasn't always like this.

What happened? Race riots in 1969 and 1971, the disappearance of economic power to the big urban centres, the decline of manufacturing industry, and a vicious circle which drove away the inhabitants, taking their local tax revenues with them. Camden ran out of dollars, and became the kind of place where city employees are expected to bring their own lavatory paper to work and policemen are expected to provide their own cars.

The time bank I wanted to see was based at the old people's project attached to Our Lady of Lourdes Medical Center in the long suburb which links Camden to Collingwood and the slightly more wealthy towns around it. Even if the faintly Roman Catholic note in the hospital's name had not allowed me to deduce that the place was run by Franciscan nuns, the vast statue of the Virgin Mary on the roof probably would have given the game away. She stares out across the car parks and railway tracks beyond, past the blackened, empty warehouses, with the word KUNT spray-painted beautifully on the walls.

The Senior Services Center was a squat brown-framed building, which looked a little like the office for a mobile-home park. But inside, the place was filled with photos of smiling children, pieces of abandoned crochet, piles of new silver pencils, pictures of St Francis of Assisi and homely notices advising that 'If you're going to take just one step make it a giant step'. The elderly lady on reception looked at me with deep suspicion, but Christine Suriano – who runs the Helping Hands project I had come to see – ushered me in with a big smile, together with a great deal of unexpected information about her new cappuccino machine.

Christine had no fewer than seven children herself, and was tremendously generous with her time. But it became clear that, while Helping Hands was doing wonderful work with older people, they had abandoned the idea of local money and time dollars. 'Only seven people ever spent them in all the years we had been running it,' Christine told me. This was rather a blow. I had assumed my search would be downhill all the way, with endless examples of new kinds of money gushing forth in the most extreme places. I had hoped to write about 'funny money' driving the impoverished community of Camden in whole new ways. It was not to be.

But Helping Hands was operating and very successful, and any organization which depends on volunteers is a confusing idea for strict economists. Who is paying, after all? It is difficult to explain in terms of market economics a seventy-year-old who comes out in the snow to drive her next-door neighbour to the library. Where is the hidden hand of the market? Who is maximizing their self-interest here?

And how do you explain one of Christine's star volunteers: a ninety-five-year-old who goes out of her way to help three mentally handicapped women visit the supermarket every week? It is an evocative example of how self-help works – and no money changes hands whatsoever. In some ways, these particular visits were too successful, because they had led to disputes about exactly who was helping who. 'I thought I was going to push the trolley,' said the old lady plaintively after their first visit.

Helping Hands goes back to 1988, when New Jersey latched on to the time dollars idea. The governor, Thomas H. Kean, found himself demanding time dollars during his State of the State address – so of course it had to go ahead. Camden was one of four centres funded in New Jersey. Each one was found an office, given a director and a computer and told to get on with it. Camden's programme director Dr Ruth Salmon told the local papers that the idea would save the state money: 'Many elderly patients could leave in-patient care sooner if doctors knew they could come back for their shots,' she said. She was right. Rutgers University, which still has a base in Camden, studied Helping Hands a few years later and found that 28 per cent of people taking part in it would have otherwise been in nursing homes or using some other expensive public programme.

By then the state was getting cold feet and an even colder budget. The money was withdrawn and three of the four centres promptly closed their doors. But Helping Hands would not give up without a fight. The local charitable trust Pew – run by the descendants of the founder of Sun Oil – came up with some good old-fashioned dollars. The only problem was that they were getting disillusioned by the idea of 'money'. 'It was moving very quickly, but not because of the concept of service credits,' said Christine. 'It was moving quickly because of the needs of the frail elderly. We would go out and recruit volunteers and then tell them about the wonderful world of service credits. And they were saying: "Well, that's OK – but I really just want to help old people". They would say: "Oh, don't worry about those for me". We came to the point where so many volunteers were giving their credits back to us, because they were under age or they had no one to give them to, so that we were putting them back in our so-called bank. It sometimes almost inhibited people's desire to volunteer with us.'

'Was this anything to do with Camden?' I asked.

'No, and I'll tell you why. Because we're nothing to do with Camden – and it *is* terrible.'

Then actually, in a roundabout way, this did have something to do with it. Although their elderly 'clients' mainly lived in Camden – and 40 per cent of them have an income of under $10,000 – all but five volunteers lived somewhere else. 'The volunteers are not people in need themselves,' said Christine. 'They are from outside the city and they don't need service credits. They don't need to call someone and say "I need a ride".' This was pure charity. Nothing wrong with that, of course, but this was not a community conjuring money out of thin air.

Nobody seemed to be calling at all, just now. Normally Christine's office was organizing about forty hours of volunteer work a week. Without them, life could be seriously bleak: especially if you are an eighty-five-year-old at home, partly recovered from surgery, and wondering how you can get your shopping and see the doctor. 'Do you know, I cannot believe this is Monday,' said Christine, listening to the suddenly silent telephones and wondering about their 190 or so recipients. 'This almost feels like Friday.'

Helping Hands is admirable and inspiring, but it is not generating a new kind of money because it is not at the heart of a geographical community. It is, instead, part of the long-running battle to get Camden's poorest people to turn up for their medical appointments. Some clinics try giving grocery coupons worth £10 to the people who turn up. Our Lady of Lourdes uses volunteers to drive them.

Yet even this is a kind of wealth, as the Helping Hands leaflet says: 'The ordinary little things like mowing the lawn, going to the grocery store, sharing a cup of coffee with a friend. You can't put a price on things like these.' And if you put a dollar price on them, the chances are nobody will be able to afford them anyway.

II

Americans have no compunction about phrases like 'you can't put a price on things like these'. Their British equivalents would worry in case this might be too gushing, or even paradoxically that it seems so enthusiastic that it must be cynically ironic. Two great American concerns – an absolute obsession about what they eat, and a laudable but slightly exaggerated concern not to stereotype people – were very much in evidence in the Camden Senior Services Center.

To keep people informed about the first, they had fascinating sheets on the walls about 'Ten Foods You Should Never Eat'. Soup from Campbell's, the local employer, had been included on the list, because of the amount of salt in the recipe. As for the second, Christine had developed a programme called Come And Walk in My Shoes – funded by a charity with the down-to-earth title of the Campbell Soup Foundation for Doers. The idea was to help health professionals, and especially doctors if they turned up, to understand what it is like being old. This involves getting them in a room, providing them with ear plugs to interfere with their hearing, taping round their glasses so that they can only see very narrowly, putting pieces of corn in their shoes, and tape round their fingers – then making them fill out a very complicated form. Sometimes they even tie them to wheelchairs. The shock can give the nurses, doctors and hospital bureaucrats a kind of claustrophobic panic, Christine told me proudly.

We were driving back into Camden for a closer look at the forgotten city, past the shuttered shops in the main road downtown. Some of them had been closed for so long that they were bricked up and overgrown. Abandoned tram-lines and cobbles still showed under the shattered tarmac in the street.

Maybe what was so shocking about Camden was the complete absence of any gentrification. Trickle-down economics might not work, but at least it keeps neighbourhoods from disappearing out of the economy altogether. Here the high-rise flats – built originally as penthouse apartments with river views – were now student accommodation or subsidized flats for old people. Knowing the way life is in cities like this, the students and old people were probably put next-door to each other. They were dangerous places too. 'I make sure I never go beyond the lobby,' said Christine.

'Why?' I asked. I was used to East End high-rise flats which were the other way round: their elderly inhabitants in London are too frightened to go outside.

'It's not safe in the elevators,' she said.

Beyond the high-rises was North Camden, Camden's slumland, and it was like nothing I have ever seen. These were original slums, brick and wood-built terraces, sometimes just wood. In Liverpool and Glasgow they would long since have been flattened by well-meaning architects and borough engineers, some of whom a generation ago could not see a poor neighbourhood without sending in the bulldozers and imposing modern concrete versions of the slums. But the neglect in Camden was almost complete: this area had never even been redeveloped. At least a quarter of the neighbourhood seemed now to be wasteland. Many of the houses, especially on the ends of rows, were burnt out or battened down, boarded up, and covered in an infestation of graffiti. One piece of distinguishable graffiti read: 'You can't come around here no more Paul'. Who was Paul? And where was he now?

'They're very frightened,' said Christine. Some of the houses had verandas which the tenants had entirely closed off behind bars, like a moth-eaten penitentiary. Fat men sat motionless on elderly chairs watching us. Children stared at us in the street, where the weeds pushed high above them through the pavements.

There were occasional signs of effort. New mini police stations had opened in the neighbourhood, known as 'sub-stations', as if they were something to do with the power supply. One house carried a massive notice announcing that it was the office of 'Concerned Citizens for North Camden'. It was this group which had recently tried and failed to set up another time dollar project for the area.

I had the cuttings. The North Camden Exchange found there was too little in the way of community to build on. More successful was the companion project, known as the North Camden Land Trust, set up to provide a home repair service to locals – who are particularly prey to cheapskate builders and fraudsters. Most of the 87,000 people who live here are virtually red-lined by insurance companies, and mortgages and home improvement loans are next to impossible, and they have to rely on what they can get.

We drove back across the city, past the forgotten tram-lines again to an even older terraced neighbourhood in an even more advanced stage of decay. This used to be Camden's Polish sector; now it just housed anybody who could no longer afford to escape. Among those was one of Helping Hand's eighty-something clients, and we drove slowly past her house, looking battered and exposed beside another burnt-out wreck next-door. Neighbours with the skimpiest mini-skirts imaginable were eating something out of plastic bags on their front doorsteps. Every window and door was grilled, yet the streets were colourful: Camden people may live in neighbourhoods so run down that you could grass them over, but at least they have bright-coloured paint.

Camden's single largest employer is no longer industry, it is health. That makes Our Lady of Lourdes – with its beige walls and large chapel – one of the city's last remaining sources of wealth. And in a city where getting on for 70 per cent of school-kids never finish high school, the hospital has played a leading role developing a whole new kind of school for teenagers who want to join the great health industry. They called this a medical-arts high school, and it provides a professional health-focused school education. For its first year, the hospital rented them space for $1 a year. Now the school is independent, with 400 pupils and a zero drop-out rate, which by Camden standards is a run-away success.

The hospital is almost an industry in itself, with a range of medical services which even includes 'wholistic prayer retreats'. I wondered why they spelled 'holistic' with a W. Maybe the nuns felt that anything to do with holes was a little indecent. I took one of their range of free publications, called *Health Talk*, packed with fascinating articles with titles like 'Getting a Handle on Irritable Bowel Syndrome'. Did you know, for example, that 11,400 American children under five are seriously injured every year falling out of shopping trolleys?

So there we were back at Our Lady of Lourdes, and I was encouraged to find that Dr Ruth Poh – who as Ruth Salmon had raised the money to keep Helping Hands going – was still a strident supporter of Edgar Cahn's ideas. She was one of those fiercely intelligent and intense American women, a little frightening in her swivel chair, with the prestigious 1995 Foster G. McGaw Award – for improving health in local communities – behind her. 'The time dollars currency is human beings – it's humanity,' she told me. 'That's what I like about it. And if you are talking about America 150 years ago, there would be no need for time dollars – people were doing this kind of thing anyway.'

That's the point. But you need some kind of social infrastructure, some kind of community, something beyond an alienating patch of waste ground and rats, to get a bank going again – and in the case of Camden, it may not be possible. Even so, volunteering is now suddenly the political flavour in the USA – where ninety-three million Americans donate twenty billion hours a year. A conference in Philadelphia in 1997 on the subject attracted President Clinton, and his predecessors Carter and Bush, who all then paraded before the cameras helping to clean up an eight-mile stretch of dilapidated Germantown Avenue. There was no sign of Reagan.

The event was highlighted by Clinton's request for £2.5 billion for one million volunteer reading tutors for children, and there was nationwide publicity about how young men are 40 per cent less likely to use drugs if they have some kind of 'mentor'. There was also coverage of the demonstrating students who joined in the conference with placards saying 'Don't volunteer me!'. The sad fact is that, although many of us are richer in money, we are – with our double incomes and childcare and commuting – poverty-stricken as far as time is concerned.

So what can you do about a place like Camden? You can send in volunteers to some extent, but can they possibly deal with the weight of need? Can cities which have run out of cash carry on running down for ever, or does there come a point when the weeds and rats take over? It is an intractable problem. Back in 1965, one mayor of Philadelphia had a go at bombing one particularly intractable ghetto from the air – rather like George Bush's treatment of Baghdad. The mayor was enthusiastically re-elected.

III

Former US vice-president Dan Quayle thinks the famous abortion test case 'Roe versus Wade' was the choice Washington faced when he took his troops across the Delaware river – so goes the old joke. These days there is really no choice at all: to cross the Delaware to get to Philadelphia, you drive over the Benjamin Franklin bridge.

It is a journey from one extreme to another, from the problems of having too little money to the problems of having too much. A million Americans are set to inherit $1 million or more in the next twenty years. A terrifying $8 trillion – the net worth of all Americans over fifty – will be passing from one generation to the next in the next thirty years or so. This is either a bounteous gift from one generation to another or a frightening burden. Probably it's a bit of both.

You can see immediately that Philadelphia is a successful city by the two towers which first broke the height restrictions there – Liberty One and Liberty Two – glinting in the morning mist. It is a conservative kind of place too, with its European-style narrow streets, its obsessive sense of history and its Quaker beginnings with William Penn, whose hat on top of City Hall marked the broken height restriction.

I had first heard about Ellen Deacon – who gives advice to people who inherit large and challenging sums of money – back in London. I was fascinated by the idea of money as a problem, and had arranged to meet her. Not only was she an experienced counsellor about issues of this kind, but she had also inherited several hundred thousand dollars herself in her twenties – which had been a serious shock, especially when she had been devoting her life to battling for social justice.

More and more people on both sides of the Atlantic are choosing to think more carefully about their wealth, making sure it is invested in ways that make the world a better place – or at least do not make it any worse. A group of New England Methodists set the ball rolling in 1971 during the Vietnam War by setting up the Pax World mutual fund, which did not invest in weapons. Now it's worth $9 billion. In the UK, ethical investment began formally in 1984 with Friends Provident. Their ethical unit trust was known in the City as the 'Brazil Fund' because it was considered a little 'nutty', but in its first year it was in the top ten performers and now there is £2.2 billion invested ethically in Britain.

The Impact Project goes further. It began when a Boston couple, Christopher Mogil and Anne Slepian, inherited a large sum in the late 1970s. They gave some of it away, and used more to set up a small foundation to work with people who have philanthropy thrust upon them. 'Many years ago, the three of us had inherited wealth drop into our lives,' wrote Christopher and his colleagues in the first edition of their newsletter *More Than Money*. 'Although we were certainly excited, we also felt isolated.'

The first time Christopher Mogil realized he had inherited a great deal of money was in 1978, when his stockbroker's secretary phoned in case he had any questions about his portfolio. 'I was haunted by the question of why I should have this privilege,' he wrote. 'I wondered whether I was selfish, pampering myself and avoiding my own insecurities about working. At bottom was a fairly simple question: should I give away my wealth?'

But it wasn't until eight years later, at a conference run by the ethical Haymarket People's Fund in Boston, that anybody else asked the same question. 'There was stunned silence, except for my pounding heart,' he wrote. 'I raised my hand and was excited to find others raise theirs also. Four of us met that afternoon to exchange stories.' It was the beginning of a long search to find others like them, and the result was a very unusual book, *We Gave Away a Fortune*. It includes people like Millard Fuller, the founder of Habitat for Humanity, who gave away everything he had earned. Or Procter & Gamble heir Robbie Gamble. Or Ben Cohen, of Ben & Jerry's ice cream, who tries to give away as much as he spends, and has done so since 1986 when he gave away $500,000 of stock to launch the Ben & Jerry's Foundation. Even the TV mogul Ted Turner gave away $1 billion to UN projects.

'I was cared for by a black woman named Gussie from the South Side of Chicago,' wrote Edorah Frazer, a teacher who gave away $450,000 – 75 per cent of her inheritance – in her twenties. 'She worked for my family from before I was born until I was in high school. I always noticed that her clothes were different and that she rode the bus while we drove. My first awareness of class differences came from her presence in our household.'

Edorah gave away her wealth in piles of share certificates two days before Christmas. 'Outside it was raining, and across the street I saw two Salvation Army men with a bucket ringing a bell. The rain was falling on me and I started to cry. It felt really clean, so simple. Although I was happy, I thought: I'm lonely. I wish I had done this with someone. Then immediately I thought:

''No, it's good that I did it alone, because it is a very individual act.'' Ultimately I am alone in this decision. It's my story. I crossed the street, took out all the money in my wallet and put it into the Salvation Army bucket.'

Most of them seem to have found giving away their money a liberating experience. As one of them said: 'It felt like the equivalent of finding a wallet on the street and giving it back to its rightful owner.' But it was also sometimes a fearful experience, as the cushion of money disappeared and they had to rely on themselves like everybody else.

'I would advise wealthy people to give to the point where they become anxious,' wrote John Steiner, who gave away most of the fortune from toy-making he inherited from his father. 'In a state of discomfort, there's a kind of questioning that goes on that's beyond the intellectual level, and that's where growth occurs.'

We Gave Away a Fortune is unexpectedly moving. As an heir you often can't trust anybody; your friends behave oddly to you; sometimes the terms of the inheritance give you less control over your money than your shadowy trustees or accountants. 'I started crying when I read about the Impact Project,' says an Arizona supporter. 'I've been dealing with my inherited wealth since I was twenty-one; now I'm sixty-four. For the first time I don't feel alone.'

It also leaves the heirs with a serious difficulty at parties. How do they answer the inevitable question, 'What do you do?' Often the ultra-rich don't 'do' anything, which makes it harder to define their place and role in the world – especially to themselves. *More Than Money* gives a range of options if you are a multi-millionaire faced with a question like that:

(a) Avoid the question ('Oh my god, do you smell smoke?')

(b) Proclaim the obvious: 'I'm a civilian.'

(c) Act as if it were still the sixties: 'I do whatever I feel like, man.'

(d) Lie: (In the heat of summer) 'I'm a ski instructor.' (In January) 'I'm a roofer.'

The Impact Project is consciously applying the teachings of many of the great world religions which unanimously advise giving. For Jews this is *Tzedakah*, for Hindus *Dan*, for Buddhists *Dana*. And the point all of them make is that giving is supposed to be something to do with joy rather than duty. 'Since giving brings a greater return to the giver than to the person who receives a gift, a person should not give until it hurts, but rather give until it quits hurting,' wrote one correspondent in *More Than*

Money. It's a paradox, and they make the most of it: giving money away makes you wealthy, they say.

IV

Ellen Deacon met me in a flowery patterned dress and a middle-aged Toyota – neither of which gave much sign that she had also inherited a considerable sum of money herself from her family's animal feed company in Texas. It's a strange paradox that radicals who believe in the perfectibility of everyone also seem to be extremely suspicious of me – though I almost certainly imagine this. But Ellen very kindly said she would take me to a coffee bar where we could talk, and on a quick tour of the city on our way.

We went down the straight streets past Independence Hall where the Declaration of Independence was signed and past City Hall, where a small demonstration against dangerous homeless hostels was meandering its way towards the city officials, shouting and carrying placards with the slogan 'IS IT BETTER TO DIE BY FIRE OR ICE?'. This was a reference to the poem by Robert Frost about the best way of ending the universe. Ice 'would suffice', he said. Philadelphia must be a civilized place if even demonstrators chanted poems. I was impressed.

But there was more evidence of Philadelphia's civilization. The demonstration was escorted by four plain-clothes policemen and women, who stood out from the crowd because of their expensive clothes. And, if you missed the clothes, they were wearing armbands which said POLICE. These were part of the city's unique Demonstration Protection Squad, set up to prevent trouble without provoking it. Bringing up the rear was a tall black policeman, walking with military straightness, sporting an enormous handlebar moustache and a white Homburg hat. Ellen was fascinated and searched the faces of the demonstrators and escort for anyone she knew. You can always tell old radicals by this habit.

As we drove on past the yellow stone steps of the Philadelphia Museum of Art, where Sylvester Stallone did his training in the first of the Rocky films, Ellen suddenly asked: 'What class are you?' I was astonished. I don't think anybody – even in supposedly class-obsessed England – had ever asked me such a question before.

'Wow!' I said as I thought quickly to myself. The term 'middle class' means something slightly different in the US: Roseanne is middle class. I claimed not to know: 'I'm not used to being asked that so directly. People try not to mention it in England.'

Ellen looked pleased by this response, and said that – although I probably had less than two pennies to rub together – I was still 'Owning Class'. Not that I own anything: the building society owns my flat. And, let's be frank, I probably couldn't give my car away for free, or most of my clothes. My fridge is older than I am, and shudders horribly every ten minutes. I suppose I own my television. But there is a flaw in this defence, because I did go to an English public school. Ellen nodded knowingly: 'Class is about more than money,' she said.

Her key concern is to show people that, even in supposedly classless America, class is everywhere. And until you accept your own class and feel comfortable with it, you can't really accept anybody for who they are either. Since one of the many aspects of American culture which Americans are proud of is its lack of class-consciousness, I felt Ellen's task to introduce it was likely to be uphill. But it is important, she says, because this hidden class-consciousness hardens people. And it trains them at a deep level to make money in brutal ways, to ride roughshod over people for class reasons.

'It is terrifying and confusing to have more than you need in a world where many people have much less than they need,' she said, speaking slowly over our cup of Starbucks coffee near the university. And that's where the class system steps in to train people differently to avoid these discomforts. 'Sometimes it is an overt and deliberate kind of change as we have in certain parts of American society or you had in the class system in England, where people are put through a deliberate educational process. Let's take a hypothetical English boy, who's taken from home at the age of six, seven or eight to this very hard place, and where over a period of the next ten years or so, he is first treated very harshly and then given a new privileged identity. In return for that, he learns to do things in the way in which they "ought" to be done. That's perpetuating a whole set of attitudes and values that are wholly exploitative of most of the people in the world. Rich people have more than they need because they equate not having with fear.'

I don't know about the brainwashing aspect. I was sent away to school, but I was also encouraged to learn for myself. On the other hand, Ellen was undoubtedly right that the mega-rich are often so because of a morbid fear of poverty. The more they manage to amass, the more insecure they get.

'Excessive wealth is perhaps harder to endure than excessive poverty,' wrote Heinrich Heine, who was evidently a member of the Impact Project in an earlier existence. 'The poor devil who has too little and who cannot help himself, may there convince himself that there is a man who is far more tormented because he has too much money, because all the money in the world flows into his cosmopolite, giant pockets, and because he must drag such a burden about, while all around the great mob of starving men and thieves stretch forth to him their hands. And what terrible and dangerous hands!'

Ellen grew up in a small Texas town, oblivious to this problem. 'I didn't understand anything about the fact that my father was the owner of the business who hired other people's fathers to work. Or that our family collectively employed them,' she told me. Her grandfather – a chicken farmer's son – had started the business during the Depression, and now it was owned by the descendants as partners. The four children in her generation have very different values, receive a percentage from a family partnership and have to fight through their differences about every money decision. 'It's just a wild thing,' said Ellen with a sigh.

'These are things which people can change and often do, but we're not given much background – often we don't find out about it till somebody dies. Then all of a sudden: Hey! you've got three million dollars. I felt terrified, guilty and confused by the whole thing.'

When she tried to refuse to pay taxes in protest against the Vietnam War, her family was horrified. They were involved in critical negotiations at the time with the tax authorities, and were afraid this would upset them. 'I was furious and I went through a process of examining all of this, and I considered saying "fine!" and giving it all away and saying "OK, I'll live in poverty for the rest of my life". And the reason I didn't do that was because it didn't feel like a real thing either. I had to figure it out. I couldn't let go of it until I figured out what this is – and that decision led to everything else.'

Ellen had met Christopher Mogil and Anne Slepian in the late 1970s, while they were all grappling with their inherited wealth, and they asked her to work with them in the Impact Project. 'The crux of the problem is ignorance, confusion, isolation – above all isolation – nobody to talk to: the only information or advice I was given was by people whose attitudes I didn't trust and whose values were different from mine,' she said.

So is money a bad thing? One of the divisions between wealth counsellors around the USA seems to be their attitude to this question.

'I think money is a valuable tool,' said Ellen. 'But you can't get more money than you need without taking other people's value away from them. That means people kicking people out of jobs when there is no way they can go anywhere else, at the age of fifty or sixty, and then getting bonuses of millions of dollars for doing that – and that is absolutely obscene. It's not really that I have the solution. It's just that I have an idea about what's gone wrong and I have somewhere I'd like to go, and getting there is a very complex process – not at all straightforward. It requires really understanding that everybody has been fundamentally damaged by being part of this – it doesn't matter if they have got the power or the short end of the stick.'

V

Waterfront developments like the one in Philadelphia, opposite Camden's new aquarium, are all descendants of the project which started them all, the Baltimore Harborplace. It had restaurants, shopping, museums and an antique ship – the USS *Constellation*, the first warship in the US Navy – and it was tremendously successful. In its first year of operation, it attracted more than eighteen million people, more than Disney World in Florida, and it made James Rouse the most sought-after developer in the world. He was called in to advise on waterfronts all the way from New York to Sydney. As we know now, the Harborplace style tends to leave out the people who most need regenerating. Like the London Docklands, it tends to leave the locals no better off, but attracts instead hordes of yuppies with windsurf boards and a penchant for bright blue and yellow paint.

But all that was in the future. Rouse had by then invented a new kind of shopping mall and coined the phrase 'urban renewal'. He was soon to invent the 'Festival Marketplace', soon to be invited into Manchester by the English Tourist Board, and soon to inspire the world of planning with the idea that arty hustle and bustle might bring more money than factories and a docile workforce. Even so, it was a message which took a long time to take hold, particularly in Philadelphia. A decade ago, the *Philadelphia City Paper* was complaining that getting a new arts centre for the city was 'like pulling hens' teeth, getting blood from a turnip, bringing horses to water and getting them to drink all at the same time'.

Being the world's most imaginative developer made Rouse an extremely rich man, but by the time he died in 1996 – leaving behind a message for his memorial service that he had 'just left on my trip to the next life' – he had also won for himself a reputation for 'unusual' views about money. At the height of his power, after the success of Baltimore's Harborplace, he resigned his job as chief executive of the company which carried his name, and set up a foundation dedicated to building affordable housing for poor people. He moved into a simple house in his first success, the new village of Columbia.

Rouse also devoted himself to building a religious organization, based in Washington, called the Ministry of Money, aimed at helping people get to their deepest negative feelings about it and feel a little better. The prescription was, and still is, a series of workshops and pilgrimages to poverty-stricken places. 'Money is a paradox,' they say. 'It enslaves, yet it also frees.' Maybe that is what they meant when they called one of their workshop seminars 'Hearing the Cry of the Affluent'.

Looking at Philadelphia in this light, you can see both of Rouse's influences very clearly. The cry of the affluent is there in the manic freeways and advertisements, but there is a water-front too – a museum, a fleet of antique ships and a large statue of Christopher Columbus for sitting around eating sandwiches. I made straight for the Seaport Museum, celebrating a city built by sea power and commerce, ever since William Penn followed here in the wake of Henry Hudson in 1682. Thousands of people from Camden and Philadelphia were employed in the Camden shipyard until 1967, the immigrants poured through here, war-ships were riveted into life and hundreds of dour commuters packed into the dark twentieth-century ferries. But not any more. Such is the power of changing capital that the two Liberty towers are tributes instead to the modern power of television and media money.

The museum looked almost deserted, except for a small band of schoolchildren wearing T-shirts with the slogan 'Yo! Philadel-phia'. And there was a warning from Penn carved into the foun-tain on the way in: 'He that would reap and not labour must faint with the wind and perish in disappointment'. Which seemed an ironic thought for a complex almost certainly built partly with lottery money. The fountain had another big notice which said 'NO WADING'.

The museum was beautifully laid out, and evocative rather than informative in the way of most modern museums, full of sights, noises, smells and photos blown up to enormous size – but very few facts. But the memorial to Columbus was a stainless steel monstrosity. And in case any of us had forgotten who he was, it said round the base in big capitals: 'CHARISMATIC LEADER, NATURALIST, MATHEMATICIAN, CARTOGRAPHER' – all of which is pretty good for a man who thought he had discovered China and ended up, according to some stories, buried under a pool room in a bar in Valladolid.

But if the museum and statue glowed with Harborplace optimism, the historic ships were in a sorry state. USS *Olympia*, the cruiser which opened fire in Manila Bay during the Spanish-American War, was painted in a strange beige, but it didn't cover up the fact that the ship was almost rusting away. Great tears of rust seemed to be pouring down her side; pieces of hardboard covered up missing parts of the fabric. 'You see, in the mother country, you take care of your heritage,' said George, the curator in overalls I tagged behind to see around the ship. I thought of Twyford Downs and felt a tinge of embarrassment.

On the other hand, I was delighted to find that you could stand on the very spot where Commodore Dewey said his famous words – probably the most famous words in the US Navy. But prepare for a disappointment because his speech was hardly Nelsonian: there was no 'England expects', no 'There seems to be something wrong with our bloody ships today'. Dewey just said: 'You may fire when ready, Gridley'. Mundane as they were, the words were carved in gold with the date: 1 May 1898.

There wasn't much that was honourable about the Spanish-American War, but for a moment the *Olympia* did seem to be a memorial to the days before absolutely everything was measured in money. But maybe that was a bit of a delusion. The war had, after all, been drummed up by William Randolph Hearst to sell more newspapers.

So I walked back across the freeway, over the remains of the rest of Philadelphia's docks, filled in and now providing the foundations for three hideous tower blocks, pointless empty places full of broken Budweiser bottles – and after just a hundred yards or so, I was in the middle of the historic city. Here were the beginnings of US government and US money. And here they signed the Declaration of Independence. You can visit the very room: almost every American schoolkid has done so.

I know this is heresy in Philadelphia, but I find it hard to generate quite the reverence I am supposed to for the founders of the USA. I find myself imagining this set of peculiar old farmers in high dudgeon, stomping around with their quill pens and beefy wives. 'There,' said John Hancock, as he signed the Declaration. 'I guess King George will be able to read that.' I could almost see it, as I stared through the sedate windows of Independence Hall.

I wonder what the signatories would have thought if they knew they would all have Polaris missile submarines named after them.

Here Congress met for the first and second time, by which time fighting had already broken out with British troops. Philadelphia let the Congress slip through its fingers just a few years later, when troops demanding back-pay – money again – surrounded the state house in 1783. American government slipped off to Princeton, then Annapolis, then Trenton, and then New York City, came back briefly to Philadelphia before finally ending up on the patch of swampy ground they now call Washington DC.

In Philadelphia you can also see the façade of the First Bank of the United States, with its eighteenth-century columns, and the Bicentennial Bell, forged in London in 1976 and rung twice a day at 11 a.m. and 3 p.m. And the Philadelphia Bank, with the kind of mid-Victorian lettering you find in St Paul's Cathedral or on memorials for the dead of the Indian Mutiny. The Philadelphia Bank needed preserving more than most: its failure in the 1857 panic almost ruined the city, and was much remarked on by Charles Dickens during his visit here a few years later. I was glad to see it still standing – a reminder of a long American tradition of bank crashes which continues to this day.

Around the corner is another very important spot for anybody seeking out the soul of American money: the site of Alexander Hamilton's office. Hamilton was the first US Treasury Secretary. He dreamed dreams of power and high finance, many of which came to pass, and was author of the compromise which took the US capital to Washington. He died relatively young, fighting a duel with the devious former vice-president, Aaron Burr, who was furious about his frustrated ambition to be Governor of New York. I wandered past Hamilton's bursting tomb later, in Wall Street, but the site of his office was marked rather inappropriately by a big ivy bush.

And here is the Liberty Bell – appropriately enough, perhaps, given that money has become the guarantor of freedom across the globe – with its great crack down one side. Like Independence Hall, I found it hard to get excited about. For one thing, it was made in Whitechapel, which – though perfectly respectable in itself – is about as American as the Roast Beef of Old England, and better known for producing Jack the Ripper. For another, nobody seems to remember what its historic significance was.

'What is it actually?' I had asked Ellen earlier, as we drove past the glass structure which houses it, packed with tourists touching the piece of old metal with reverence. 'I suppose it's something terribly anti-British?'

'Well, absolutely,' she said, but a few seconds later I couldn't remember her explanation.

The explanation of the uniformed official inside the building was equally forgettable. 'What is it?' I asked her, with a gesture towards it.

'It's a bell,' she said.

The truth is that the Liberty Bell was rather an obscure metallic object for producing a ringing noise, and then it was adopted as an anti-slavery symbol in the 1850s. But then symbols are important and have a value beyond anything which might be written on the face. Look at banknotes.

VI

'The universal regard for money is the one hopeful fact in our civilization,' wrote George Bernard Shaw in the preface to his play *Major Barbara*. 'It represents health, strength, honour, generosity and beauty, as conspicuously and undeniably as the want of it represents illness, weakness, disgrace, meanness and ugliness.' Shaw was enjoying shocking the sensibilities of his middle-class audience, by saying how they might have behaved, even if it wasn't how they thought – still less admitted. He may well have visited Philadelphia and Camden: I don't know, but if he had he might have underscored the point.

'The first duty of every citizen is to insist on having money on reasonable terms,' Shaw went on, and his influence on us all is only too apparent at the other end of his century. 'The crying need of the nation is not for better morals, cheaper bread, temperance, liberty, culture, redemption of fallen sisters and erring brothers, not the grace, love and fellowship of the Trinity, but simply for enough money.'

Benjamin Franklin, Philadelphia's most famous son, would have agreed completely, but he had his own solution – he printed more of it. He is thus a key figure in the American ability to conjure money out of nothing, and downtown Philadelphia – where Uncle Sam meets Covent Garden – is a round-the-clock celebration of American beginnings which seems to resurrect him round every corner. There are 'Fun with Franklin' entertainments for kids. There are celebrations of 'Ben Franklin's greatest hits' ('Young, middle-aged and Old Wise Statesman Ben sings about work, politics and life in Philadelphia. Running time: twenty-five minutes. Venue: Second Bank of the US').

In 1729 at the age of just twenty-three, Benjamin Franklin

wrote a little book with a long title, *A Modest Inquiry into the Nature and Necessity of Paper Currency*. Two years later he had a go at printing some himself for the first time. It wasn't actually his idea. Americans had been experimenting with money since arriving on the *Mayflower*, and settled eventually on tobacco, which had great advantages – you could grow it, after all – but it had some disadvantages too. One of these was that the colonial governments were endlessly attempting to limit its production. Another was that people tended to smoke the good money, and use the lung-wrenching stuff for paying debts. Bad money, as Gresham's Law says, drives out good.

The first paper money emerged in the Massachusetts Bay Colony in 1690. The notes were issued to soldiers back from an unsuccessful raid on Quebec, and each one promised an eventual redemption in gold and silver coins. It occurred to the colonists that printing money could cause a little mild inflation, which stopped prices falling and seemed to make everybody a little better off. Franklin was an enthusiastic supporter of the idea. His *Pennsylvania Gazette* apologized for not appearing on time because he was 'with the Press, labouring for the publick Good, to make Money more plentiful'.

'About this time there was a cry among people for more paper money, only fifteen thousand pounds being extant in the province, and that soon to be sunk,' wrote Franklin in his autobiography immediately before the Revolution. 'I was on the side of an addition, being persuaded that the first small sum struck in 1723 had done much good by increasing the trade, employment, and number of inhabitants in the province, since I now saw all the old houses inhabited and many new ones building: whereas I remembered well, that when I first walked about the streets of Philadelphia, eating my roll, I saw most of the houses . . . with bills on their doors "To be let".'

The richer people thought this was a terrible idea, of course – for the same reasons that they have ever since. Partly because they wanted their debts repaid in 'proper' coins and partly because the resulting inflation would lower the value of what they were owed. Back in London, Parliament banned the American colonists from printing money, and in 1766 Franklin defended the idea in person in the House of Commons. He failed to persuade them, and the rest – as they say – is history.

To find the centre of the continuing, bubbling Franklin industry, the spot he carried on printing in his later years and the 'Good House' he dreamed about during all his years in London, you have to walk down an alleyway and into 'Franklin Court'.

It is rather a sad story, in fact. Ben Franklin's wife waited for him for fifteen long years, while he was in London putting the case for the states of Pennsylvania and Massachusetts. She finally died in 1774, just weeks before his return.

And here it all is laid out before you, together with a succession of tourists and a number of women of varying shapes and ages dressed in yellow eighteenth-century dresses, and with what looked like lace handkerchiefs on their heads. But I was in for a slight disappointment. Franklin's house had been demolished by his grandchildren in 1812, and what you actually get to see is a big white frame showing where the house used to stand and some piles of bricks – one of which turned out to be the remains of his bathroom.

Not that this was an unimportant spot. Franklin spent a great deal of time there, having a warm bath every day to relieve the pain from his gallstones. I listened to the story of these being enthusiastically delivered by one of the young women in Ben Franklin costume with a peculiar accent which I couldn't place. It sounded almost like Somerset. I was intrigued and listened to her telling the admiring Americans around her that she came from London and missed her family. At first I thought this was part of the act which went with the costume, but I realized after a few fond reminiscences that this was definitely late twentieth-century homesickness.

After some weeks in the USA, I was beginning to have fond memories of London myself. It is amazing how the memory of life in London can grow on you while you are abroad, even traffic wardens, chemical smog, Prime Minister's Question Time and drunks spewing up on the Underground. So I told her we were fellow-citizens. This news did not seem very welcome, and when I asked her what part of London she came from, she was positively embarrassed.

'Er, Suffolk,' she said. I was gripped by the kind of embarrassment you feel when you unwittingly catch somebody out in a minor fib.

'Where do *you* come from?' she asked.

'Oh, Crystal Palace.'

She looked nervous for a moment: 'Very posh.'

But as any Londoner knows, Crystal Palace is about as posh as Alexandra Palace or the Hackney Empire. I smiled reassuringly. I suddenly worried that she might be completely bonkers, and – as in *Fatal Attraction* – break into my home and boil my rabbit, so I escaped downstairs quickly. Why downstairs? Because in the absence of Franklin's actual home, the Philadelphia decision-makers have built a large underground bunker packed with unusual exhibits about Franklin's life. There are a number of the kind of things you expect in a museum: knives and forks, old telescopes, ancient letters and shopping lists, but also a large model complete with a sound and light show to dramatize Ben Franklin's confrontation with the House of Commons. And, strangest of all, a bank of fifty telephones on sticks, known as the 'Franklin Exchange'. Using these phones you can dial up historic people from the past, and hear what they have to say about the man whose basement we were in.

I dialled D. H. Lawrence on 041 249 3422, which seemed to me to be a Glasgow number, but still. A recorded voice in an unconvincing English Midlands accent accused Franklin of trying to 'take away my dark freedom'. John Keats was no more complimentary. Franklin was 'full of mean and thrifty maxims', he said. I also dialled David Hume, the famous Scottish philosopher, and found myself listening to a woman with an Irish accent.

The reason for their complaints was Franklin's *The Way of Wealth*. For a quarter of a century, he published an annual calendar called *Poor Richard's Almanack*, with collected proverbs urging thrift and diligence. These were stitched together into one text for the 1757 edition, and later republished. *The Way of Wealth* stayed in print for almost 200 years and was republished as far away as China. Strange when you think this evangelist of thrift was busily slaving over a hot press printing money at the time.

But for all this, Benjamin Franklin is one of the great creators of the modern world, and you can't help but admire his energy and imagination. I found this opinion was shared by some alternative-thinking Americans as well. 'I really like Franklin – much better than the others,' said the journalist I stayed with that night. 'George Washington was a bit of a putz, quite frankly.'

The good news is that the tradition of printing new kinds of money in Philadelphia continues. A new currency called EQUAL$ has been launched by a local charity called Resources for Human Development. The currency circulates like time dollars, and when it was featured on one of Philadelphia's black talk radio stations at its launch in October 1996, as many as 200 people phoned in asking for details. The tradition continues.

VII

There are three ways of increasing national wealth, according to Franklin. War, which he described as robbery. Commerce, 'generally cheating'. And agriculture. And this, he said, was 'the only honest way wherein man receives a real increase to the seed thrown into the ground'. It was 'a kind of miracle'. It was slightly hypocritical of Ben, who spent much of his life writing little maxims for tradespeople, to condemn commerce as cheating, but he was right that commerce is not perhaps the natural basis for growth. Economic growth – like any other kind of growth – has its roots in the earth.

We have the same agonized debate today, but in slightly different terms. Growth is possible through war, but – as Hitler discovered – counter-productive. And it is clearly possible through commerce, but there are limits which – if you are not careful – cheat you of real wealth: money can be won at the cost of the environment or the sanity of youth. Quality of life for all of us is affected more and more by these so-called 'limits to growth'. 'Industrial humanity is behaving like King Midas,' said the radical economist Paul Ekins. 'He turned his daughter into gold before he realized the limitations of his own conception of wealth.'

Is there a natural way for wealth to increase, like the miraculous growth of seeds in soil, as Benjamin Franklin was suggesting? His own solution was to get on his printing press and print some more – not as a solution in its own right, but as a kind of fertilizer to wealth. He knew that printing currency which had no corresponding increase in economic activity would cause hyper-inflation and make everyone poorer, but he did sense that society needs a means of exchange to survive.

But then Americans really believe in wealth: they know it is different from the limited number of coins, notes, cheques and counters we use to measure it. Keeping those two ideas firmly separate – a feat Bernard Shaw didn't manage – made Franklin a great man.

Chapter 4

New York: money as religion

'Every time a child says "I don't believe in fairies" there is a
little fairy somewhere that falls down dead.'
J. M. Barrie, *Peter Pan*.

I

As New Jersey Transit's elderly train juddered me into New York
City, Dennis Rodman – the six-foot-six star basketball player for
the Chicago Bulls – was in the newspapers again. He famously
carries out TV interviews in a leather slit skirt and sequined top,
but had also just head-butted the referee in a recent match. By
doing so, he seemed to have demonstrated that Edgar Cahn was
right that dollars can have a 'toxic' effect on society, because the
head-butt seemed to have enhanced Rodman's already healthy
financial situation. He had been swamped by endorsement offers
after the incident. Nike and McDonald's were both joining the
queue and by the end of the year, he looked set to earn an
extra $1 million. A ghostwriter had been signed up to write his
autobiography, entitled *Bad As I Wanna Be*.

The problem is that high-pressure marketing to young people
these days often means developing a rebellious atmosphere
around your product, which is why the big marketing departments are on the look-out for role models they can get to promote
them. If Al Capone were still alive, he probably would have
been signed up to promote double-breasted suits to adolescents.
It makes life more colourful, but equally it means that the power
of marketing money is sometimes being shifted to encourage the
louts – and that costs even more money to deal with later.

This is one of the paradoxes of modern politics. The bill doesn't
end up with the marketeers, but with the local taxpayers who
have to fund the prisons and juvenile courts. Except that they
don't want to pay – hence John Kenneth Galbraith's famous
catch-phrase 'private opulence and public squalor'.

Galbraith's inspiration for this phrase was obviously New York

City, which had been teetering on the edge of bankruptcy for a generation, and where shiny bloated automobiles have to pick their way between the potholes like ballet dancers in a minefield. The commuter train ride from where I was staying in Princeton was a curtain-raiser for some of the squalor, as we swept through nondescript New Jersey towns, through the crumbling heart of Newark, under the Hudson River and into Pennsylvania Station.

However fond of the idea of Penn Station you may be, because of its appearance in the song 'Chattanooga Choo Choo', it is – like Victoria Bus Station – really only for the initiated. There are no sensible lists of destinations, no easy timetables; just the occasional inaudible announcement and one surly purveyor of information behind a long queue and a thick window. But then this is part of New York's paradox which Galbraith was trying to communicate: the private facilities are breathtaking while the public ones struggle and might have been designed to irritate and confuse outsiders. If it wasn't for the grid system of avenues and streets in Manhattan, I'm sure many tourists would still be in there somewhere trying to get out, too frightened to ask for directions to the airport. The newspaper that morning carried a cartoon of a New York cab, with a recorded message for passengers as they get out, which went: 'So leave your *@+! belongings in the cab, ya moron!! Ya think I give a &*O@!#??'

Somehow this is also part of New York's charm, because it is a vast, brutal, angry, tremendous place: an international city like London, but thrilling in a way that London is not, with its broken streets, its dirty pieces of retired chewing gum like black snow on the pavements, and its rusty water tanks on the roofs, like long-forgotten Apollo moonshots. It has tremendous energy: New York is like London on speed.

I walked in the general direction of Wall Street, past some Koreans with red bandannas on bikes, a one-legged bedraggled tramp in a wheelchair, a fearsome old lady in long floral patterns, a bare-chested gay couple, a furious family in a van – 'I don't give a shit what you think', roared the husband over his screaming child – an elderly Hasidic Jew, and a little girl in a T-shirt with the slogan 'GIRLS KICK ASS'. There is a heady sense of 'in-your-face' about New York, and an endless range of unusual people sharing the same cracked and badly-mended sidewalks.

Perhaps it is not surprising, in these circumstances, that Wall Street has more life and sheer chaos than the staid, clinical, choking City of London. But then Wall Street is not run by a decadent collection of semi-appointees, as the City is. And, unlike the bare polluted streets of the Square Mile, Wall Street has managed to retain Randee Elaine's hair salon, and Sam's Falafel III ('Best in town or your money back') and the Foot Doctor ('bunions, calluses, warts and spots') – and the fine mesh of family business which brings a place alive.

If I was searching for America's new alchemists, I had to look up the old ones as well – and Wall Street's old alchemists have certainly been able to conjure money. Look at Manhattan itself: the island was bought from the Indians in 1624 for a little under $24 in beads and old furs, Wall Street's very first good deal – and now look at its financial power. Such power, in fact, that it has become almost a substitute religion, where the cathedrals of commerce tower above the older spiritual cathedrals. This parallel was pointed out by the pioneering futurist James Robertson – incidentally the man who drafted Harold Macmillan's 'Winds of Change' speech many years before. He wrote in his book *Future Wealth*: 'Today's army of accountants, bankers, tax-people, insurance brokers, stock jobbers, foreign exchange dealers and countless other specialists in money, is the modern equivalent of priests, friars, monks, nuns, abbots and abbesses, pardoners, summoners and other specialists in religious procedures and practices.'

They are, and they apparently have the power to forgive sins too. It's not such a fanciful parallel given that about 10 per cent of the working population in the Middle Ages was employed in some religious branch or other: a similar proportion of the British is now working in one or other of the strange byways of financial services. Religion has always perceived money as a potential rival, and many of the well-known clichés began there. It wasn't just the Beatles who pointed out that it can't buy you love. St Paul lambasted the love of it as the root of all evil. Read most religious texts from the great world religions and you find they are filled with economic advice, some of it rather archaic stuff about sheep and goats, but some down-to-earth economic policy too. Most of it is about being careful not to cling too tightly to money. 'The superfluities of the rich are the necessities of the poor,' said St Augustine of Hippo. 'When you possess superfluity, you possess what belongs to others.'

The problem is, as King Midas discovered, money doesn't quite fulfil our needs. That is fine as long as you realize it, but if you don't – and you expect money to provide every kind of wealth – you are liable to be more than disappointed. Or turned into metal.

But if money plays the kind of role that religion used to, the key parallel is in the area of belief. This is especially so in Wall

Street, where you find yourself wondering whether all the pomposity is quite real – never mind the money. This is, after all, a place where many of the people find it hard explaining exactly what it is they do – as Sherman McCoy found explaining it all to his son in *The Bonfire of the Vanities*; where the derivatives market can be described by one writer as a 'phantasmagoric world' which deals in over 47,000 different options but no touchable products at all. The New York Mercantile Exchange in 1994 was trading 200 million barrels of oil a year – four times the real amount produced in the world – 'Like trading ether,' said Nick Leeson. So what underpins the vast international money system? It certainly isn't gold.

I began to see the whole thing differently when I was reading a fascinating book by the Japanese expert Karel van Wolferen, called *The Enigma of Japanese Power*. He thoroughly upset Japanese leaders when it was published in 1989 by claiming that, at the heart of Japanese society, there is actually nothing at all. He describes the Japanese establishment as a kind of religion, calling for a 'secularization' of their society, and quotes a revealing response by one Kyoto professor about foreign criticism of Japanese business methods. 'The *Japan Times* and the Kyoto professor, along with numerous other commentators, do not know it, but they are defenders of a faith,' he wrote.

This is a value judgement, beyond the reach of economists, but the same may be true of the Western money system. And there is some more evidence for it in *The Enigma of Japanese Power*. Take a look at the real reason why Japanese business was able to fund their worldwide expansion in the 1980s. Not by saving up – nobody does that in these days of mega-debt – but by massively increasing the value of Japanese land, especially in Tokyo. By the mid-1980s, the Japanese banks were encouraging their clients to raise the value of their assets, and because there was no real division between the public and private sectors in Japan, this bubble did not burst. By 1987, the value of all Japanese land was four times as much as all US land – even though the USA has fifty-seven times more habitable space than Japan.

Japanese business had – theoretically, anyway – enormous assets against which to borrow: and they did so. By 1987, land in Tokyo was worth ten times land in Manhattan, and its value was increasing at the rate of around 90 per cent a year. By 1990, the top ten banks in the world were suddenly all Japanese. It's not surprising, in those circumstances, that they were able to buy almost whatever they wanted. This belief at the heart of Japanese expansion – because it *is* a belief – managed to survive the 1987 crash, which is more than American business did. The crash wiped $400 billion off the value of US business, just as Black Wednesday wiped 25 per cent off the value of British business in 1992.

Nothing had otherwise changed. They still had the same assets, the same offices, employees, contracts, company cars, pencil sharpeners, but the belief in their value had changed. The value of companies is now a measure of our belief in their potential: Microsoft's fixed assets amount to only 6 per cent of its share value – the rest is belief. In the same way, the stock markets of the world are also massively intricate measurements of belief – belief which can destroy money just as easily as it can create it. The share price of a company is a measure of what investors believe a company is worth, and the price they are prepared to pay to receive its dividends, so this is not a new idea. It was Heinrich Heine who first said that money was the religion of modern life.

Arthur Miller's musical *The American Clock*, about the 1929 Wall Street Crash, plays with this same idea. The main character keeps all his money in his shoes, and his lack of belief in the system spreads until it brings down the whole edifice. 'My God,' says a ruined millionaire he is lending to, as he takes off his footwear. 'You don't believe in anything.'

America has a long record of spectacular crashes, building on a tradition which began with the speculation in Dutch tulip bulbs in the seventeenth century, John Law's thrilling French inflation and Britain's South Sea Bubble in the eighteenth century. It culminated in the disaster of the 1929 Crash: between then and July 1932, stocks on the New York Stock Exchange lost 83 per cent of their total value. Half of the $50 billion in new securities offered in the 1920s turned out to be worthless. I saw Arthur Miller's play performed at the National Theatre a few years after its first production in 1980, and it seemed amazingly farsighted. 'There's never been a country that hasn't had a clock running on it,' he wrote, just seven years before the ruinous 1987 crash. 'So I keep asking myself – how long?'

It's an uncomfortable question which somebody should ask pretty regularly. More recently, the frightening dip in the world's stock exchanges in October 1997 – crashes nearly always seem to happen in October, for some reason – depended not so much on whether the Asian financial turmoil would force markets down, but on whether people *believed* it would force them down. The facts didn't matter nearly as much as the perceived belief about the facts. And most dangerous of all were unexpected disappointments, which can drive the markets down; that is why – in the moment of danger – *Fortune* magazine reminded its readers of J. P. Morgan's famous long-term market prediction. 'It will fluctuate,' he said.

II

The idea of 29 October 1929, and the Wall Street sky darkened by suicidal millionaires flinging themselves from ledges – plus their other financial earthquakes before and since – are active fears in the American imagination. And in mine: I kept a weather eye on the sky myself, just in case the shares had carried on plummeting. If an American asks 'Is this the big one?' he is probably talking about a catastrophic loss of belief in the markets. Unless he is from California, of course.

There are many more safeguards these days. If the market drops by 250 points, it closes automatically for thirty minutes to cool off. The Stock Exchange does not admit to having closed in any circumstances since the outbreak of the First World War, though actually it did close in 1929 – ostensibly to catch up with paperwork. It also fell by 508 points during the 1987 crash.

As for the points system, that is better known as the Dow Jones Industrial Average, the brainchild of two New York financial journalists, Charles Dow and Edward Jones, during the Gold Rush. The Dow Jones had just celebrated its centenary and was rising at a fearsome 1,000 points a year, fuelled by the record funds we were all investing in pensions, sloshing around the markets looking for the best returns. This would certainly worry Arthur Miller if he knew – as he probably does – that it took seventy-six years, until 1972, to break through the first 1,000 barrier. The stock market rose a fearsome 30 per cent in 1997 alone.

Looked at with a century's hindsight, there is another worry. Only one of the original companies listed by Charles and Edward in their Wall Street office back in 1896 still exists: General Electric. All the other great names have been broken up, dissolved or dispersed by the corporate raiders, their once-powerful board-rooms demolished and their thunderous names forgotten. When you think that quite ordinary multinationals these days are bigger than many nations – the top one hundred companies in the world control assets of \$3.3 trillion – this is a small reminder of just how vulnerable these omnipotent companies are.

Whatever happened to all that power and enterprise? Were they swallowed up? Did they depend too much on Mussolini-style leaders at the top, or were they just too rigid to deal with a changing world or dwindling resources? Or like Tinkerbell in *Peter Pan*, maybe people just stopped believing in them. The phenomenon seems to be continuing: as many as two thirds of the Fortune 500 companies back in 1956 have disappeared as well, some by merger or acquisition, some simply by good old-fashioned bankruptcy. 'My name is Ozymandias plc,' they might have said. 'Look on my works, ye mighty, and despair'.

The papers had been asking the 'is-this-the-big-one?' question forty-eight hours before I got to New York, because of a disturbing two-day slump on the New York Stock Exchange – over 160 points on the first day, and the same again the day after, before it began to claw its way back. 'I was so nervous I couldn't eat,' one magazine executive told the world. 'I made call after call to the 0800 line to find out how much I was losing.' On Wednesday she found she was down $4,000 and took her holdings out of stock. She wasn't alone.

Why had the market started to slide? It wasn't because of a fresh White House scandal, poor economic news or growing poverty figures – quite the reverse. It was because there was *good* news about falling unemployment. The markets interpreted this to mean that there would shortly be a rise in interest rates, and they sold – or went 'bearish' as they say on Wall Street. But why did the market fail to recover in the days that followed? That was less clear and the shaking investors kept a close eye on the market hour by hour. Was this the beginnings of a new crash? 'Relax', said one trader in *Fortune* magazine. 'That's not a pattern we are seeing right now.'

Recognizing patterns is what Wall Street is all about these days. You can stick to the tried and tested ones and buy before the famous 'Santa Claus Rally', which usually takes place between Christmas and New Year. Or you can try to sell before the Jewish New Year, because this inspires people to turn over a new leaf – which tends to mean selling. Or immediately before the stock market reaches a worryingly high round number. You should also sell before the inauguration of a president, because they normally take added steps to conquer inflation shortly afterwards. Nine times out of ten when a president is re-elected, there is a bear market. Ronald Reagan – never very interested in reining back the juggernaut – was the one out of ten exception.

It's a good game, and you can choose to search for your own patterns. It isn't really about intelligence, according to James Buchan in his brilliant book *Frozen Desire*, but 'a peculiar concentrated stupidity, such as one admires in a woman we remember wearing this year's fashions last year'. The logic of Wall Street is not so much blind allegiance to the market, but the thought that someone out there is just a little bit ahead and therefore knows better than the market does. Which is why every generation of traders finds new iconoclasts and heretics they can follow. Two recent leaders of the heretical pack called themselves the Motley Fool, giving hard-hitting advice on the Internet, based on the idea – worrying for investors – that 80 per cent of mutual fund managers perform worse than the market. 'Be a FOOL and be proud of it,' said their online website.

Actually any pattern will do. This is why Wall Street trading houses are buying the services of experts in chaos theory, fuzzy logic, genetic algorithms, neural networks, data visualization, fractal theory and even the movement of the stars. Fibonacci sequences, where each number is the sum of the previous two, are said to appear in market behaviour, just as they do in snail-shell spirals, daisy petals or galaxies. Or the experts are studying, like the French physicist Jean-Philippe Bouchard, the movements of detergent molecules. California clairvoyant Terrie Brill listed the mutual fund giant Merrill Lynch among her clients; one Wall Street astrologer claims to have 15,000 clients. Even Vanderbilt and Morgan regularly consulted clairvoyants and the US company AstroAnalyst recently claimed it had an arrangement with an international bank in London. Former maths professor Rebecca Nolan publishes detailed predictions in her newsletter *Financial Astrology*: she quotes the manager of one Japanese securities house as saying that 70 per cent of her foreign exchange predictions come true.

In spite of these peculiarities, the New York Stock Exchange is astonishingly smug about its contribution to all our lives. I queued up for my free ticket to the visitor's gallery to get a whiff of the money-conjurors halfway through an uncertain week. 'Nosmok-ingnophotographyenjoyyourvisit,' said the lift attendant as we filed out. A notice outside the lift informed us that we should not chew gum either. It is not, of course, considered good form to chew gum inside a church, and in a sense that is where we were.

The NYSE, as they call themselves – motto: 'The world puts its stock in us' – began in 1792 when the new US government first sold bonds to repay their war debts. And on May 17 of that year, the first twenty-four brokers met under a long-forgotten buttonwood tree on Wall Street. It was known as the Buttonwood Agreement and it led to the street we know today. History doesn't relate what happened to the tree. I thought of asking the rows of porters smoking outside the Stock Exchange in their coloured jackets, but knowing how New Yorkers react to stupid questions, I decided not to.

We were all herded into a small cinema and shown a video about the work of the Stock Exchange, packed to bursting with product placement. It was self-satisfied beyond belief. 'The opening bell is not just the start of business at the New York Stock Exchange, it's really the start of business around the world,' said the smug voice-over, ignoring the fact that the London Stock Exchange would already have been open for five hours and the Tokyo Stock Exchange for fourteen hours. An enormous man in what looked like a child's orange T-shirt munched his way through an ice cream in front of me, as the video showed a leather-clad girl on a motorbike exclaiming: 'Who says you can't take it with you!' Was this a reference to portability or a theological statement? I didn't know.

I could stand it no longer and went to look at the trading floor, past displays explaining that if you had bought a share in McDonald's when they were first traded at $32.75, your investment would now be worth over $2,800 – not bad for studying the swirls on the back of a snail. The floor itself was strangely calm, bright with a faint whiff of coffee. Or I felt there would have been if there hadn't been a thick pane of glass in front of me.

The market was recovering slightly from the previous day's losses, though not permanently – share prices carried on slipping in the days that followed. As I walked in, the clock said 11.00.53 and the big display boards were announcing the Rocky Mountain chocolate results. This seemed to ignite no great flurry of buying. In the biggest trading area, seven complicated modules were apparently suspended from the ceiling by a massive gold-painted metal frame. They had been lowered into place from there in 1980 so that there would be no expensive interruption in trading. Each one looked like a borrowed lunar module, with desks and screens showing share prices, and more screens held out in arms from each desk.

Around them on the floor were the meandering specialists, brokers – the modern pardoners and summoners – talking and moving around with the characteristic New Yorker loping gait. And further out around them was the confetti of trading in the previous hours, the abandoned yellow, pink and white slips of paper – as if this was the biggest betting shop in the world, and heaven knows, maybe it was. Above all this were a set of vast NYSE banners and the motto, EXCELSIOR, plus the Stars and Stripes and clocks showing the time in London, Mexico City, Hong Kong, Tokyo, Sydney and Zurich – in case anybody wanted to call the famous gnomes. Above that was a long-forgotten ornate ceiling, irrelevant in an age which measures only money. The men below greatly outnumbered the women: one man below me with half-moon specs and a pot belly was discussing business with a girl blowing bubble gum, and around them was the detritus of keeping the economy moving: flashing lights and screens, half-eaten pretzels, plastic cups of coffee, crumpled copies of the *Daily News*, sticky calculators and bottled water.

There was also something tremendously seductive about it. 'Have we got any stocks, Dad?' said a little boy in a baseball shirt to his embarrassed father, as we crowded out of the public gallery.

'No,' he snapped.

'Can we get some then?' The father ignored him. He looked as if he had been asked some frighteningly intimate question about his manhood.

'Why not?' His father visibly shrank as we glanced over at him. 'Why not, Dad?'

I'm not sure which of them had the right attitude, but you certainly have to be careful, because Wall Street shares another important attribute of religion. Like the 'Kingdom of God' – which Jesus famously described as a place where 'the last shall be first and the first shall be last' – Wall Street is also an upside-down kind of world. For lots of reasons, the share markets of the world are not really the hidden hands of the market they are made out to be, rewarding the best, punishing the worst, a beacon of the capitalist world. For example:

Upside-down world 1: Investors and shareholders tend to be over-valued by society, claiming the lion's share from the markets. You might even assume they are creating the wealth and providing the capital for business expansion. Actually, they don't. If you 'invest' in a company like Microsoft, the money doesn't go to them, it goes to other speculators. Only new issues get money to the corporation. Since the 1987 crash, US corporations have bought back more equity than they have issued – but they have still shelled out $1.2 trillion in dividends to shareholders.

In the UK, the Tomorrow's Company inquiry set in motion by the Royal Society of Arts cast some doubt on the all-powerful role of shareholders. They even floated the possibility that directors might be breaking the law if they *only* considered their interests. But it is still widely believed that corporations exist purely to maximize the return to shareholders, without much thought about whether this return might include the way in which corporations treat the people and planet.

Upside-down world 2: Traders and their employers are also over-valued by society – almost embarrassingly so, as former Salomon Brothers trader Michael Lewis described in his best-selling exposé *Liar's Poker.* 'My father's generation grew up with certain beliefs. One of those beliefs is that the amount of money one earns is a rough guide to one's contribution to the welfare and prosperity of society,' Lewis wrote, explaining why he gave the trading business up for journalism. 'It took watching his son being paid 225 grand at the age of twenty-seven, after two years on the job, to shake his faith in money.'

Don't forget that Michael Milken, whose junk bonds were responsible for plunging American business into unsustainable debt, earned $550 million from his company Drexel Burnham Lambert in 1987 alone. He was eventually sentenced to ten years in prison for securities law violations. But then, since traders don't have to take account of the social impact of companies, of course it is trading – rather than stewardship of assets – which gets the lion's share of the proceeds.

Upside-down world 3: Far from providing a sober-minded direction for the large corporations of the world, many of the people making the key trading decisions in London and New York are entirely detached from reality.

When I got back to London, the papers were dominated by the latest asset management scandal in the City, still reeling from the collapse of Barings Bank at the hands of rogue Singapore trader Nick Leeson.

Star fund manager Peter Young – earning £300,000 a year – had been suspended by his German-owned bank Morgan Grenfell, who announced 'irregularities' amounting to £1.4 billion. It became clear that Young had been going slowly round the twist, obsessed with inventing a rocket-launcher and building a mathematical model for the way termites burrow. And this wasn't a bizarre search for patterns either. 'I asked Peter to go shopping,' his wife told the *Financial Times.* 'He came back with thirty jars of pickled gherkins. My husband does not see that as strange.'

Upside-down world 4: Neither Wall Street nor the City is providing a service to the big corporations. In fact, the chief executives are no longer masters of their world.

The *New York Times* carried a fascinating review by business journalist Joseph Nocera, who described watching two senior executives giving a presentation to mutual fund rising star Christine Baxter, aged twenty-seven. At the end of the meeting, the chief executive said plaintively: 'May I ask you something? We've been through here a couple of times now and you've never given any indication you don't like the company or that we're doing something wrong. But you haven't bought any of the stock. Is there anything we're doing that's preventing you . . .'

It's a strange phenomenon, said Nocera: 'Prior to the 1980s, chief executives did not spend time hawking their company's shares to fund managers in their twenties, pleading with them even, to buy their stock.' But now that's exactly what they do, and their enormous salaries depend on it.

Upside-down world 5: Wall Street has encouraged the virus of corporate down-sizings, mergers and contortions which have hit Western corporations – sometimes disastrously. A similar phenomenon has been going on in the UK: according to one study, Britain's top 1,000 companies shed 1.6 million jobs – two thirds of the whole unemployment burden – in one year between 1992 and 1993.

In Wall Street and the City, the whims of the investors count, because boardroom salaries are linked to corporate share price. Which is why, at the height of the down-sizing trend in corporate USA, the chief executives of the biggest corporations were earning on average $2,100 an hour. Walt Disney Inc managed to give its retiring president $90 million, after only fourteen months in the job. In 1995, AT&T's Robert Allen took $5.85 million in pay, plus stock options worth over $10 million more. On 2 January 1996, he announced that another 40,000 AT&T employees were being given the push.

One other peculiar side-effect of down-sizing has been the sudden surge of interest in cosmetics among American executives. You wouldn't have caught my grandfather glancing at a special suit to make him look slim, or even considering simple facial surgery. But in the new corporate world, fifty-year-olds are competing with thirty-year-olds, and these things count. Men's Choice hair colour sales had risen by a third in the USA in three years of heavy down-sizing, and as many as 200,000 American men had hair transplants in 1994. Why do men make up a quarter of all American facial surgery patients? It's so they can keep their jobs. Local plastic surgeon Thomas Romo III told the *New York Times*: 'The concepts down-sized corporations are dealing with are lean and mean. They don't want guys who look fat and happy.'

Upside-down world 6: Share trading is often computerized and carried out automatically across sectors, rather than by choosing the successful and innovative within them. Sometimes one fund manager's whim can push share prices down for no particular reason other than mood – and because they happened to hold a large number of shares. Many of the big hi-tech shares, like Motorola, have suffered in this way.

This is just a small symptom of the basic problem: that the people who run the financial markets have more to gain from world volatility than from stability. It is change that makes them rich. The markets have a vested interest in global crisis.

Upside-down world 7: You probably thought the big financial institutions were there to protect the interests of their customers – who are, through our pensions, all of us. The descriptions of life on Wall Street by former Morgan Stanley trader Frank Partnoy in his book *F.I.A.S.C.O.* would finally disabuse you. His bosses encouraged him to think of clients as the enemy. 'When an account called to say hello, I needed to be prepared to blow his head off and make a sale,' he said, describing the sale of the notorious Mexican peso-linked derivatives issued by a company based in Bermuda, which collapsed together with the peso in December 1994.

If all those examples of the upside-down world of finance aren't enough, there is the biggest example of them all: the US budget deficit, now running well into the trillions, which is borrowed each day by the US government to keep their wheels turning. 'In God we trust', say the notes. In fact, dollars are underpinned not by gold or even money in the vault, but by the world's collective belief in the US government's promise to pay its gigantic debt. A running national debt indicator nestles - appropriately enough – among other symbols of conspicuous consumption in Forty-Second Street near the corner with Sixth Avenue.

I was determined to see it, and pressed through the rush-hour crowds in Times Square to get there, past the other indicator boards – one with the latest news and financial results, and the other with more personal messages: 'Sharon: I love you to the moon and back, Dave dht@zvh.com', it read as I passed.

I tripped over one of the new purple automatic pavement cleaners I had read about in *Time Out New York*, known as Felix 1 and Felix 2. They come up behind you and a disembodied voice says: 'Nehhh! Nehhh! Move it please!', as they pulverize bottles and cigarette ends into dust. The ones used in Windsor Castle and the Vatican apparently say 'Caution!', but this wasn't considered truly American. 'Who says "caution" round here?' asked *Time Out*.

I was about to give up, but a few yards further, threatened by weeds from the broken brickwork and above a sign which offered deli salad, was the National Debt Clock. The figure was racing beyond $5 trillion, and the last three digits were moving so fast they were unreadable – as you would expect when it is increasing at the rate of $10,000 a second. Another clock underneath, called 'family share', stood at $66,953 borrowed per American household.

Nobody is quite sure what the US national deficit means in practice. The first US Treasury Secretary Alexander Hamilton famously said that national debt 'if it is not excessive, will be to us a national blessing'. Benjamin Franklin clearly felt the same, but he might have had a different attitude if he had known the annual interest payments were running at nearly $300 billion – getting on for a fifth of the government's annual budget and by itself more than the total US debt at the end of the Second World War. It might cause inflation. It could cause world financial meltdown. It could be completely irrelevant. 'Blessed be the young,' said the US president Herbert Hoover, 'for they shall inherit the National Debt.' They may also have to inherit a solution.

III

New York's Upper West Side conjures up images of Officer Krupke, meeting a Girl Named Maria where ignorant flick-knives clash by night. But thirty years after Leonard Bernstein's show *West Side Story* was written, the West Side is not the same any more. Past the Lincoln Center and the Metropolitan Opera House, the West Side was colonized by the slightly more down-at-heel bohemians who found themselves priced out of Greenwich Village. Even Bernstein lived there for a little while, in his 'radical chic' days. The New York liberals followed, and behind them the pastrami bars and dinky cafés. The Sharks and the Jets found themselves defeated by market forces and the power of inexorable gentrification.

And among those moving into space vacated by them were caterer Jane Wilson and Diana McCourt – a carpenter – plus Diana's actor husband and their five children. Jane and Diana have invented a new kind of money specially for women, and a currency system known as Womanshare.

Diana told me that the neighbourhood still has a healthy ethnic 'mix', and to that extent it is a microcosm of New York City. But in spite of the influx of painters, writers, philosophers and the sort of people who never miss an exhibition at the Guggenheim, it can be a tough place too. 'Fairly dangerous,' as Diana put it. 'My youngest son was mugged three times. Perhaps that's why he became a cop.'

There was little evidence of this as I took a cab up West Side Avenue. Elderly ladies were exercising very small, very long dogs, women in shorts were clambering out of video rentals with their evening's entertainment, and the road was up again. One of the peculiarities of life in the Upper West Side is that the road is normally up. The area round Eighty-third Street, where Diana McCourt lived, appeared particularly safe. Everywhere I looked, large steady brick-built apartment blocks sweated in the muggy afternoon heat – an air-conditioning system sticking out of every window, like their own personal rabbit hutches. Every pompous-looking front door was shadowed by an awning, providing a little blessed shade. I was late as usual, and dashed under a particularly stripy awning, through the front door, past a fat doorman with a Zapata-style moustache, and into a lift decked out with port-holes and brass like the *Lusitania*. I was surprised to find Diana McCourt's front door open, but decided to ring the bell anyway and found myself ushered into a labyrinthine West Side apartment.

Her spare bedroom doubled as the Womanshare office. It was full of books about radical economics, together with family photos on the walls, lists of things to do and pigeon-holes of press clippings – including a spectacular photo of Jane and Diana, shown carrying a power drill rather as James Bond held his pistol in *Thunderball*.

The idea of a currency just for women began in 1991, when Jane and Diana ran into each other in a local coffee shop. They hit it off immediately. Jane had just sold her catering business and Diana was phasing out her woodworking business, and was – as she put it – 'looking for new ways to be in the world'. They began meeting for breakfast at Diana's flat every Tuesday.

Jane and Diana went together on an international retreat to the south of France, where the Vietnamese writer Thich Nhat Hanh urged them all to go home and change the world by working together and supporting each other. 'On our return we found ourselves as a community of two,' Jane told one magazine interviewer, 'sharing yoga, apples and cats every Tuesday morning, telling each other our dreams, and doing research on how we could become more directly involved in our communities.' They also started to exchange their skills of carpentry and cooking.

Womanshare emerged as a response to them both stepping back from full-time work, and to the particular life of the Upper West Side. Although the neighbourhood is increasingly affluent, that doesn't necessarily go for the people who live there. It is often an isolating place for women who find themselves trapped in flats with a shrinking pension: or alone without husband and children, who have gone their various separate ways; or who have determinedly independent careers. Inner-city angst is not just for poor people, after all.

Womanshare was designed to do something about that. It would bring people together to help each other out – and every time they did so, they would earn a credit which they could then spend on services from somebody else in the group. It was like time dollars or LETS in this respect: people would go into debt to each other, and by so doing conjure up a new kind of money. But there was no 'moral' agenda here, as there is with time dollars – the idea was to tackle loneliness. 'We had both organized women's groups all our lives, and women's training groups,' Diana told me. 'We did quite a bit of reading about it, then we presented it to a group of several women. That and a couple of friends became the core.'

The first Womanshare newsletter appeared during Bill Clinton's first presidential election campaign in November 1991, urging the new members to get trading with each other: 'Meanwhile start connecting and sharing skills among those of you who have each other's numbers,' it said. 'The sooner we start, the more momentum we will have and we will be enriching ourselves and each other.'

The idea was an immediate success. By 1993, the *New York Times* was writing that they 'moved from friendship to social revolution'. Jane and Diana used the quote in their leaflet, and suddenly they were the darlings of the media. After one article in the *Chicago Tribune*, women wrote to them from forty-eight of the fifty states of the USA. One letter came from someone who helped battered women in Israel.

'Sally needs a wedding cake,' wrote one New York cultural magazine, explaining how the system worked. 'She peruses her Womanshare "yellow pages", which are updated four times a year, and finds Lucy, who makes the confection and gets three hours' credit in the "bank". Lucy can then trade in her credit for, say, three hours of psychotherapy from Anna, or any of 180 available skills.' One application form quoted breathlessly in the *New York Times* listed one applicant's skills as 'sewing, embroidery, crocheting, knitting, macramé, quilting, découpage on rocks, candle-making, tie-dying, calligraphy, ballroom dancing, cooking, kitchen renovation advisor'.

The same person listed her needs as: 'Help in decorating and decision-making especially with rug size and club chairs and colour, electrical work, installation of tile bathroom floor, wallpapering of bathroom, more efficient space utilization of closet, exchange or trade clothing, jewellery or non-household items, make-up consultation, acupuncture, someone to come to my home and do fitness training with me.'

Wedding cakes, psychotherapy, closet space-shifting? This was hardly the nitty-gritty lifts-to-doctors currency of Edgar Cahn. But it seemed to work. Membership rocketed very quickly from an initial thirty to seventy-five people, but this was not intended to be the kind of new money which takes Manhattan by storm. The group decided to cap the membership at one hundred, and let anyone else join a waiting list. This is still how they organize it – people who want to join are encouraged to set up their own organization. Bringing people close together means you have to have a smallish group.

The thing about ordinary dollars is that they are exchangeable with anyone you meet. It's a kind of *ersatz* trust: Edgar Cahn says the only strangers you let into your home are those you find in the Yellow Pages. Womanshare credits were going to be different. If someone offered you one, you could know you could trust them in a completely different way. The group wanted to keep it that way.

Although similar Womanshare systems are popping up all over America, its main purpose goes beyond anything economic. It is a self-help system which provides members with friends, support, pride, skills and power. It is supposed to change lives, because Womanshare is not just about exchanging, it is also about sharing – or 'joyous living' as the seven Womanshare principles put it. The last one of these is empowerment: 'Womanshare encourages women to reclaim their rightful roles as leaders, healers, mentors and visionaries . . . We women are a force!'

'We're discovering that doing tasks together has a beauty and power that goes far beyond the work,' Diana told me. 'We're also finding that some shares are just about being in the presence of another – having the comfort of another person on hand when you have an onerous chore to do.' When Jane slipped on her oriental rug in 1994 and fractured her pelvis, doctors said she would take three months to recover. In fact she took six weeks, by going heavily in 'debt' to Womanshare – splashing out in credits to get people to read poetry to her.

Isn't this just a group of people doing each other good turns, you may ask? It is, but because good turns generate credits – a kind of non-money money – these can circulate around the community. Every time somebody passes them on, they generate another good turn. It uses the power of money, but in a quite different way. There was also something tremendously anti-puritanical about Womanshare, which I liked. This was not about eking out a living, it was about unashamedly inventing a new kind of currency which makes people's lives more friendly and liveable – more luxurious even – 'I suppose there are other ways of being poor than just having no money,' I said.

'You're talking about the invisible poverty of women,' said Diana, warming to me at last. 'There are so many women in our group who you'd think of as affluent or something, who are on the edge of being terrified because they're just living on a fixed income with small savings. I guess what we're saying is that Womanshare is middle-class in culture, but there is a real need. People really need these services. And then there are others who are freelance writers and artists, who work alone. Or there are people like me who grew up in huge families and feel depleted.'

Or as I heard Jane say later to a group of fascinated political activists: 'You can be high-tech or high-touch. We believe in high-touch.'

The money isn't used just for services, it is used to fund classes. Like Diana's class for teaching women to use power tools. Or others about how to deal with the menopause, stick-shift driving, desktop publishing or t'ai chi. And what they call 'brokering'. Members help friends who are organizing a big project like a party or wedding, and are too depressed to make the phone calls. This may well be a specific Manhattan problem – *Time Out New York* that week had a feature on where you could get therapy for free, but I would probably prefer to put myself in the hands of Womanshare than the New York State Psychiatric Institute.

'Brokering can make a big difference,' Diana told me. 'Before the wedding we had cooking teams and delivery teams and flower teams. We once organized someone to move house, packing up in Connecticut and unpacking in Long Island. I just brokered for somebody who was in the middle of her dissertation, and she needed help with her survey mailings.'

They even have an 'emergency response team'. Or there is the ultimate in Womanshare luxury, when – by paying in credits – you make a friend 'Queen for a Day' on their birthday, organizing dinner, massage and poetry readings. 'Queen for a Day takes Womanshare to new heights,' said their newsletter in March

1994. It is vital to the whole idea, like time dollars, that everybody's time is worth the same. Womanshare works strictly to an hour for an hour. They are also strict about men: they can't join.

'I was much more of an activist. I had a much more political agenda, and I changed a lot as Womanshare evolved,' Diana told me. 'But then, as it evolved, I realized that it was in a deeper sense much more revolutionary. The radical changes that were happening to us, you couldn't measure in terms of credits and dollars, but it was so effective in other ways. You could watch people's lives changing, people who were so isolated, even antisocial. Or people who were career people, determined to be independent, not meeting anybody. A lot of people had never been involved in groups before or come to meetings before.'

For one thing, it gave people permission to ask for help. For another, it introduced a different system of values which was enthusiastic about the kind of skills women happened to possess in the Upper West Side. 'Culturally, women haven't ever had their skills valued,' Jane said later. 'When we talk to new members now, they say – "Oh that's a skill . . . ?" "Oh, you consider that a skill . . . ?"'

Womanshare is run without grants of any kind, but it still costs up to $5,000 a year in old-fashioned cash to run. And it charges membership fees of $50 a year, plus six hours in credits owed to the organization. The problem is that the bulk of administration falls on Diana, made even worse when her mother came to live in the bedroom we were sitting in – from where Womanshare was administered. 'That's why Diana has a gazillion hours of credits,' said Jane later.

But the organization has survived this crisis, which forced members to set up an administration which worked, and to think about the future. There were plans to buy a kind of 'retreat house', or a support place for freelance therapists to run courses, even a scheme for a revolving credit system – lending money in dollars to members. After I managed to heave copies down in an enormous cardboard box in a cupboard, I found that the newsletter painted a picture of a thriving organization. It included notices of meetings of the Womanshare self-marketing group, their self-expression group, and their rather evocatively named Dream Group, which allowed them to discuss their dreams.

It was also packed with tributes from grateful people, including one member, thankful for all the help organizing her daughter's *bat mitzvah*: 'It wasn't only the huge amount of money that such personalized services would have cost (and which I could never have afforded) but also the constant support and encouragement from so many people – worth more than I can say,' she said.

So what does Womanshare mean? In the earliest days of money, one of its functions was simply to bring people together. Nobody really agrees about the origins of money and there were probably many different ones. William Bloom in *Money, Heart and Mind* comes down firmly on the idea of money starting as gifts and exchanges between tribes, or recognizing ceremonies, building people's social and creative relationships. 'The simple truth,' he wrote, '. . . is that money emerged in order to facilitate human relationships – not to facilitate trade and business.'

Womanshare seem to have stumbled on a memory of this. They have invented a 'funny money' that brings people together, improves their relationships, beckons them to rely on each other. And, what's more, they have managed to hang on to what is important: they don't let the rules of the new money get in the way of the relationships. So in a different way to Wall Street, Womanshare money is also creating an upside-down world. Their money seems to make its users behave completely differently.

'Do you have a problem of people taking a lot and not giving a lot?' I asked Diana. 'Or maybe if they do it so much, will they stop using the money altogether?'

'No, actually, we have the problem of people giving a lot and not taking,' she said. 'I think it comes from a feeling of abundance: that they can get what they need in the group, because the group is there. It is self-destructive in a way, because it's teaching people a new way of living and sharing and giving – so maybe you don't need the system after a while. It's really a natural instinct, in our memory or something like that.'

When I listened to Diana and Jane at a meeting a few weeks later, a man in the audience asked what would happen if a member bought one of Diana's new pots through Womanshare and then sold it for £200.

'Well, I've never thought about it,' said Diana, slightly taken aback.

'Typical question from a man,' said a woman in the audience. I felt a little ashamed for wondering something similar myself.

IV

The following morning, I was up early to investigate one of the most successful time dollar banks in the country – Brooklyn's Member to Member. Member to Member was so all-embracing,

I had been led to believe, that you could even pay for your health insurance in time dollars.

New York has a special atmosphere in the early mornings. Normally it feels a bit like a stale, brightly-lit motel bedroom: the pale early morning light adds a kind of grumpiness. At times like these, the difference between WALK and DON'T WALK can be all the difference between life and death. You know that the drivers waiting for the lights to change, all looking ahead intently like Norman Bates in *Psycho*, would not slow down even a fraction if you happened to be in the road in front of them. There is a barely suppressed violence about the place.

I had previewed Member to Member by taking part in their telephone bingo. This was bingo for Brooklyn's old people, funded not by grants or big bucks but by imaginary time dollars. The organizers, the callers and the prizes – a small selection of bookmarks and picture frames – were all paid for in what Edgar Cahn had called 'funny money'. But even telephone bingo was a tough world, as I discovered by hanging on to the receiver to listen in.

'Did you say N2?' said a strong Brooklyn accent down the line.

'She hasn't called anything yet.'

'No I haven't. Now clear your boards everybody,' said the bingo caller in a New York version of Joyce Grenfell. 'Have you cleared your boards? Mother, have you cleared your board? OK, the first number is G-fifty-nine.'

There was a sound of writing and heavy concentration. The players meet the same people every week at this time, but unlike similar social gatherings, they have grown past simple exasperation with each other and allowed it to blossom into active loathing. After a few minutes and a surprisingly small list of numbers, there was a result.

'Bingo,' said a rather tentative elderly voice.

'Who's this? Rose?'

'She doesn't know what she's talking about.'

'She's very confused.'

'Excuse me, but did you call fifty-eight or fifty-nine at the beginning?'

'Your Bs and Gs sound alike.'

'She's just too old.'

'Rose, we're talking about the letter L. Down the Bs and across the bottom.' Poor Rose: I didn't think I would ever have the nerve to call bingo if I had to run this kind of gauntlet. And indeed, Rose did seem to now be worryingly quiet. Maybe she had done the decent thing and gone outside with a pistol.

'I give up,' said another player.

'Come on, don't get so upset – they don't understand, that's all,' said another one, secure in the knowledge of her own sanity in an increasingly peculiar world.

And so on, until thirty minutes or so had gone by and we all put our receivers down, and the various players congratulated me for living in London – which rather touched me. I got the strong impression that half an hour's healthy exasperation with each other was the main point of the exercise. It certainly couldn't have been the bookmark they won. I had listened to what may well be the world's only alternative currency bingo game, which was something for the notebook – and it provided me with an excellent introduction to Member to Member as I battled through the New York subway to get there.

Everyone warns you about the New York subway, as the place where New York's famous aggression gets out of hand – though actually the city's lurid crime statistics have been dropping for some time, partly because of the determination of its mayor, and partly because of simple demographics. There are just fewer young men of criminal age – about nine upwards these days.

Even so, New York has a different attitude to crime than fear-gripped Washington. In New York – rather like London – the shades of neighbourhood are so inter-mixed that there is really no chance of avoiding it. Each city has its own mythic horror stories too. In Washington it was the morbid fear of car-jacking. New York has its pride at stake in such contests, which may be why I heard two or three terrifying tales of baby kidnapping.

So visitors are urged to travel together on the New York subway system, and there are even signs beside the ticket offices where lonely passengers can wait in safety at night before the trains arrive. It anyway takes ages for a Londoner to understand how the subway works, because a number of our assumptions – that all trains should stop everywhere, that lines should have easy-to-remember names, that all stations should be called something different – are completely flouted underneath New York.

Riding the silver subway trains is a bit like travelling in an aluminium army-issue food tin. They are cleaner these days, but ancient, and the advertisements are particularly revealing. I liked the one for New York's Channel 13, the upmarket TV channel which beams the produce of the BBC into the homes of New Yorkers: 'Take your mind off the dumb stuff', it said.

As it turned out I found myself staring at the posters more than I would have wished. I had got on the wrong train, couldn't make out what the announcements were saying, and we just waited and waited. I had crossed the famous Brooklyn Bridge, which claimed the life of its creator John Augustus Roebling in 1869, gazed down at the closely-built parallel streets, re-entered the tunnel, and after an hour and a half of bad advice, wrong trains and sheer bad luck, I finally realized that we were not going to Bay View in Brooklyn at all that morning.

I was an hour late for my appointment and somewhere under the middle of Brooklyn, and there was nothing as useful as a local map. For all I knew the landscape above me might have come straight out of the Lost World. 'Well at least we don't have bombs down there like you do,' someone said to me after I found they didn't know where they were either.

'We hardly ever have bombs,' I protested. He seemed to feel this proved his case. In New York they put up a monument to each explosion – there is a particularly tasteless one by the World Trade Center.

So I emerged into the morning heat around Brooklyn's Thirty-ninth Street, and found myself in a terrain a little like the Whitechapel Road – but with two key exceptions. There were no cabs, and nobody seemed to speak English. Passers-by were all speaking Spanish, all the signs were in Spanish, everything in the corner shop was in Spanish, all the newspapers blowing around the pavement were in Spanish. It could have been Guatemala City.

I found a battered old jalopy owned by Dominican Cabs and asked the driver to order a cab for me. 'No English,' he said. But he grabbed the radio anyway and made a number of excitable remarks into it. Despite having done a Spanish course many years ago, mainly because I was smitten by somebody else in the evening class, all I can do is request a map of Cuenca, demand whether there is a toilet nearby and ask for directions to the Hanging Houses – Cuenca's celebrated local marvel. After about five minutes, another elderly taxi with the Dominican Cabs slogan on the side dashed by. I waved furiously.

This driver seemed tremendously pleased to see me, but spoke very little English. 'Dominican cars are best,' he told me with an enormous grin, his eyes nowhere near the road as we zipped past the usual suburban shops and gas stations. 'Other cars pass, nothing – you take Dominican. Even if you have no money.'

This seemed a great joke to both of us – though maybe for different reasons – and soon we were moving into a different kind of area where most of the signs seemed to be in Chinese, and small Chinese garage workshops lined both sides of the street. There were large trees on the pieces of waste ground, the corrugated iron long-since rusted away. On the verges I read the brand names on the litter: Häagen Dazs, Wrigley's, Snapple. This was not exactly the litter of deep poverty, but then maybe Brooklyn people like it. I hope so, because they certainly seem to get through a lot of it.

Brooklyn is actually involved in a long-range waiting game. They refused to join with New York at all until a closely-fought local referendum in 1898. It was probably the wrong decision, because over the century their thriving port silted up, their blue-collar jobs disappeared, and the investment swept instead into the Manhattan money markets. Faced with a vital decision in the 1960s, the New York Port Authority – set up originally to prevent competition between the two ports and to damp down armed conflict between the rival police forces – decided to invest in money rather than ports.

Money tends to chase money under our current system, and Brooklyn's loss meant that New York has that modernistic twin-towered horror known as the World Trade Center. Brooklyn's vast rusting grain terminal remains empty, though there are signs that New York's politicians seem to be coming round to a scheme to revive Brooklyn's port as a way of competing with Newark across the state line in New Jersey.

My cab was rumbling along what looked like a back alley, strewn with rubbish and old cars, opposite Bay View Auto Body and New Way Fashion Inc – both evidently Chinese businesses – and drew up beside a modern brick building marked Jewish Medical Center. We had arrived at New York's most advanced time bank.

V

An enormous receptionist with a big green sweatshirt presided over the bland, empty waiting-room. I leant against the window-sill and took notes. Police sirens wailed in the distance. A vital staff meeting was in progress by the time I got there, and the organizer was busy. But her assistant showed me in, past the forest of other notices, the strangely luxuriant indoor plants – offset alarmingly by a green carpet and bright purple chairs.

This was the home of Elderplan, one of only four Social Health Maintenance Organizations (HMOs) in the USA. HMOs were set up as a way of giving some financial incentive to the health-care industry to keep their patients in good health, rather than just treating them expensively when they get ill. Social HMOs take this one stage further, concentrating on peer education in nutrition, stress management and exercise.

Anyone can join Elderplan as long as they are over fifty-five, and enormous efforts will then be made to keep them healthy. The copy of their newsletter *Your Health Matters!* was full of advice about keeping cheerful. 'Create a smile file,' it advises. 'Fill it with humorous clippings, cartoons and funny photos. Turn to it from time to time when you need a lift.' There was also an enjoyable article about how you don't have to live with depression, urging members to watch out for classic symptoms. These ranged from 'unable to sleep' to 'have thoughts of death and suicide' – you have to watch for this kind of thing.

Then there were Elderplan's walking clubs and telephone programmes, plus a nutrition discussion group, a current events discussion group, the phone fitness group – and that was just in May. Not to mention the Birthday Club – a phone group for people born on the same day. And telephone bingo of course. But what made these so exciting for me is that many of them are again funded not by old-fashioned dollars or pounds, but with time dollars. Each time dollar earned by members looking after each other, visiting, giving lifts, teaching each other or just making supportive phone calls, fuels this whole other economy which they can rely on. It provides the counselling services, the training, even house repairs. The dollar economy can't afford to do this, but because they have invented their own currency, and the people who use it accept it, earn it and believe in it, the whole thing works.

That's not all. In Brooklyn, members can even pay part of their medical insurance in time dollars. Or they can if they have to pay it. It takes 109 hours of volunteer work to pay a quarterly insurance bill. 'Elderplan benefits because volunteers . . . are doing for free what the plan would otherwise have to pay a home help attendant to do,' explained the *Brooklyn Daily News*, in my pile of cuttings. They could have added that earning time dollars seems to keep people healthier.

Member to Member was one of the first time banks, set up in 1987 with a grant from the ever-present Robert Wood Johnson Foundation. Ten years on, their programmes have been such a success that they are expanding out of Brooklyn and into Queens and Staten Island. By the time I got there, Member to Member volunteers – of which there are 1,100 – had carried out 60,000 hours of time dollar credits, I was told. 'Within the population of older people, there are several generations and significant

differences. Obviously we try to focus on the weller members –
we look for people who can provide support services, visiting for
isolated people, escorts to see the doctors, things that will erode
someone's independence if they are without them. If you can't
see to read the mail or pay the bills, then you will eventually be
evicted. That's the core of the programme,' said my guide.

'How long are they allowed to keep their credits?' I asked.

'For ever. If the programme closes or things change, we have
made arrangements with other organizations to carry on the services. It's also inflation-proof: an hour is an hour. In ten years
from today, a dollar is going to be worth a percentage of what it
is worth today, but a credit will still be worth an hour. It's the
great equalizer.'

I asked the magic question for time dollars: does it change
people who take part? Does it make them nicer? Does it transform
them?

'Well, one of the biggest things about the time dollar programme is that they're feeling needed,' she said. 'We also have
more women than men, and many of them have never really
worked before, and are discovering skills that they never knew
they had – that they never had an opportunity to develop before,
like leading workshops.

'To me it's really – and I don't say this very often – it's a sort
of communist approach. People volunteer and they give what
they can, and they get what they need: from each according to
his ability and to each according to his needs.'

I looked at her with new eyes. Americans are not in the habit
of quoting Karl Marx very often. Neither am I. I only ever think
of the old monster when I wander past his squalid flat in Dean
Street in London, and think of him eking out *Das Kapital* word
by word while his children screamed around him.

But it was time to sample a time dollars self-help group. I chose
the group of recently bereaved. 'Oh, they love to talk to people,'
she said reassuringly. How right she was. The Jewish community
centre in Brooklyn was a homely building which looked like
a municipal swimming pool in a small Yorkshire town. It was
embedded in a neighbourhood of large blocks of flats, the inevitable graffiti, and signboards for organizations called things like
'Saving Jewish Souls from the Perils of Assimilation'. And dentists. There were dentists everywhere: advanced dentists, general
dentists, cosmetic dentists, Russian dentists. And of course, Jewish dentists. Brooklyn people must have some of the most tended
teeth in the world.

The same homely whiff of Yorkshire could be found inside the community centre, with its worn marmalade carpets, complete with years of coffee stains and long-forgotten umbrellas. I crept into the widows' self-help group with trepidation. Would there be hostility, despair, hysterics? I simply had no idea. But I had reckoned without the down-to-earth charm of elderly Jewish ladies from Brooklyn.

'You sit right down there,' they said straight off, as I steered myself past the pile of coloured wellies on to a free chair in the circle of nine widows and two widowers. I smiled inanely.

'Look at his dimples. Has he got a girlfriend? Ask him if he's got a girlfriend.'

'He looks just like my youngest son in Philadelphia. I'm going to give him a hug at the end.'

'You just sit there and we'll look at you. I think he's a shy one,' said a delightful lady, who seemed to have struck up some kind of romance with the very shy-looking elderly man next to her.

It really was disturbing. It is rare at the age of thirty-eight to be lionized in quite this way, but to be lionized simultaneously by a phalanx of recent widows was scary. They all seemed much tougher than me. I tried to imitate the Mona Lisa with my facial features – for all I know that explains her mysterious smile – and look generally welcomed and unobtrusive.

This was actually the self-help group which had graduated from the bereaved group. They were supposed to have survived the first flush of despair, and were now being encouraged to talk about what they had been doing, with the general assumption that it was good to keep busy. The proceedings were organized by Grace, a brisk but welcoming woman in purple slacks and brand-new sports shoes. She was being paid in time dollars.

'Well, I've just graduated from arthritis self-help,' said one woman in a yellow headscarf. 'That means I can do this,' she said, tapping each finger in turn against her thumb.

'If you can do that, you don't need us,' said the woman sitting next to her.

Many of the others had been actively visiting people even older than themselves, and earning their own time dollar credits by doing so. A widower in a white baseball cap had a mother aged 105. 'She don't remember, but she's alive,' he told us.

One of them played the violin in an old people's home – the very words gave the group a collective shudder. 'Some of them can't even applaud,' she said. 'At the end of the performance, this woman grabbed my arm and said "play!" She was blind, and it meant so much to her. There were tears running down my cheeks.'

'You know when you tour those places,' said Grace, 'you have to go down on bended knee and thank God you're not there.'

'They take your independence away,' said another in the group. 'Your mind tends to go down.'

Then more mundane problems. One woman wanted advice about her valuables at home. 'I worry about going out. I live all alone,' she said.

'Everybody lives alone. We all live alone,' said somebody else tetchily.

The man with the baseball cap also had a problem. 'I've had a catastrophe, really bad. My VCR broke. You people talk about tragedies: I got real problems.' The group responded to this as if it was a flirtation – as indeed it was in a way.

'Now my TV's stuck on Channel 13,' he said – Channel 13 is New York's intellectual channel, with wall-to-wall David Attenborough and BBC costume dramas. 'I put it on when I get back and a lion is walking, a giraffe is walking or there's the Three Tenors. You don't want to see that kind of thing again and again.'

You certainly don't. But there was by now a rustle and the session was clearly over, not because it had reached an end, but because there was a special cheap lunch elsewhere in the community centre. The ones that were left fumed, but at least had time to talk to me about Member to Member. Some of them got their repairs done with time dollars. Somebody else had her shopping done for time dollars by a time dollar 'volunteer'. 'She's my angel,' she told me.

They even asked me out to lunch with them, but I had to get back into Manhattan for my final New York visit: to see the supposed source of the old kind of money, and to go where Jeremy Irons entered so explosively through a tunnel in *Die Hard With a Vengeance* – the Federal Reserve of New York. But I had been moved by the whole encounter. The new kinds of money somehow didn't matter to the Brooklyn widows, though not because they were unimportant. They were just part of life's plumbing, so to speak – providing what was needed reliably and pretty unobtrusively.

My grandparents have long since died, and we London yuppie types have very limited contact with older people. Meeting them and reading what they had written in Member to Member's newsletter *Volunteer Voice*, I felt the poorer for it. The memories they wrote about there were particularly vivid: their dancing

Victorian grandparents, their father killing a pet chicken by Sara-
toga Lake, all a lifetime before. And the continuing sense of
uncertainty:

'So much beauty still to gaze on,' wrote one old lady in a poem:

> *'Task unfinished, hours so few,*
> *If I set my task with vigour,*
> *Make my plans and stay the route:*
> *Will I realize all I dream of,*
> *Plant the seed, then pick the fruit?'*

VI

The Federal Reserve of New York has immense power and influence. So much so that I had to book my tour in advance: I am
not yet on chatting terms with the formidable governor Alan
Greenspan, whose every word seems to twitch the markets. So
it wasn't until the end of my stay in New York – having met
Womanshare, played phone bingo in Brooklyn and watched the
stock market plummet – that I was finally able to visit.

It is also a peculiar institution, founded out of a compromise
in 1913. American political traditions couldn't quite swallow a
central bank, so the Fed is financially independent of the US
government and is organized as a network of twelve reserve
banks around the country. The New York Fed covers New York
state, the north of New Jersey, the south of Connecticut, and –
for some reason – Puerto Rico and the US Virgin Islands. But it
has some other vital roles which the others don't have. For one
thing, it provides the main engine of US government borrowing,
which means this is the place where the money which pops out
in dollar bills and on the National Debt Clock is conjured into
existence.

Treasury Notes and Treasury Bills – known as T-Bills – with
varying dates of maturity are auctioned here day after day to
keep the engines of government whirring. In order to put dollar
bills into circulation, the Federal Reserve must buy these bills
and notes to underpin the cash – buying government debt, in
effect. The mighty dollar, like the pound, both backed by gold
within living memory, is now backed by debt.

The other speciality of the Federal Reserve of New York is that
it holds in its vaults, a hundred feet below the surface, a leftover
from the bygone age when money really *was* money – about one
third of the world's gold reserves. Jeremy Irons' gangsters entered

the Fed via a tunnel, a feat which nobody has ever achieved, either here or at the Bank of England. In *Die Hard With a Vengeance*, the gangsters had to explode a bomb in the Wall Street subway station and then dig – remarkably easily, I thought – right into the vault.

But I went in through the front door, marvelling for a moment at the unusual brick monstrosity I was entering, with its hideous black metal bars and fearsome ironwork lamps. Architect Philip Sawyer designed the bank like the Florentine palaces he had studied in Italy. He had a particular penchant for the Palazzo Strozzi, which is why there are now 200 tons of wrought ironwork decorating the outside. And I thought it was just extra security.

I walked past the notices banning smoking and directing people to the day's auction of T-Bills, and entered into the fantasy of the place. Because although the Fed is a thoroughly modern institution, there is a kind of nostalgic game played with visitors like me that it is still sixty years ago and gold is still the key to everything. As if money – like Father Christmas – was still real. The notice about the T-Bill auction was the last mention of the Fed's modern role during my tour: everything else was devoted to the piles of metal in the basement.

The security guards were looking pretty relaxed in the lobby as I delved into their small exhibition of letters, designed to show the crucial role the Fed had played in building the world's financial system. There was a photo of all the great central bankers of the past, taken on Long Island in the summer of 1927: Strong from Washington, Schacht from Berlin, Norman from London and Rist from Paris.

This was the meeting which had to face the first consequences of linking currencies to the value of gold in 1925 – a saga which seems to be re-enacting itself with the single European currency. They fudged the issue and probably paved the way for economic collapse. Montagu Norman was looking tall and elegant in his hot Edwardian suit, just two years before the Wall Street Crash and four years or so before the Great Depression for which he is held partly responsible.

Further down the corridor, past some oppressive paintings of the Connecticut countryside, were the current prices for Treasury Bills and Notes and some desks where you could buy your own. I declined, but I did pick up some of the Fed's unusual literature explaining their role in simple metaphoric and glowing terms: unusual, because I felt sure the Bank of England would not deign to explain itself – 'Never Apologize, Never Explain' might be the

Bank of England's motto – and certainly not in comic-book format, as used by the Fed.

My bag had been X-rayed and locked in a cupboard just in case, and I found – by some administrative oversight perhaps – that I had not joined the visitor's tour after all, but twenty-nine new Federal Reserve employees on their induction course. 'Do we get to meet Bruce Willis?' said one of them, as we shot eighty feet below the surface in a lift. The fact that we were not likely to is why around one hundred governments, central banks and other organizations around the world keep their gold here, in anonymous blue-painted cages in the vault. The gold justifies the employment of enough security guards to populate a small town.

The gold is held in trust for other countries around the world, but instead of moving it around the world for trade, where it might get lost or stolen or goodness knows what, all you need do is call up the people at the Fed and they stamp your gold bars and move them to the cage belonging to the government you owe them to. About 9,000 tons of gold live below the Fed, so if Bruce Willis or anyone like him did get in, there would be diplomatic chaos. The US government's own gold is kept in Fort Knox.

'Most of it was sent here before the Second World War,' the guide told us. 'We don't charge for this service because it is good public relations and good for the US. And it also means that if we are in dispute with other countries, we can freeze their assets. More gold is leaving than is coming in,' he added sadly. 'We don't know why.' He shook his head at the fickleness of foreigners. But if they do too much asset-freezing, I could have told him why the gold is leaving: Americans tend to be blind about how they put people off with their occasionally noisy determination to get their own way.

We passed through a series of blue-painted rooms, with pump-action shotguns in glass cases, and half-drunk plastic cups of coffee resting on the top of them. Then finally the enormous circular airtight vault doors were swung open – there is just enough air in the vault for one person for three days – and there was the gold piled in front of us. It was an extraordinary sight, because although it no longer underpins the world financial system, it remains frighteningly valuable. When each bar is worth $150,000, I calculated that the smallish five-foot pile was probably the equivalent of Britain's annual budget for the NHS.

The staff being inducted were silent as well, as a businesslike manager in a skullcap opened the inner gates and we could see the little rooms and the piles of gold snaking away into the distance. 'Since you're all staff, we'll let you handle the gold,' said a brisk woman who seemed to be in charge. 'But don't drop it.'

The guide went white and slipped me his own security pass. 'Just in case,' he whispered nervously. And after a few moments the gold bar was passed to me. I half-expected a big hand to grasp my shoulder with the words: 'Hang on, son, are you with the Fed?' But no: I was allowed to hold it. It was extremely heavy, as if it packed the weight of a car wheel into the size of a box of chocolates, and it looked old and gnarled with its different stamp marks to show when it had been passed from cubicle to cubicle. I realized it was worth considerably more than my London flat.

It was a disturbing moment, and I wasn't quite sure why. Holding a gold bar seemed to recapture those moments of childhood when you did something furtively adult, like drink beer or handle large sums of money by mistake. And there was something childlike to it, as if – in our topsy-turvy world of financial relativity where nothing is quite what it seems – this was real.

But I'm not absolutely sure it was. There is a paradox about gold, after all. To start with, money was linked to gold because it provided a clear standard. In the end gold remained valuable because it underpinned money – and we all carry with us the folk memory of those days. Yet when you realize that all the gold reserves in the world piled together would only measure fifty-five feet cubed, it becomes clear why the right to exchange your money into gold on demand just couldn't last. The final vestiges of the gold standard were swept away by Richard Nixon in 1971, but for all practical purposes, the dollar had long since been delinked, as the pound had been a generation before.

Gold has always been valuable, but it wasn't until the sixteenth century when the Spanish brought it back from the New World, exchanged – against the best efforts of Christopher Columbus – for bits of old leather and broken plates, that one medieval religion began to make way for another. Keynes said that British capitalism began in 1580, when Sir Francis Drake returned on the *Golden Hind* carrying vast quantities of gold stolen from the Spanish. Queen Elizabeth I was a major shareholder in the expedition, and with her profit she was able to pay off the whole of the national debt and still have £40,000 left over. With this she set up the Levant Company, and out of the profits of that, the East India Company began and so on and so on. Keynes calculated that that £40,000 invested at average rates of interest, less a percentage of profits brought home, would come out more or less exactly to the £4,000 million which British foreign investments were worth when he was writing in 1930.

'Every £1 which Drake brought home in 1580 has become

£100,000,' wrote Keynes in 1930. 'Such is the power of compound interest.'

You can't do a similar computation for American wealth. It had its beginnings with the chickens and seeds brought over with the *Mayflower* pilgrims, and that has somehow been conjured into the towers of Manhattan or Houston – partly through theft from the Indians, partly through knowhow and sheer hard work, and partly through wild and imaginative belief in currencies, money and debt. And by rickety banks lending reckless non-existent sums to win the Wild West. Americans seem to understand this stretchable aspect of money – its benefits and pitfalls – more than we do. 'Plain men with commonsense views about money,' wrote Keynes about the British, 'are often the slaves of some defunct economist.'

This stretchable aspect of money increases its mystery. Like God and the bread and wine, money can be in lumps of metal or pieces of paper one moment and then suddenly not. Somehow it makes its religious nature all the more apparent when you're in Wall Street – described by the legendary journalist H. L. Mencken as a 'thoroughfare that begins in a graveyard and ends in a river'. Halfway down, you run across the St Nicholas Greek Orthodox church, almost swallowed up by the alternative gods and looking like a municipal lido – with the sign advertising the times of services dwarfed by two massive notices next to it displaying the charges for the car park which now surrounds the church.

It's a matter of what you believe is important and real. And right at the heart of the American money religion is this element of belief. When belief fails, as Arthur Miller wrote in *The American Clock*, everything comes tumbling down. 'This is what I've been trying to tell you for a long time now, doctor,' says his hero. 'The market represents nothing but a state of mind.'

Which leaves me with rather a worry, because we know what religions do to unbelievers. The medieval church killed the heretics and early atheists, not just because they felt a bit differently about life, but because the existence of unbelief threatened God's tenuous and tolerant relationship with the world. Letting atheists wander around infecting things could bring about a response worthy of Sodom and Gomorrah. When they accused the dissolute playwright Christopher Marlowe of being an atheist, it wasn't just an insult – it was a serious threat.

So it struck me, as I put pen to paper: maybe it's the same with money-atheists. Those of us who don't believe there is anything at the heart of our money system could have the same effect on the gigantic bubble as Arthur Miller's hero did on Wall Street. We threaten a long pin and an absolutely massive pop. Maybe this book will generate the same response from the City of London as Salman Rushdie's *The Satanic Verses* attracted from the Ayatollah.

But perhaps there is another kind of money we can believe in. Like people's time in the case of Brooklyn's old people, or people's support for each other in the case of Womanshare, because they both seem to work. Or something else. I walked across Washington Square in the Sunday sunshine, past the fat elderly men with bare chests, the wizened old ladies reading books about finding husbands, and a group of Hassidic Jews with long black curls giving out leaflets. I took a longer than usual glance at their stand full of pamphlets and this attracted their attention.

'Sir! Hi! Are you Jewish?' one of them asked. I told him I wasn't.

'Here,' he said. 'Have this anyway. And have a nice one.' And he gave me a small credit-card-sized piece of cardboard, called The Good Card. I was rather pleased.

Americans are fascinated by images of money, like the forty-foot greenhouse painted like a dollar bill that weekend in Battery Park, and this 'credit card' was no exception. It came from a radical Jewish group called Chabad Lubavitch Centers, with a phone number to call to find out more (514-842-GOOD), and introduced the World of Good Campaign, calling for acts of kindness to bring about the arrival of the Messiah.

'Use your Good Card as a reminder to include more good deeds in your daily life,' it said on the back. 'This is the ultimate credit card. It won't burden you with debt – the more you use it, the more credit you get.'

Chapter 5

Ithaca: money as lifeblood

'My boy, he says, always try to rub up against money, for if
you rub up against money long enough, some of it may rub off
on you.'
Damon Runyon, *Furthermore.*

I

'I was short of money and it occurred to me to print some,' said
Paul Glover during our first discussion over the phone – though
he didn't sound exactly overjoyed to hear that I was coming to
Ithaca to see him. Still, it was a thrilling statement to make – and
an excellent sound-bite – with just the right element of rebellious
indifference and shock value. It also described exactly what he
had been doing for the past few years. But he left out the guts
of the story: most people who print their own money are arrested.
So the next step in my search was further north, to find him in
Ithaca in upstate New York. I felt a little like Odysseus.

I hired a car to get there, complete with hideous red upholstery,
biscuit crumbs, and irritating automatic dimmable sidelights
which I spent ages trying to turn off. Like most American hire
cars, it was considerably bigger than I expected, with a bonnet
like a tennis court, and I struggled to make the monster do my
bidding – I'm one of those people who can't change the channels
of a car radio without the car swerving over the road.

I crossed the border into New York State, past whole villages
of service stations and the forests of billboards that straddle
American freeways, and the large chunks of car and dead deer
strewn along the hard shoulder, their legs sticking out in a very
undignified kind of *rigor mortis*. There were so many along one
stretch of road that it looked as if they had been taking part in
suicidal pranks in front of the passing trucks.

I resisted the temptation to follow signs like 'Endless Mountains: next six exits' and listened to an appalling talk-radio station
populated by offensive slow-talking shock-jocks. 'I sometimes

wonder if these southern Baptists understand the American way,' one of them drawled, so slowly that I could have written it down and picked my nose between words. 'If they don't like what Disney is doing, why don't they just buy it and make their own films?' I began to have a sneaking and unexpected sympathy for the moralizing southern Baptists. The jingle for the show was: 'Bill and Mike KICK ASS'.

By now I was driving through a series of identical, down-at-heel, whitewashed townships – Caroline, Slaterville, Richford, which turned out to be the birthplace of John D. Rockefeller – not that it has done Richford much good. There were sad, obscure signs by the road by grass patches, indicating that something historic no longer stood there. 'Cabin site,' said one. 'Cabin built by Maria Earsley, 1794, first settler in Caroline, first trip from Roxbury, New Jersey, on horseback with son John.'

I passed valley after valley of old shacks, run-down story-book farms, with silver caps on their silos and rusty hulks and evocative signs by the road: 'Woody's Small Engine Repair', 'Hog Hollow Road', and one small building which offered both 'Home Cooking for Rent' and 'Viking Vermin and Pest Control'. One church by a big road intersection said: 'If the sermon doesn't rouse you, the trucks will.'

The financial glow from Wall Street did not reach out here. The money had flowed down to New York City and the people had followed, leaving peeling porches, old machinery and all the paraphernalia of agricultural distress. The problem is, as Edgar Cahn and Jonathan Rowe explain in their book *Time Dollars*, that 'money can defect' – like some of Britain's inner city estates, where the milk has long since stopped being delivered and the only remaining economic activities are the weekly arrival of Giro cheques, followed shortly afterwards by the loan sharks. Economists barely recognize the defection of money from communities as a separate problem, but communities *can* run out of cash – rural communities as well as cities, and some of them do. Some American economists estimate that seventy-five cents of every dollar the government pours into Indian reservations flows straight out again within forty-eight hours.

One alternative economist who has been grappling with this problem is David Morris of the Institute for Local Self-Reliance. 'Neighbourhood investors in downtown Chicago had deposited several million in local banks, but received back only $150,000 in loans,' he wrote. 'Of the $35 million the 30,000 residents of Carbondale, Illinois, and Northampton, Massachusetts spent on oil, gasoline, natural gas and electricity, more than $30 million left the economy immediately.'

Money also goes straight into the tills of the big out-of-town stores, which is one reason for the political backlash against superstores in the USA – what the *New York Times* called 'America's quiet rebellion against McDonaldization'. It's a criticism from the left, but echoed by the right as well in Pat Buchanan's condemnation of big business and footloose capital. In the UK, economists reckon that almost half of everything we spend will go to just 250 companies by the year 2000. In the USA, there is more of a surviving fine mesh of smaller businesses, but they have also turned out-of-town shopping into a fine art. A generation of vast K-marts, elephantine Barnes & Noble bookstore, acres of potholed parking lots, are sucking what remains of the local economy out of town-centre shops.

As many as 80 per cent of Americans live outside cities. They resist the spectre of identikit small towns with throttled local economies, as we all do.

Concern about the issue on the east coast focuses on Wal-Mart, the monster chain stores which made Arkansas businessman Sam Walton one of the richest men in the USA. Every Wal-Mart in the USA sends its takings down to Arkansas every evening: a massive flow of money away from small towns. Wal-Mart now has 2,800 stores and annual sales of $93 billion, but met its match in a vociferous community campaign in Hamilton, outside New Jersey's capital, Trenton. Other New Jersey and New York neighbourhoods followed suit, one of them a small town of 30,000 called Ithaca.

I can't say that Ithaca was the most interesting town in the world. Actually it isn't even in the top couple of thousand. It has a dull concrete city centre, crumbling cinemas and unimaginative car parks, but it was relaxed, somehow, and there are important points of interest. There is City Hall, a satisfyingly tiny block, five windows across. There is Cornell University and there are lakes. 'Where else can you get libraries of tens of thousands of years of human knowledge, and down the road be able to go skinny dipping?' someone asked me later. And reaching right into the centre from the university, there are the gorges – with massive jungle waterfalls, a hundred feet high. Some of the Tarzan films were shot there, which gives some indication of how strangely out of place they seem. 'ITHACA YOU'RE GORGES' said one bumper sticker I passed. Like many centres of counter-culture, Ithaca people set great store by bumper stickers.

And finally there is Ithaca's revolutionary method for revitalizing the local agricultural economy and fighting off Wal-Mart at the same time – printing their own money. As a result, a closer look at the town shows that although parts are clearly crumbling and its concrete town centre isn't exactly thriving, Ithaca is certainly hanging on. There were at least three small bookshops in the main shopping street, and secondhand clothes shops and craft shops which would have long since been forced out in similar British or American shopping centres. Something about Ithaca's economy seemed to be working.

I needed to find my lodgings, and was directed out along Meadow Road – or Route 13 as the state government would call it – past the shopping malls, K-mart, Dunkin Donuts and all the rest of them, gleaming on potholed tarmac, just as they do outside almost every other city in the United States. I found the road where I was staying down a beaten track past two competing tyre depots. It had few house numbers, and the two passers-by I asked for directions seemed unable or unwilling to help – or maybe they just didn't understand what I was saying.

After fifteen minutes of knocking on doors with no reply, I found a rusty old Volvo, with a telltale bumper sticker bearing the slogan 'BUILD COMMUNITY POWER WITH ITHACA HOURS'. My host Marty arrived shortly afterwards, with tied-back hair and a big smile. She glanced at my deeply unfashionable grey socks under my shorts, and said: 'You must be David Boyle.'

Her wooden house had a balcony, rickety stairs and exiting clutter inside: spices, notices, drawings, old computers, six guitars on the wall, some half-completed weaving – probably an Ithaca speciality in honour of Odysseus and Penelope – a piano and a marmalade cat stretched out on the bed. And unusually for an American household, who all have showers instead these days, a proper British-style iron bath. Down the stairs to the basement, past the videos of *The Sound of Music*, the glue and step-ladders, was my bedroom, normally the venue for a group of local herbalists. I felt a little embarrassed about my gleaming white hire car with its New York plates and blood-red upholstery.

Feeling more relaxed, I set out to explore Ithaca and to track down Paul Glover who, I had to admit, sounded a little less enthusiastic about my visit every time I called him. 'Paul is a great guy, but he doesn't like academics much,' said Marty from the veranda, as I set off into town, my black briefcase looking badly out of place in the early evening haze. 'I just thought I ought to warn you.'

'But I'm not an academic,' I said hopefully, my heart sinking a little.

II

Paul Glover is one of those angry, multi-talented people who flit from enthusiasm to enthusiasm, and suddenly find themselves – rather unexpectedly perhaps to some people – bang in the middle of a success. He has degrees in advertising, marketing and city management and might as well have one in protest. During the Vietnam War, when Ithaca was almost in open revolt, he had to use a false name to avoid the FBI. 'I have a long and diverse background,' he told me later, evasively, when I asked him about it.

But protest turned into positive action. He founded a group called Citizen Planners in Los Angeles in 1978, which led to the publication of his study about how to rebuild the city sustainably over twenty years. He even walked across the USA, through valleys and woods from sea to shining sea, a bit like Forrest Gump. But Glover is no Gump. You wouldn't catch Forrest Gump getting a grant from the Fund for Investigative Journalism in Washington; it was this which brought Glover back to Ithaca to write a report on the local energy supply, and then another about the region's economy.

Like so many places in depressed agricultural areas or no-go cities, Ithaca had a problem with cash, and moving from energy to money made this obvious. Once you looked at the local economy as if it were made up of energy flows, you realized the cash was disappearing almost as fast as it was appearing – which was increasingly rarely. The local businesses and small farmers were being squeezed and money was going to big corporations or utilities, who took it straight out of town.

So here was his idea. Imagine for a second that Ithaca had its own money. The big chains and banks wouldn't accept it, and it would stick around being re-used locally, providing some kind of income for people on the fringes of the local economy. In short, it was a win-win deal – the only people who would lose would be the Wal-Marts and K-marts of the world. But could it work?

Paul Glover found himself doodling cartoons of Ithaca money with his girlfriend in early 1991. They stuck in his mind when he was lying in bed listening to National Public Radio – a bit like Radio 4, Classic FM and Radio Oxford all rolled into one – and hearing about early local money experiments in Massachusetts. 'That was the immediate spark,' he said. 'I rolled over and made a sketch.' The designs for the Ithaca money notes came quite early in the scheme, as did the characteristic slogan 'IN ITHACA WE TRUST' – a parody of the motto on the dollar. Four of the designs – of salamanders and gorges – were by local artists, while one note has a couple of cherubs taken from a British bookplate. The local currency was to be called 'hours'.

Paul had been involved in setting up a LETS project in Ithaca in the late 1980s, but only about thirty people had participated and it had folded when the organization which owned the computer – called, rather sadly, the Self-Reliance Center – closed down in 1988. So there was both interest and suspicion about local money, and with his designs burning a hole in his pocket, Paul began to take advice. He tackled two locals about it: Cornell economics professor Dave Wharton, and Patrick Jennings, who had written a thesis about LETS and was keen to find a new kind of money which anybody could use, rather than just members. Something beyond time dollars, in other words.

Professor Wharton later wondered in an interview, with the kind of honest ignorance you don't usually find in an economist, why Ithaca Hours seemed to be working. 'I'm not quite sure why you can't sell your services for dollars if you *can* sell them for hours, but for some reason there are people who seem to get left out of the dollar network,' he said.

But that was in the future, and all this was new territory, and there were a large number of possibly insurmountable problems ahead. First, there was the problem of the currency itself. It had to be creditable and it had to be legal. It also had to be impossible to forge. In fact it had to be 'better than dollars', said Paul later.

Then there was the problem of how to promote it. 'A newspaper seemed to me the best way to keep everyone informed,' he told the alternative economist Richard Douthwaite. 'Moreover, like other newspaper editors, I'm not responsible for supplying the tax authorities with information about the business affairs of my advertisers.' The first notes were issued to businesses advertising in the paper, and organizers decided early on to advise people using hours that they should be counted as taxable for the tax authorities, if they were used for professional services. We don't want to 'provoke the sleeping IRS giant', said Paul in a 1992 memo.

Then there was the major problem of persuading people to accept the notes. Paul went out hammering on doors and found as many as ninety tradespeople willing to accept hours and list themselves in his new *Ithaca Money* newspaper. The biggest coup was persuading two local cinemas to accept them for the full price of tickets, earnings they would spend on cider from Littletree Orchards, one of the farming co-ops which backed hours early on. In return for advertising in the paper, Paul issued them with the first notes. Littletree, incidentally, now pays some of its staff entirely in hours.

The first issue of *Ithaca Money* appeared at the end of 1991 with the headline 'Better Than Bucks', listing the benefits of the new currency. According to the paper it:

- Creates new jobs by connecting people with those who need their skills and products.
- Recycles waste within Ithaca, rather than exporting or land-filling it.
- Finds new customers.
- Creates interest-free credit.
- Protects our savings from inflation.
- Insulates Ithaca from the shocks of the national economy.

'Hours is money with a boundary around it, so it stays in our community,' Glover told the television interviewers. 'It doesn't come to town, shake a few hands and then wander out across the globe. It reinforces trading locally.'

Five out of the six original objectives seem to have worked out. But the penultimate point, protecting savings from inflation, has fallen by the wayside for the time being. The original idea was that one Ithaca Hour would be worth an hour's work. Paul had made the currency worth $10, because that was a little above the average agricultural wage for an hour's work. If they were shrewd about it, Ithaca Hours might also raise the local wages. But in practice the link with the value of the dollar has been important, because it allows businesses to accept hours for purchases, and in the end this has been far more valuable. Still, the inflation-busting aspect of hours is held in reserve. If there were ever to be mega-inflation – and with the U S budget deficit running at $5 trillion, that may not be impossible – then hours could theoretically take the value of a 1998 dollar and ride out the storm.

The first *Ithaca Money* also included an article about the local economy in Tompkins County, of which the city is part. 'Tompkins County industry has been fumbling our lives for years,' wrote Paul. 'Since 1980, nearly 3,000 manufacturing jobs, paying on average $473 weekly, have been lost and replaced by service jobs paying about $210 weekly.' There was the problem in a nutshell. The old jobs of making and selling were being increasingly centralized, taken over by big international chains. The new jobs in a place like Ithaca, two to three hours away from Wall Street, were dependent and low-paid. Local economic self-determination was flowing away, and people were feeling more and more insecure.

The local paper, *Ithaca Times*, was supportive, carrying a picture of Paul looking like Robert Shaw in *Force Ten from Navarone*. 'Paul Glover has honest blue eyes and the sort of gaze that couldn't lie,' they said, and as someone who was intending to break the monopoly of the dollar by force of personality, he needed them.

Not all the local coverage was positive. Local columnist Scott Samuels painted a lurid scenario where Ithaca Hours were the first step back to wearing racoon pelts. Ithaca Hours are 'more communist than Big Red Bucks or Greenbacks', he said. 'The currency, which may even be illegal, is accepted at only a handful of stores for now, and if it ever catches on, will catapult Ithaca back into the prehistoric age.'

Paul Glover replied with characteristic irony in the following issue. 'The commie rag *Sales and Marketing Management* suggests barter should be "an essential ingredient in the long-term plan" of Fortune 500 companies, and that "bartering is increasingly seen as a sophisticated tool for building sales". They are dragging us back to the Stone Age,' he wrote. 'Even worse, these phony hours are backed by nothing but promises by local people. Give me dollars, by God, that are backed by our Congress, the Savings & Loans, the majestic debt and trade deficit of the United States of America . . . You and me have a lot of work to do, Scott, to protect America from Ithaca.'

The Savings and Loans were the US equivalent of British building societies – as fans of James Stewart will remember in *It's a Wonderful Life*. They disappeared at vast expense to the US tax-payer in a financial scandal still being investigated by nibbling journalists.

In spite of Scott Samuels' cynicism, which must have been shared by many others in Ithaca at the time, Ithaca Hours began to work. The first restaurant meal was bought with hours on 29 October 1991 at the Cabbagetown Café. The receipt is now in Ithaca's museum. By issue three of *Ithaca Money*, Paul was grow-ing more expansive. 'Strength of Hour Grows While Value of Dollar Declines', said the headline. By issue four, the tone was even more confident: 'We're Richer When We Hire Each Other', proclaimed the front page. 'We're Making a Community While Making a Living'.

By 1993, eighteen months into the great experiment, hours

began to attract serious interest from outside. Small grants began to arrive, from Ben & Jerry's and the New Road Map Foundation, the alternative economics think-tank in Seattle. Ithaca Hours organizers were also making their own interest-free loans. Nine loans, up to fifty hours each, had been issued by 1996, and twenty-seven local charities and non-profit projects have now received grants in hours.

The grants are made by whoever turns up to their 'Barter Potluck' meetings held in the local wholefood supermarket, GreenStar, on the fifteenth of every month. This amounts to 9.5 per cent of the monthly issue of cash, and one of the main ways the money is put into circulation. Grants have been made over the years to the Local Task Force on Battered Women, Offender Aid and Restoration of Tompkins County, and MAGPY (Mothers and Grandmothers Protecting Youth), whose self-appointed job it is to hold big parties to keep local young people away from drugs. (Barter Potluck, incidentally, is derived from the North American Indian *potlatch* ceremonies – massive community exchanges, dancing and initiation festivals – eventually banned by the Canadian government in 1927.)

In the same year, 1993, the scheme received its first piece of major nationwide publicity in the alternative newspaper *Mother Earth News*, which gave a glowing account of Ithaca Hours in practice. 'Restaurant owner Michael Turback swears that he can practically hear people smiling over the phone when he tells them that he accepts Ithaca Hours for payment at his restaurant,' said the article in big letters across the two-page spread. The manager of the local credit union, Bill Myers, was also complimentary: 'When you put an extra $50 in someone's paycheck, they often use it to pay off a bill. When you give someone extra hours, they do something special with it.'

This did appear to be the secret. Hours were making ordinary dollars stretch further, and encouraging people to buy services or goods which they never usually used – which is why those people providing services on the fringes of the economy seemed to be helped in particular. There was a sense of something rather illicit. When you spent hours – and I found this myself – there was just a little thrill of getting something for nothing.

When I arrived in Ithaca, the *Ithaca Money* newspaper was on issue twenty-nine, and 5,700 hours – representing $57,000 – were in circulation. The amount of money traded in the five and a half years since the launch was estimated to be somewhere in the region of 150,000 hours, or $1.5 million.

To somebody like me, used to the marginal way in which new

currencies work, the range of services you can buy in hours was pretty astonishing. Under 'B' in the twenty-ninth edition, you could find the usual services like bath salts, baby-sitting, belly-dancing, book-keeping. Then there were Bonsai lessons and Bosnian translations, which are probably even more specialized – though who knows in a place like Ithaca? But there were also bank fees, bed and breakfast, bicycle repair, building, bowling and bricklaying. Not a bad selection. There was also a range of different kinds of psychotherapy: everything, in fact, from accounting to zipper repair, and a great deal of practical necessities like food, plus some enjoyably basic adverts like 'Joe's Truck'. The costliest item available, according to the paper, is a meteorite costing 8,260 hours. This may be difficult to achieve when you remember that only 5,700 have ever been issued.

By the time I arrived to track down Paul Glover, hours had received the ultimate accolade. A local restaurant had been robbed and the thief had gone out of his way to open a separate compartment of the till and take the hours as well as the dollars. Ithaca's local money had truly arrived.

III

'Yeah, I'll tell you about that,' said Paul Glover ominously, as I turned on my tape-recorder, balancing the microphone on a burnt-out candle, and mentioning I'd heard he wasn't too fond of academics. 'It would be good to start with that.'

We were sitting on his porch in the university area of Ithaca, just as the students were wandering up to the tapas bars and pizza joints at the top of the hill. It was one of those balmy hot summer evenings and already quite late. I had been afraid he would avoid me altogether, but here I was and here he was – in a 1995 Ithaca Festival T-shirt and an aggressive-looking spiky red beard, like a caricature of George Bernard Shaw in his prime. He was relaxing on a battered yellow sofa, surrounded by old boxes and what looked like a retired dentist's chair under a blanket. It was the kind of place I might have been offered a joint, except that he didn't look that friendly. I laughed nervously.

'Academics are paid salaries, and activists get garage sales,' he said slowly and deliberately. 'I could get more money to study Ithaca Hours than to co-ordinate the system. If I went poking around at it, analysed it, critiqued it, I could get myself a grant to do that. But to accelerate it, it's difficult to find the money. Also the academic process is very conservative. It doesn't take a bold leap of imagination. It doesn't take the risk of failing.'

It wasn't just academics he disapproved of. He didn't like tele-vision either. 'I would credit most of the Ithaca Hours idea to the habit of not watching television,' he said. 'Ideas are very normal. Some people have approached this as if it was an astonishing inspiration, but when one doesn't watch television, having ideas is commonplace.'

A deep suspicion of TV is quite common in Ithaca. In the Ithaca Hours 'bank' in Autumn Leaves Bookshop, where I exchanged my first hours – beautifully printed in yellow and pink with a line drawing of a salamander – I found stickers for sale showing a man beating his TV to death. Marty had no television either. One entry in the latest *Ithaca Money* offered 'TV collection and destruction'.

Number three on Paul's hate list was cars. In fact he hadn't even been a passenger in one – except once during a family crisis – since his famous walk across the USA. He cycles everywhere, and I often ran into him in his shorts and cycle helmet as I wandered round Ithaca. In fact, being ever-present on his bike, cajoling, reassuring and generally smiling at the users of hours, has been a key feature in their success.

Number four was the cult of personality. Paul had been refusing to let people photograph him, because he doesn't want to take the credit for Ithaca Hours. Their success, he says, is down to the community. And he particularly didn't want to talk about the days of the Vietnam War. 'Is it true you were forced to use a false name to escape the FBI?' I asked. He grimaced and changed the subject. But for all his shyness, he spoke in carefully crafted, perfectly grammatical, eminently quotable sound-bites. 'So much media attention has sought to focus on me. I'm not the Charles Atlas of local currencies,' he protested, distancing himself from the 1950s muscle-man. 'This community has made this happen. They have to make it work. It's like a community magic act. It's due to the boldness and acuity of hundreds of people. I publish the newspaper, I try to keep the list accurate, but 99.5 per cent of the actualization of this programme is to the credit of the public.' But still, even this determination did not prevent Paul from being voted 'Unsung Hero' in Ithaca's local paper in 1995.

I wanted to know what the challenges had been to the system as it grew, but this was the wrong question to ask. 'Well, first of all, nothing goes wrong,' he said. 'Economics is 85 per cent psychology, therefore the newspaper is about promotion. There is no bad news in it. It is an entirely self-fulfilling prophecy. When there were ninety people who agreed to take this money and three stores, the money was presented as being powerful, totally solid and totally wonderful. And by insisting on that for four and a half years, it has gradually come to be perceived as reliable – so that people will hold on to it – so desirable that people will prefer to be paid in it. It is a cultural process.'

This is all undoubtedly true. But isn't it interesting that, no matter how radical you are – from local money promoter to Chancellor of the Exchequer – you find yourself talking up the economy. Clearly Paul Glover is more successful at it than, say, Norman Lamont – who famously tried to talk up the pound as it sank inexorably through the floor on Black Wednesday 1992.

But there is another side to all this. If you want people to copy you, and carry on setting up hours systems around the world, you need to tell them the truth, don't you? Don't you need to look the mistakes full in the face? I asked.

But Paul was having another go at the academics. 'The academic is going to dissect this like a living cadaver, and is going to extrapolate – to pin it down like a bug on a specimen sheet,' he said, his chin jutting out. 'Part of my aggravation with the academics is that they pile on to this as a phenomenon, a novelty, something they can study, write papers about, pass the papers back and forth to each other, getting comfortable salaries. And I'm out here up to my neck in it day to day, translating what I learn into actual programmes – not as a lifelong incubator to protect myself from a coarse and hostile world.'

I didn't like to think of myself as escaping from a coarse and hostile world, so I pressed him about the difficulties. These are urgent issues, I said, and people needed to be able to try the same as he has. 'Ha!' he said. But rather to my surprise, this meant he agreed with me.

Luckily for Paul, there are other things to worry about. Like inflation. 'Everyone knows that if governments print too much money – or people distrust the currency – the value starts drifting down. Of course there is no chance of the kind of wheelbarrow hyper-inflation which we have all seen pictures of: not enough Ithaca Hours have been printed. But if people stop trusting its exchange value, they would end up accumulating it or refusing it.'

So how do Ithaca Hours control their money supply? For someone who wants to change the world, Paul Glover turns out to be enjoyably conservative in his monetary policy. Apart from keeping detailed figures – 50.5 per cent of the first issue notes from 1991 have been returned, he told me – the real work is keeping his ear to the ground, pedalling around on his bike, making sure the notes are not accumulating anywhere. As a result, there is a demand for hours which he likes to keep unsatisfied until the system has grown a little more.

'There is now generally a far greater demand for the money than supply. And hours are issued far more conservatively than are dollars. The original big notes are now worth anything up to twice their face value as collector's items. I have myself been offered one and a half times its value for one of the first ones. Hours are issued at a reasonable relation to the rate of expansion and the diversification of the list.'

'What is reasonable?' I asked, growing a little bolder as the conversation went on.

'Reasonable is that it works,' he said. Gut instinct counts in Ithaca.

Their phone survey showed that about $60,000 in hours is being traded in Ithaca every month, which makes it the largest local currency system in the world. Every note is moving once or one and a half times a month. Paul does his own survey, rather like an ornithologist tagging swans. Whenever he gets paid with an hour, he writes the date on it. Some have been back seven or eight times, and they are speeding up now they are being printed wallet-sized. 'I encourage other people to write on them what they have bought with them,' he told me. 'Not that many people have done that, though some of the regulars do. I think it's a tribute to the maturity of the money that it doesn't pile up in the retail sector. Most of it transacts among people who call each other up.'

Which brought us to the big question – what underpins Ithaca Hours? It obviously isn't gold. Nor, like dollars, is it debt. Hours are backed by the belief of the local community. 'I think the US money is backed by the US marines more than anything else,' he said with determination. 'We have enormous military power, so we can enforce access to raw materials. If the Japs became too powerful applying the rules of the game, this country would just step in and say we're changing the rules of the game now. That's all. Dollars are issued at a rate of $830,000 additional national debt every minute. We regard US money as funny money, under-pinned no longer by gold and silver but by less than nothing – by the trillion dollar national debt. And Ithaca Hours, by contrast, are backed by a specific market basket of goods and services.'

'Do you have any economics qualifications?' I asked.

'I'm a community economist,' said Paul bullishly.

'Does that mean self-appointed?'

'Yup . . . that's where all authority comes from – from assertion.

So I am a community economist, with all the rights and privileges associated therewith.'

Of course, he said, as I wandered down the steps to find my way home, even community backing can be vulnerable. 'All it takes is for Henry Kissinger to pronounce that this threatens the integrity of the dollar on which we all depend, and that's that,' he said. He made a squidging movement with his foot, on the top step, as if disposing of a snail.

IV

'You know what we call them now?' said Marty with a mischievous grin, waving an hour vaguely in the air. 'The Untraveller's Cheque. Because you have to use them here. You can't take them with you.'

On the face of it, that is the disadvantage about local money like hours. People will choose them only if they get some other benefits themselves – like more business or a better zing in the local economy. And looking at Ithaca more closely, I realized there was something just a little unusual about it. The biggest restaurant I found in the centre was vegetarian, and – unusually for the USA – the main shopping mall was in the middle of town. The other Ithaca malls were pretty paltry. The one near where I was staying was dwarfed by the out-of-town K-mart and Computer World, and sold almost nothing but cigarettes, chocolate and beer, presided over by a sharp elderly woman with a baseball cap and cheroot.

The Ithaca Commons mall in the centre was the kind of hideous concrete business we all decry in England, but it was busy. 'At least the shops are full,' said Marty. 'Some towns had one and it failed because of the out-of-town malls.' Among the shops there was Autumn Leaves, the secondhand bookshop which also serves as the Ithaca Hours bank. Joe, the manager, turned out to be the man advertising TV destruction in the *Ithaca Money* paper. I called him up about it later, and he said that although TV destruction wasn't exactly lucrative, he did get a steady couple of requests a year. Two of the four shops I asked said they took hours. 'I'm thinking of it,' said one. 'Maybe I will when they can pay for city taxes.'

The first store to take the risk was the GreenStar Co-op, just the other side of the railway. America is criss-crossed with these wholefood supermarkets, and they really are wonderful, with their air of hummus and enlightened capitalism. Some of the pâtés look ready-chewed and the indefatigable sense of lentils can be a little overwhelming, but they are friendly, varied and above all organic. Which means they don't contain chemicals which reduce your sperm count, and at the age of thirty-eight you have to consider these things. It is one of those peculiar aspects of life in Britain that we have failed to develop much along the same lines yet. We have piles of health-food shops, but somehow the custom has yet to build them into health super-markets. The English remain slavishly tied to Asda and Tesco.

Ithaca's GreenStar Co-op even has the word 'Peace' above the door to the manager's office, and a long chain of shoppers with push-chairs or wellies – occasionally both. The car park was filled with large rusty cars with bumper stickers – 'STOP WAL-MART', 'MAGIC HAPPENS' and 'HATRED IS NOT A FAMILY VALUE'. In the tills ahead of me, great bundles of hours were changing hands along with the dollars, in return for roast red pepper hummus and vanilla bean creme shampoo. I could see the notes peeping out as the tills opened.

'It's a great way to help strengthen the local economy,' said Alison, one of the Co-op managers, as I sat her down with an insipid cup of GreenStar tea and a gargantuan muffin. 'It also helps remind people of the importance of how you spend your money.' Which is why most of the GreenStar staff were paid partly in hours. Not very much: Alison's pay packet probably included about $520 in hours a year. 'But I know people who earn a significant part of their income in hours,' she told me.

Where does she spend them? 'Mostly on food, and I just used a half-hour on my new shoes, which normally cost $50. Then my partner and I bought a little crafted furniture, a bit of jewellery – movies, different things like that.'

GreenStar is obviously a friendly kind of place. I found myself smiling at the woman behind what would normally be the meat counter, which is not something you catch yourself doing in Tesco. And then, as I was queuing up to pay for a couple of pieces of liquorice, I got talking to a local landscaper. 'I think it's wonderful,' he said. But then he would: he pays between 10 and 15 per cent of his employees' wage packets in hours. He even gives his daughter her allowance in hours. 'I also sell plants for hours, and maybe buy honey and vegetables from the Farmers Market vendors. It's a pretty small loop, really. But then my bank takes it in return for what they charge me for bouncing a cheque.'

The small midweek version of the Farmers Market was taking place in the centre of town, with a row of stalls selling anything from cabbages and jewellery to hot Indian meals. The stallholders ranged from middle-class people after the Good Life to completely monosyllabic former hippies. 'Don't take a picture of me, take a picture of him,' said Paul, indicating one of the latter. I had run into him on his bike, checking up where the hours were flowing.

'It's a sort of like shiatsu massage,' he said. 'You have to search for the blockage.' And having found it, he goes through the list of places it can be spent and tries to bring the two sides together. And if he has to, he can sometimes buy the hours back to keep them in circulation, using his small regular volunteer's grant from the federal government. 'I pay my rent in hours and buy much of my food. In fact my appetite for hours is so huge that, when I get the money from the government, I ask round to see if I can buy any more.'

The big Farmers Market, where Paul buys his food, takes place on Saturdays under an enormous 300-yard canopy a little way out of town by a creek, where yachts with names like *Warr-en Peace* bob in the breeze, and sirens sound on the other side of the inlet. It was completely empty when I drove out there, except for the bare tables, and notices saying 'We Accept Hours' pinned to almost every one. On the hill behind, I could make out the pompous buildings of Cornell University, looking like an ancient Greek town.

It was the Farmers Market which provided the inspiration for how hours could work. 'I remember really clearly when Paul came up to me in my craft show – which is what I was doing then – and said "I've got a great idea",' said Marty. ' "We're going to print money and use it to exchange between ourselves." '

'I immediately clicked about how valuable the hours idea was: it was a great idea, because I bartered all the time at craft shows, but what if the people didn't want what I had?' Paul had then asked her what she thought of having a picture of a waterfall instead of George Washington on the notes. 'I said it was a great idea. He said, "Would you really accept that?" I said, "Great, 100 per cent. Do it." I was one of the first published backers, and then I got my hours – and I decided to buy goats' cheese with them, which was a bit of a luxury.

'So I went to the Farmers Market, and the guy who made the goats' cheese was signed up. We had this kind of idea that an hour represented an hour of work, but people aren't really using that. They are just translating it into dollars, and there's still a little confusion about it. He was describing all the things he had to do to make goats' cheese, and he said, "This is supposed to be worth an hour of my work?" So when we were finished, there were about fifteen people standing around, so I suggested that he just translate the dollar price into hours. I was the first person who had ever wanted to spend some with him, so that was our first time. It was a bit of a leap of faith. I never had any trouble spending it. And it's got easier and easier to use it at a variety of places. You can't store them: they've got zero interest, so you've got to use them.'

Marty had been involved with LETS, and she wanted Ithaca Hours to give people easier access to loans. 'My concern was that I didn't want it to be just a miniature version of our federal dollar economy, which has poverty and so on. Life for many people now would be extremely difficult without hours money,' she said.

'I think that is a responsibility which is probably only going to be enlarged. People have said some really interesting things to me about it too. One man said this had really loosened him up about money. It makes it really obvious what a symbol it is.'

'What did he mean by that?' I asked.

'That the money itself is just paper. You can't eat it. You can light a fire with it, but that's it. But the fact that it's worth something to other people is what makes it valuable, whether its dollars or hours.'

Another friend of hers had been carrying hours when he was mugged in New York City. 'You've got the wrong guy,' he said, showing the mugger his Ithaca notes. And they had a peculiar effect: the mugger was so astonished that he started chatting about the economy. 'It doesn't benefit people, does it?' he said.

V

'We have been gradually becoming respectable,' Paul told me. 'And at the same time we have been changing the definition of being respectable.' For one thing, hours were getting the enthusiastic backing of the mayor and the local chamber of commerce. For another, there were now four big envelopes kept in the Ithaca Museum, which made up the hours archive. This was my next stop, and it was a definite downside to Ithaca-style parochialism. I was charged $5 to consult the local history collection because I wasn't a resident of Tompkins County.

The museum itself is disposed of in about the time it takes to heat a cup of tea in the microwave. The only exhibit which I can remember was the very first cloth cat, which you still see advertised everywhere, and which emerged out of Ithaca in the 1890s.

Once I had the hours archive spread out in front of me, I found I had a whole range of smiling cartoons of people passing on the notes. Cartoons of manically happy people have been a key feature of the whole hours idea since the beginning. Paul told me he was careful not to draw these himself. 'I had to have someone else draw the people,' he said. 'Mine looked crazy. Nobody would have wanted to trade with them.'

Even so, there was usually some smiling authoritative character in the cartoons wearing an Ithaca Festival T-shirt. Sometimes a 1982 T-shirt, sometimes a 1995 one – sometimes both in the same cartoons. But always uniformly delighted by the whole thing, except when they are reading the disastrous economic news in the cartoon's local paper, the *Ithaca Gerbil*. And if the people aren't smiling wildly from the pages, they are paying tribute to hours in print.

'My five-year-old daughter Jade's pet rabbit recently had a hair blockage which was causing her to slowly fade, and death was a possibility,' wrote one satisfied reader of *Ithaca Money* in 1994. 'Not being able to afford to pay in US dollars, we turned to Ithaca Hours which my husband Charles was paid for the drum he made.'

Or like local restaurateur Michael Turback: 'I will tell you quite honestly that by accepting Ithaca hours for the full price of meals I have introduced my business to a large number of new customers,' he wrote. 'I shop with hours at the Farmers Market for fresh locally-grown produce. We have paid for carpentry, plumbing, cleaning, painting and trucking and other odd jobs with hours . . . I find myself using hours for small luxuries I could not otherwise afford.'

Or like Cheryl, giving Spanish lessons for hours in the public library. 'It's really nice. I hired someone to make a little cat door, I get a regular massage, had some electrical work done and pay hours at the health club.'

Or like David who 'does chimney sweeping and trucking, and he handcrafts fine canoes and paddles'. For some reason local currencies seem to do better in places where people are multi-talented like this – one of the reasons they have taken off in countries like Australia and New Zealand where, rightly or wrongly, everyone seems to believe they can do their own plumbing.

'I trust a person more who has Ithaca Hours in their wallet,' wrote Susan, who was employed full-time with three child-care jobs paid entirely in hours. 'It means they've invested in Ithaca, that they're willing to be open-minded about the value of labour.'

Reading through some of the success list made me realize that the 300 or so businesses which were accepting hours were underpinning the whole fringe economy by doing so. For people on the edges, hours definitely made life better. But there is something for the better-off too. As one local lawyer wrote: 'Every time I spend some I smile and feel as if I have just gotten away with something.'

Paul Glover has documented hundreds of these success stories, and a number of them are printed in his self-published book *Hometown Money: How to enrich your community with local currency* – dedicated 'to Ithacans whose trust in each other has created this money'. The same book also has some good advice for any others going along the same path. Don't, for example, start with serial numbers like 0001, it makes the whole project look dangerously pioneering. Paul also suggests how you deal with the issue of waggish friends who say: 'Printed your own money? I bet you swipe a few for yourself.'

'This is their joke, not yours,' writes Paul. 'Offer amiably to show them the disbursement sheets. I allocated myself a forty-hour founder's fee (paid at ten hours per month) announced in the first issue of *Ithaca Money* to deflate speculation about theft.'

Also in the library archives were examples of some of the wide publicity hours had received around the world – though not in the UK, for some reason. I happened to know there had been only one article about hours in Britain, because I had written it myself.

Even *Forbes* magazine had given Ithaca Hours a favourable mention in an editorial the week before I arrived. I brought the cutting with me to Ithaca, and Paul hadn't seen it. 'My Gosh, *Forbes*!' he said with one of his explosive laughs. '*Forbes*!' There's few enough business magazines quite so conservative as *Forbes*. But then, just as Edgar Cahn was appealing to nostalgia to promote time dollars, so Paul Glover was appealing to conservatism with hours. 'Of course it's conservative. We want to conserve things,' he said. And not just local business: hours organizers want to conserve trees; they plant five of them after every issue of *Ithaca Money* until they can find a supply of recycled newsprint.

The designs are a wonderful way of making other points. Like the picture of the mega-lefty beetle, one of the tiny beetles which create the topsoil – this one discovered in Cornell in 1986. Glover is, of course, a mega-lefty himself, and not just in his ability to recreate Ithaca's topsoil. The two-hour note has a picture of the indigenous local Finger Lakes people, whose existence was burned out by George Washington two centuries ago. 'They danced with flutes, under stars, beside fires,' wrote Paul idealistically.

The notes are beautiful, glowing and jewel-like somehow, and on bizarre dream-like kinds of paper. Some are on cattail paper made from a local shrub; the original half-hour notes were printed on hemp paper. Some of the new ones are on paper made from local angora rabbit fur. The quarter-hour notes are the ones you can't colour-copy, because if you touch the pink with the heat of your thumb, the colour disappears. Very clever.

'Paul's got an obsession with counterfeiting,' laughed printer David St George when I tracked down his small print shop down an alleyway near an undertaker's called Bang Funeral Home: 'These are safer than dollars.' The new ones are kept in the safe before Paul comes to collect them, put the numbers on them and turn them into money. 'You can print a garage full of it, and it doesn't matter until you put the serial numbers on,' he said. This is presumably part of the community magic act Paul was talking about earlier: amazing to think you can take paper and turn it into money.

'Paul's got all kinds of things up his sleeve,' said David, shaking his head. 'That's why it's a success – because it's got him.' David's print shop had been the main focus for television crews covering the hours story, because one of the obvious TV shots for jaded producers is of printed notes pouring off the machine. He offered to put them through the feeder just for me, but I felt too embarrassed. Still, maybe constantly faking the printing process for journalists had made him a little less serious about it.

'We always like it when we're doing a job for Paul,' he said. 'It's more fun. And I've got a drawer full of the things in my office. I always give them to visitors and say "see if you can find someone who takes it!" They usually can though.'

This wasn't quite what I wanted to hear. I suppose I had hoped for deadly seriousness from a printer, awed by the process of being Ithaca's very own mint. Still, perhaps it was a useful prick to my growing triumphalism about the whole thing. Money is fun, after all, and I reminded myself quietly of this. You can get too serious about it.

'Hours are harder to counterfeit than the US dollar,' Paul told me. 'If somebody did so, they'd be doing us a favour. It's a lot of work printing them ourselves.' Luckily, hours now have the protection of the law. A judge prosecuting an Ithaca couple for forging $20 bills mentioned during their trial that if anybody tried to counterfeit hours, it would be a felony punishable by seven years in jail. Printing your own money is clearly an Ithaca hobby.

The next stop was the bank which has done most to make hours respectable. The Alternatives Finance Credit Union (AFCU) is a big fish as credit unions go. They have $22 million in assets for one thing, and their own Visa cards with pictures of the various Ithaca waterfalls. The AFCU makes sure it lends to people who otherwise find it hard getting the time of day from their bank manager.

'I sometimes wish I had followed the 3–6–3 banker's Golden Rule,' said the latest edition of their newsletter. 'Pay 3% on deposits, charge 6% for mortgages, go golfing at 3 p.m.' But as their editorial writer points out, banking has changed since then. 'Citibank uses the 2–19.5–500 million rule: pay 2% on savings, charge 19.5% on credit cards, make a $500 million profit.'

The AFCU is different. For one thing, they let dogs into the bank. For another, their headquarters looks like a half-timbered semi-detached house. As I drove up, I could see the bare pedalling legs of Paul Glover disappearing into the distance, part of his ceaseless quest to keep the hours flowing.

'We strongly support Ithaca Hours,' Carol Chernikoff told me in the bank, 'because Ithaca Hours make a commitment to the community and acknowledge that people want to keep their money within the community.' Which means that you can use Ithaca Hours to pay interest on your loans at this bank, and bank charges. The bank uses them to pay some of their suppliers: printers, gardeners, computer consultants – and staff. 'Most people here take a percentage of their pay in hours,' Carol told me. I thoroughly enjoyed that thought, imagining the staff at my own rather dour bank in Paddington accepting their salaries in 'funny money'.

They can't take hours as deposits which you can write a cheque against, because Federal Reserve rules say they can't mix hours with federal money. They can only take hours as loan payments because they look at the interest they charge as a kind of fee. In fact, the board of directors limits them to holding only $5,000 in hours at any one time. 'But we never get anywhere near that, because we spend them,' said Carol. 'Though we get them regularly, daily. The stronger the hours system is, the more it's around, the more people believe in it, the more they'll take it.'

Were there any problems? Not really, she said. But there was a problem giving twenty-five cents change to the smallest denomination hours note, which is worth $2.25. Their computer boffins are looking at ways they can keep the twenty-five cents on the screen to build up for later.

'I think Ithaca is a richer place for some people because of it. There's a whole string of conventional business which is done in hours. But then there's a whole string of other people who might not be able to earn $30 on a Saturday helping out somewhere, but can earn three hours – so it's a casual kind of thing. It's a less formal way to earn than federal currency. You don't have to just barter: you help me, I'll help you, pay me in Ithaca Hours – then I can get my chiropractor. I think for the under-employed and the less conventionally employed, then it does boost their buying power. Does it make a huge difference to the rest? No, I don't think so. But it's a great system, and when you see all the people who take them, it is important and really adds up.

'Kids are also very aware of Ithaca Hours because they can earn them. It's easier for them to help at a farm or help at the Farmers Market or whatever – and in Ithaca Hours. And when my six-year-old son got a new wallet, he said: "Oh look, Mum, there are three different places for money – one for dollars, one for coins and one for Ithaca Hours." '

'What do other bankers think?' I asked Carol.

'I don't know what other banks think. I never go to other banks.'

But this was a question I really needed the answer to. And, more to the point, what did the Federal Reserve think? 'That's something I wouldn't be able to answer,' said the press spokesman for the Federal Reserve of New York, when I phoned them – the New York Fed covers Ithaca. 'That would be the responsibility of governor level in Washington.'

So I dialled the Federal Reserve in Washington DC, and a spokesman called Bob Moore – having nowhere else to pass the buck – washed his hands of it. I explained what I was interested in and asked if the Fed had a position on it.

'No,' said Bob.

'Are you going to have a position on it?'

'No.'

'So you're just not thinking about it,' I said, hoping for a little more and feeling exasperation creep up my spine.

'No.' There was a difficult silence for a second. Then Bob decided to get more expansive. 'I suppose if people want to do something like that, they can do,' he said. Then a little guffaw as he warmed to his subject. 'I mean, if you want to buy a car with chickens, and somebody accepts chickens, that's OK.'

VI

'When thus coined in large quantities, this paper currency is circulated in every part of the Grand Khan's dominions; nor dares any person, at the peril of his life, refuse to accept it in payment.' As Marco Polo discovered, medieval princelings who stumbled upon the idea of paper money were able to enforce its circulation. There was no 'If you don't mind, I think I'll take my change in gold and jewels'. These days people will only accept money if they believe it has value and will stay valuable for as long as they need to pass it on to somebody else. They will accept it if it works.

Although Paul Glover knew nothing of this history when he embarked on the hours project, he may have inadvertently picked up a folk memory of local currencies from half a century or more ago. The cities around Ithaca had been particularly active printing their own money during the Depression, especially Syracuse, Seneca Falls, Norwich and Binghamton. And what's more, in places like Waterloo, Iowa, Harlem and Richmond, Virginia, the notes were even called hours. The hours name seems to have hung in the ether, so to speak, until it popped into Paul Glover's head as he was doodling cartoons.

It was all pumping blood into the system. After the Wall Street Crash, the initiative had passed to Austria, where the stage was set for a famous local money experiment by the mayor of the skiing town of Wörgl. Mayor Michael Unterguggenberger was a follower of the former Argentinian trader Silvio Gesell. Gesell, who counted Keynes among his other admirers, had urged the world to adopt currencies with a 'negative interest rate'.

In other words, if you put this money in the bank, it wouldn't earn interest like ordinary money. Like crops or meat or most of the natural world, it would decay. This would be bad news for Scrooge, but good news for anyone who depended on the local economy, because decaying money needs to be spent – and quickly.

It was a desperate time: Wörgl's unemployment was running at getting on for a third of the local workforce, and Unterguggenberger organized himself a 32,000 schilling loan and used it to back an issue of his own range of Wörgl notes. But there was a snag for anyone who wanted to put them under their mattress, because – following Gesell's instructions – you had to pay 1 per cent of the face value to stamp each note every month, otherwise they began to lose value.

In August 1932, he used the new notes to pay half the wages

of the council staff. Local traders accepted them rather unwillingly, but they knew they could – for a fee – exchange them for 'real' money. They could also use them to pay local taxes. In the first month, local tax arrears were almost paid off, and the town could suddenly afford to employ fifty people to asphalt the roads and extend the sewerage system. By January the mayor was building a ski-slope and reservoir, and without incurring any debt. By September, the Austrian Central Bank – terrified of losing control over the supply of money – had started legal proceedings to close the project down. It was a brief, tremendous success, though of course it never had the chance to go badly wrong.

On the other side of the Atlantic, the phenomenon was being watched closely by one of the most famous economists of the day, and soon Yale economics professor Irving Fisher was publishing his own version of the local currencies idea. Fisher had made a great deal of money from his invention of a card index file, and lost up to $10 million in the Wall Street Crash, so he had his own reasons for new measures. Within months, about 300 US communities were printing their own negative interest money.

Then on 4 March 1933, it was all over. President Roosevelt – advised that the monetary system was in danger – outlawed any more scrip systems, and gave the existing ones a short time to wind themselves up. Though, as he did so, he also created the conditions for a final flurry of activity. Fearing a complete collapse of the American banking system, he closed all the banks – and all over the country, communities and companies had to provide some kind of alternative to money.

American attitudes to this kind of thing are coloured by American history. By the time Abraham Lincoln acted to create a national paper currency, less than seventy years before the Depression, there had been 7,000 different kinds of bank notes in circulation in the USA, issued by 1,600 different banks, and every business kept a copy of *Counterfeit Detector* next to the till. Some were completely reliable; some were issued by tiny banks in remote trading posts, in the hope that nobody would ever come back and redeem them. Some were not what they seemed: one Massachusetts bank with $500,000 in circulation was found to have a reserve of just $86.48. 'A modest backing,' said Galbraith.

'Sound' economists have traditionally disapproved of this chaos, almost as much as they disapproved of the 'greenback' notes the federal government issued afterwards. But actually, as

Galbraith explained, it served the pioneering West very well by making capital available, turning it into farms and businesses and eventually into sound economic success. 'Then as still,' he wrote, 'what is called sound economics is very often what mirrors the needs of the respectably affluent.'

And so it was in 1933. By the end of that year, half of all the banks in the USA had failed, and Congress was clamouring for more money in circulation: 'I care not what kind – silver, copper, brass, gold or paper,' said one senator from Oklahoma. But Roosevelt, who famously declared that day in March that 'we have nothing to fear but fear itself', was also trying to assuage the fears of his 'sound money' bankers and economists. As a result, local money disappeared for two or three generations or so.

Now it seems to be back, because Ithaca's experience has been an inspiration to local activists around the USA, who realize that the increasing economic insecurity they see around them makes people interested in this kind of underpinning. They are following in Glover's footsteps by printing their own hours money. His *Hometown Money Kit* includes extracts from letters from all over the world and pictures of some of the notes which have followed his lead: San Antonio Hours, Ka'U Hours from Hawaii, Mountain Money from North Carolina, Kansas City Barter Bucks, Cascadia Hours from Eugene, Oregon.

'Could I ask you to send a *Hometown Money Kit* to Mongolia,' wrote one understated missive. 'I would appreciate it very much.'

'Well, here it is, our first money,' wrote Suzy Hamilton from Nelson in British Columbia. 'Some people are wildly enthusiastic. Others haven't a clue what I'm talking about.'

'I'd like to organize Folsom Prison Hours,' wrote John Gann from Repressa, California. 'They'd be a local community currency which would allow prisoners to offer hours of artwork, legal work, etc. to people outside.' I have wondered since what happened to Prison Hours, which is a wonderfully subversive idea, ripe for outraged condemnation at a Conservative party conference.

But a century or more further on, hours are not the same. Not even Paul Glover wants them to *replace* the dollar, and there is absolutely no chance of their doing so yet awhile. They are simply underpinning an aspect of the economy which this current late stage of capitalism seems to be ignoring – local life. Or to put it another way, they are providing blood to extremities of the body.

Ithaca Hours have lasted a good deal longer and circulated a good deal further than any of the Depression scrip currencies, but still every small extension of the scheme opens up a whole new world with whole new challenges. Nobody really knows how local currencies will work as they develop. One criticism is that they might turn a community inwards, small-minded and self-obsessed, so that they replace the goods they used to import with their own versions. But Glover rejects that idea: 'Import replacement does not turn communities inward and take trading and jobs from other regions,' he told one local community development organization. 'It makes each community more productive than ever, wealthy enough to export and import more than before, enabling communities to reach each other from positions of strength.'

Another imponderable is the problem of money supply. The alternative economist Richard Douthwaite spent a week in Ithaca while he was researching his book *Short Circuit* – Paul refused to let him take his photograph – and he pinpointed at least one pitfall for the future. You can control the issue of hours into the economy, but you can't necessarily call them back, which is one of the reasons why Paul cycles round town every day, checking on thrombosis in the system. But it might not be enough one day, and then you would get inflation, which means that the value of the currency goes down. Maritime Hours, which circulate in Nova Scotia, are already reported to have faced these kinds of difficulties with inflation.

The problem is that – just like dollars – the supply of hours has to match the amount of exchanges going on in the economy. Too much and prices go up; too little and you get deflation. Goodness knows what deflation would mean for hours, and perhaps Paul Glover has wondered this as well. Because, like any central banker, he errs firmly on the side of deflationary caution.

This is a problem all those time dollar banks don't have to face. The amount of time dollars or LETS money in circulation is exactly the same amount outstanding, and when people pay it off, it just disappears. Running an economy on a computer – like running anything on a computer, actually – is a good deal easier than running it in real life. Time banks don't have to guess how much work is going on in the system, and issue the right number of tokens. Hours banks and Banks of England do have to and, as we all know, what suits one place can be ruinous for another.

By the time I left Ithaca, I was completely convinced by the argument that some places can run out of cash without their own local money. But hours are also a kind of antidote to one-dimensional culture, where everybody has a local McDonald's and Safeway, everyone's town centre looks exactly the same and nobody knows anybody else.

The latest economic research says the same. The most successful places, according to the American economist Robert Putnam, don't necessarily have low taxes or low inflation, but they do have lots of 'civic activity'. After studying towns in Italy, he formed a great affection for Emilia-Romagna, which he describes as 'among the most modern bustling, affluent, technologically advanced societies on the face of the earth'. 'It is,' he went on, 'the site of an unusual concentration of overlapping networks of social solidarity, peopled by citizens with an unusually well-developed public spirit – a web of civic communities.'

The most successful places turn out to have more newspapers, more people involved in local politics, more local pressure groups, more local football supporters and scout troops and so on. They are not places where everyone shops at one Wal-Mart and then goes home to sit in front of *Blind Date*.

'The regions characterized by civic involvement in the late twentieth century are almost precisely the same regions where co-operatives and cultural associations and mutual aid societies were most abundant in the nineteenth century, and where neighbourhood associations and religious confraternities and guilds had contributed to the flourishing communal republics of the twelfth century,' wrote Putnam.

Ithaca wasn't around in the twelfth century, but it certainly has a continuing tradition of 'civic activity'. Hours may just be a tool here: what is really circulating isn't so much money, it is spirit. And where the spirit and creativity circulate, the money follows. 'We'll be able to insulate from the national sector, reduce the loss of money to utilities and the damage to the environment, and be able to install transport alternatives, like a trolley system and bikeways,' wrote Paul Glover about life after hours have been even more widely accepted. 'We'll be able to do anything that the government is not disposed to do, and without waiting for their approval.'

VII

I drove out of Ithaca past the same unkempt rural villages, through the enormous mist-enshrouded hillsides – once the haunt of Iroquois, Cayuga and redcoats – feeling excited about Ithaca's experiment, but also a little fearful about what people will think, just as Paul was fearful of the coruscating academic do-nothings. In Britain, the Asdas and Abbey Nationals which make every town centre identical are just pale reflections of the Wal-Marts and K-marts of the USA. The bland Dunkin Donut culture is taking the economic heart out of towns like Ilchester as much as Ithaca.

What happens when Ithaca Hours becomes such a success that it begins to irritate the big boys? Will they accept the need for this kind of balance? Ithaca Hours may be no bigger and no more irritating than a gnat to Wal-Mart or the Federal Reserve, but that still might be enough for them to act against it or even take it over.

I was interested to find out whether there was anybody in the mainstream world of finance who appreciated what they were doing. So when Paul Glover mentioned a Wall Street broker who had shown interest, my ears pricked up. I called him at his prestigious Madison Avenue address, hoping to fix up a meeting, and he called me right back.

'Glover's a great guy,' he said, deftly deflecting my proposed meeting. 'I tell you what: if you've got a pencil and paper I'll give you some references. Then when you get back to England, you can send me what you write and we can swap ideas.' Clearly no meeting then: I had hoped to describe what I imagined to be his marble portico. 'I'm a member of the English Speaking Union. So I probably contributed part of your grant.' He guffawed and gave me some references to books by the economist Benjamin Graham.

'Both me and Buffett studied under him. You know who Buffett is? B-U-F-F-E-T-T.'

Warren Buffett is the most famous and successful investor in the world, and one of those rare investors who has become wealthy by turning his back on the usual short-termism of Wall Street and the City of London. Instead, he invests in 'large blocks of a few securities we have thought hard about', and hangs on to them. 'Gin rummy managerial behaviour (discard your least promising business at each turn) is not our style,' he wrote.

My broker outlined his own alternative currency idea. That the Federal Reserve should buy a basket of commodities, and use that as a basis for a currency which – because it was tied to real things – could hold its value during hyper-inflation and thirties-style deflation.

'It's no newer than the Bible,' he said. 'Joseph did it during the seven years of plenty to get through the seven lean years.' Another guffaw. 'Keynes liked the idea, but he died. Glover is doing the sensible thing in an isolated area. But you need a wider structure to have validity for the whole country. Keynes was quite right that gold is a barbaric relic: you need to use something you have to eat or wear or use as the basis.'

And this is the nub of the argument about Ithaca Hours. Of course, Paul doesn't want it to be a nationwide currency – then there would be no way to distinguish the local greengrocers from Wal-Mart. But should it still be based on something? Paul Glover would say that hours are based on more than the dollar is. But to survive inflation and official disapproval, hours may have to be based on more than just people's work and people's belief.

There are at least forty similar systems in the USA and Canada now, all of them probably in areas of enormous local pride. Everyone involved has put love and effort into the design of their notes and psychic effort into building confidence in their new currencies. If they work, perhaps the mainstream system will find that hours are useful to keep around.

Passing the window of one rather tawdry magazine shop before I left Ithaca, I saw they were advertising some kind of sub-Monopoly game in the window, and had spread the play money out all over the display. It reminded me how thrilling it was playing Monopoly as a child, before my constant failure to develop Mayfair turned me off the whole idea.

Thinking about this as I bombed down the freeway past the Endless Mountains again, the achievement of Ithaca Hours seemed all the more amazing. By an immense effort of will and by sheer hard work for half a decade, they had succeeded in getting Monopoly money accepted as valuable. And by doing so, they also managed to turn some of the community's forgotten skills into more wealth – the creativity and civic complexity which is not recognized by the international dollar monoculture. This was the collective effort of will which Paul Glover referred to as the 'community magic act'.

When I got back to London, I heard that the Federal Reserve had slightly shifted its position. They decided to send a researcher from Cleveland to Ithaca to check the whole thing out. Paul Glover swung into action and drafted a fearsome statement, outlining the riots and bombings which could happen if the Federal Reserve didn't stop money drifting from rural communities to Wall Street. It was put on the Internet.

'Rather than inflating national currency supplies, local currencies can add the proper amount of trading medium to communities which do not have enough dollars,' he wrote. 'Healthy communities depend on the vitality of small communities, just as healthy lungs depend on the vigour of tiny air sacs which form them.'

The Fed's representative sat on the same porch as I had, while she talked to Paul and other Ithaca Money people, about their policies and hopes and how the whole system was run. While she was in Ithaca, she stayed with some friends. When they realized she was coming to investigate Ithaca Hours, they called her up. 'You can only stay if you promise you're not coming to close it down,' they said.

She promised.

Chapter 6

Minneapolis: money as information

'Is this a business! You got, you sell it, you still got it!'
Mrs Lubavitch, an enthusiastic member of the oldest
profession.

I

I sat in the emergency room at the Princeton Medical Center
feeling stupid, and realizing I must be one of the few people in
the Western world capable of ending up in ER from trying to
open a bottle of Mexican beer. I needed five stitches, a simple
process which – such are the peculiarities of American health
economics – involved four enormous invoices, two from the doctors and two from the hospital.

A nurse brought in a strange map of my bloodied finger, drawn
by the registrar, looking like a long isthmus with contours, and
asked me what I was doing in the USA. I told her I was looking
for new kinds of money. 'Well, let me know when you find one,'
she said in a matter-of-fact kind of way.

The stitches were the culmination of a weekend of thirty-
something doubts. Could I face going back to London without
the relationship, just when everybody else I knew was leaving
to live with their partners in small cottages a long way from
London? How did I get to be thirty-eight without getting married?
And of course: what on earth am I doing searching for a new
source of wealth when I barely understand the City pages of the
newspapers? I did once meet the City Editor of a major broadsheet
who told me he didn't understand how share prices work;
remembering this cheered me up.

To avoid these and other questions, I spent the weekend preparing for the next stage of the search, and poring over the financial section of the *New York Times* looking for inspiration, and
quizzing an investor I met about Treasury bonds. What really
underpins the dollar, I asked him? Is it gold, T-bills, the marines?

'Oh, none of those. It's just our belief in it,' he said, which is really what I suspected.

I felt satisfied about this as I sped, together with my suitcase and stitches, on the bus to Newark Airport, driven by a man who looked like John Wayne. A crucifix on a green plastic necklace was hanging from his driving mirror. I had never flown on a US domestic flight before, and fumed slowly as we sat on the tarmac for nearly an hour, the pilot explaining that there was 'a lot of weather south of our route'. My seat was right at the back of the plane, in a heady atmosphere of body odour and a queue for the lavatory which exchanged loud intimacies in my ear. 'Well, I want to be a dentist,' they said, inexplicably.

Lunch was flung at me in a plastic bowl and turned out to be a pretzel, a sachet of mustard and a plastic bag of small wet carrots called 'Bunny-Luv'. There was a warning that this was protected as a registered trademark. I racked my brains to think of anyone who could possibly want to steal it.

Sometimes American sincerity is so intense that it is impossible to swallow. As Minnesota appeared lush through the clouds, parcelled out in small perfectly square zones, the pilot informed us that 'it has been our sincere pleasure having you with us on board today'. I'm a sucker for things like that – when shop assistants tell me to have a nice day, I believe them. But in the Midwest where I was going, they really do mean it – there is an old-fashioned open-heartedness about people who live there. This is a region of generosity and ancient Scandinavian traditions, populated by characters from Garrison Keillor novels and large men with enormous bonhomie, firm handshakes, big smiles and a light touch of polite xenophobia.

Ed Lambert from the Minneapolis Consortium of Community Developers certainly had the open-hearted generosity, because he came all the way to pick me up at the airport in his jeep. I had met Ed before, at a conference on local currencies in Milton Keynes, where we had sat round in a semi-circle and listened entranced as the various organizers of local currencies around Britain and Ireland compared balances and folk tales. Ed had been impressed with the thrillingly whimsical names of the LETS currencies. In Milton Keynes, they had a local currency called concrete cows – after the strange sculptures you see in fields in the approach to the town – but which must take newcomers by surprise when first offered some of it. You can imagine some bizarre choices for the names of currencies if the same idea caught on in the USA. Apples in New York, Tombs in Tombstone, Gibbets in Baton Rouge, and goodness knows what in San Francisco.

Although it was swelteringly hot when I arrived, the Twin Cities of Minneapolis and St Paul spend much of the winter under a heavy layer of snow, which means that shopping is done indoors, along long carpeted corridors and walkways between indoor shop-fronts – which would be impossible in London, of course: where would people spit?

Minneapolis looks like a clean gleaming version of the city of Oz from a distance, but when you're wandering around inside, it's more like Glasgow – with broad streets and dour red-brick hotels like Victorian warehouses. It is also set in the so-called 'Land of 10,000 Lakes', and Minneapolis has at least three of these, complete with fishing lines, yachts and bounding dogs. And lots of theatres: Minneapolis is second only to New York in its number of theatres per head – all of this *and* Minnehaha Falls, which once inspired Henry Wadsworth Longfellow to write what must be the dullest piece of doggerel in the English language. This is, after all, a city which boats among its list of tourist attractions something called the Museum of Questionable Medical Devices.

Apart from that they have some of the best public phones in the USA, and some of the worst taxis. The phones very sensibly take credit cards, unlike almost every other public telephone you come across in the country. The others take small change, or strange phone cards, issued by almost as many organizations as used to issue bank notes in the last century. And American change really is small. They haven't seen fit to issue any coins more valuable than twenty-five cents, so phoning the next-door state means dragging a Santa Claus sack of coins along with you, and funnelling them into the slot while the operator insists you need another $2.25 to get in another sentence.

Minneapolis also boasts large numbers of old red telephone boxes from London. Some are used for plants in people's front gardens; some have retired as attractions in suburban bars. So if you wonder where all those evocative, urine-smelling, art deco phone boxes went to – they are in Minneapolis. As for the taxis, most drivers had not the slightest idea where they could find the street you wanted to go to. The ones I used meandered haltingly down wrong turnings, while the meter powered ahead. Some drivers simply shrugged their shoulders and pointed at the next cab in line.

I was in the Twin Cities partly to meet Ed Lambert, who is one of the few people who understands the progress of local currencies on both sides of the Atlantic, but also to track down an ambitious new kind of money project designed to end poverty, known as Commonweal, which I had heard about from Ed when I met him in Milton Keynes.

Ed was immensely hospitable, and I set myself up on a shiny brown sofa in the corner of his flat, with his books on community development and the meaning of dreams piled around me, together with my crumpled shirts. 'Here's a steamer my ex-wife used,' he said, peering into the larder as we searched for an iron. 'I don't know how it works . . . no, nothing else . . . what's this . . . aha!' On the fridge – a slightly smaller version of the vast kitchen warehouses Americans seem to prefer – was a sticker which made me particularly warm to him. It said: 'Guys just don't get it'.

II

Minneapolis is an unexpected hotbed of radicalism. The influential Institute for Local Self-Reliance is based here, spreading many of the tenets of alternative economics. So is the headquarters of the strangely-named magazine *Utne Reader* – called after its founder Eric Utne, though it also means something deeply significant in Norwegian – and packed with subversive ideas about traffic-free cities and television-free homes. Minnesota's senator Paul Wellstone also has a reputation for being a 'liberal' – which in American parlance is only one step away from being a communist. People like me find ourselves supporting him when we watch his opponents' adverts, accusing him of outrageous backing for the environment, and outrageous lack of backing for the death penalty.

This was going to be a place where new kinds of money could thrive. Not far away is one of the most successful time dollar banks in the country, MORE in Grace Hill, St Louis. MORE provides a vast yellow pages of services paid for in time dollars – emergency call-out services, a network for watching over children at risk, literacy training, career advice, shelters and a neighbourhood centre – and now has 10,000 volunteers earning time dollars to pay for them. The St Louis bank Boatmans has decided to bank time dollars by issuing a dual-track time dollars/cash debit card – and it was something along similar lines that I was chasing to Minneapolis.

There were two time dollar banks in Minneapolis, in fact. One is a very local project which works door-to-door in the south-east area of the city, but they failed to answer their phone. So I went to the Time Bank. Or, to give it its full title, the People Helpers

Community Time Bank. I heard about it from a much photo-copied local newspaper cutting I had been sent in London. One reason I wanted to go there was that one of the organizers appeared to be called Bjorkman-Bobb. I pictured an enormous Finnish-American man in a baseball cap, and was determined to meet him just so that I could relate – at dinner parties in years to come – that I had met the man with a name like that.

I was wrong, unfortunately. Bjorkman-Bobb was Gunilla Bjorkmann-Bobb, one of the two women who ran the Time Bank, and she was on holiday. Instead I met a heavily-pregnant Gina DeNardo, who had been running the project with Gunilla from the offices of Senior Resources since 1994. Gina had applied for the job because Ed had told her to: Ed seemed to be every-where. 'Ed had been talking about this concept for ages,' she told me. 'I understood it, but it is very difficult for people new to it to understand. And with seniors, there's also a wariness of strangers.'

Still, they seemed to have managed. When I climbed down the stairs at the Senior Resources Center to see the Time Bank computer, they had 182 members earning time dollars – though 108 of those were from one group, the Temple of Israel, who get involved once a year and don't get to keep their earnings, choosing to operate on a traditional volunteer basis.

'So how have you explained it?' I asked.

'How do I explain it?' exclaimed Gina: she evidently hadn't been asked this before. 'Well, I try to remind people the way communities used to be, helping their neighbours out because they needed help. Also everybody knows that, in farming com-munities, if somebody needed a barn built, then the whole com-munity helps. And if people were brought up in the sixties, it clicks just like that.'

The Time Bank was different from some of the stricter projects I had run across before. It was multi-generational, and the first members weren't old, but they had come to specialize in what old people can give young people – providing children with surrogate grandparents, for example. It worked both ways, said Gina: 'One of the "grandchildren", Tony – he's nine or ten – told Mary, "Do you know, since I've started to talk to you, I'm not lonely any more". Saying something like that is just wonderful. Having young people is a great benefit for the seniors.'

As always with time dollars, an hour is worth an hour, and the older people pay their way. 'They can offer things like sewing, mending, teaching, different crafts, cooking, country story telling, mentoring – well, other seniors don't need something like that.

We really believe that when someone contributes to something like this, it gives them more self-esteem, more energy.'

I was getting to be an expert on this kind of thing, and Ed was keen for me to spread the word. And since he seemed to know everybody, the next thing I knew, I had been invited on to a local radio station – KYMN Radio in nearby Northfield, the town where Jesse James had his career brought abruptly to an end.

'We have to break right now,' said my interviewer after a first burst of questioning about time banking. He somehow just had to be called Wayne Eddy. 'But after the ads I'm going to be asking you whether this isn't a *socialistic* idea.' He stressed the word 'socialistic' rather in the way Senator McCarthy might have done, like 'cancerous' or 'semolina'.

'I'll try and be ready then,' I said, and scribbled a reply for myself furiously as the ads rolled: 'We sell fun, fun, fun at Leo South on route 9: but remember – always wear a helmet.' What seemed hours later, Wayne came back on.

'Well, I've met people of every kind of political persuasion who are involved in local money,' I said rather haltingly. I was expecting a deluge of righteous indignation about sapping America's moral will. 'Some of them are pretty radical, but some are concerned that they want to keep their communities the way they used to be, with local shops and people helping their next-door neighbours. Some of them see this as a way of keeping things as they are against the kind of international forces which are pressing against us.' I felt myself turning slowly into a Midwest conservative as I spoke, but it seemed to satisfy Wayne. Edgar and Gina were right: the appeal to nostalgia really works.

'Well that's fine, David. Now how are you liking the Twin Cities?' I'd been expecting this one. Everybody in the USA asks things like that, and there's really only one acceptable answer: you absolutely adore it and will shortly be filing immigration papers. I talked about being excited to see the Mississippi – which I was. I was only disappointed that alligators never ventured this far north.

'I guess it's like us going to see the Thames in London,' said Wayne, pronouncing the river as it is spelt. 'Have I pronounced that right?'

III

Joel Hodroff is a former radical campaigner with a mission to abolish poverty. He aims to do this not so much with a new kind of money – though he has invented one called Commonweal Service Dollars or C$Ds – but by finding a way of using currencies like time dollars to buy things in the 'real' economy. The key to his Commonweal project is a new kind of credit card, which carries both ordinary dollars and time dollars at the same time. It was an enjoyably subversive idea that you could earn time dollars and then put them on your credit card.

I knew almost nothing else about Commonweal, except that it had still not been launched and that Joel had devoted almost five years of his life to getting it off the ground as a profitable business. This kind of new money was intended to pay for itself with a transaction fee paid for in good old money.

Ed had arranged for us both to find out more at a popular open-air restaurant, called the Black Forest (gateau a speciality). But Joel intended to throw us in the deep end because – without ever having met me before – he brought along some of his backers. He had even arranged a meeting with the local council for later in the afternoon. People were already dealing over lunch as early as 11.30 a.m. – they do lunch early in Minneapolis. The businesspeople were poring over contracts, a few people seemed to be embarking on affairs and there were a couple of obviously estranged husbands and wives hammering out a divorce settlement. We all rubbed shoulders under the vines in the sunshine.

Joel's associates had arrived before him – a banker and Kevin Ryan, an ebullient Irishman who would be Commonweal's chief executive officer for the launch later in the year. We all sat down in a flurry of business cards. I handed out the cards given to me for the purpose by the Churchill Trust, who had kindly given me a grant for the journey. I was always glad to do this face-to-face, because they were emblazoned with a portrait of Sir Winston Churchill himself, complete with a watch-chain and a bullish expression. And much as I admired the picture, I didn't want people to think it was supposed to be me.

Kevin had been a key figure in Commonweal. He came to Minnesota, via New York, when his parents emigrated from Ireland, organizing new product marketing for 3M and then heading the research and development department of Tonka Toys. He set up a consultancy called Cincinnatus – after the Roman general who led the army and then went back to the plough when he'd finished

– but sold all his shares to join Joel in the Commonweal project. 'He's fun, hard-working and I love him,' Joel told me later.

Joel Hodroff finally arrived, a gaunt driven figure with stress marks round his eyes, a big smile, an even bigger suit and an absolutely vast Filofax – the kind that has to be delivered ahead of you by fork-lift truck. He heaved it on to the table and introduced us all again, urging Ed and me to talk about other new kinds of local money we had run across around the world. He listened, excited and rather breathless, breaking off to scribble diagrams on a pad of paper.

'I'll just be in the background and let you talk,' he said. But the temptation was too much, and soon the diagrams were coming thick and fast – graphs, explanations, metaphors, a drawing of a street corner with too many restaurants.

My head spun. The whole idea was impossible to categorize. It envisaged the real hope of an end to poverty, yet it used the mechanics of credit cards to do this. Joel himself was equally hard to categorize – he was a former union activist and drew his inspiration from a list of sources which includes twelve-step programmes, Marxism, libertarianism, meditation and corporate barter – an unusual list. He still wanted to change the world: yet here he was doing so in the Minneapolis suburbs with the active support of the Mall of America, the biggest shopping mall in the USA.

As I worked through my lentil and pasta soup, he set out the issues. The economy has long since solved the problem of production. The difficulty businesses face is not how to produce more, but what to do with their over-capacity when times are slack. What do twenty-four-hour restaurants do on a Sunday morning, for example? What do clothes stores do with their winter clothes stock in the summer? Usually they use this capacity to market the business with special offers, two-for-one dining or 20 per cent off, but advertising these offers is expensive. What if – asked Joel – they could sell that over-production instead in return for local currency, time dollars, service credits, funny money, baby-sitter tokens? What if we could use the over-capacity to put economic power in the hands of people who don't have it at the moment?

'Society has modelled money on the basis of production and ownership,' he said, getting increasingly animated. 'We have to change that. We don't have a problem of production, we have one of distribution. You have got to step into the enormous confusion of it all if you're going to understand.' He could see the enormous confusion of it all on my face.

'You mean,' said Ed, 'that you are putting purchasing power in the hands of baby-sitters, and turning the over-capacity of businesses – which they usually just discount – into a tradeable asset?'

'Bingo!' said Joel. 'At the moment they just have to sell it off cheap, in competition with each other, and the main beneficiaries are the newspapers because of all the special offer advertisements they have to take out.'

Among the other organizations which had swung behind Joel's big idea was a team of local government officers at Hennepin County – in charge of local welfare, and therefore interested in anything which might help – and Minneapolis' exciting new organization for local renewal, the Neighbourhood Revitalization Program (NRP), and he had taken the risk of asking them to talk to me too. So Ed and I dashed off to meet the council officials, passing acres of car parking and the new wire mesh walls on either side of the street, ready for the Grand Prix event over the holiday. 'Here we are racing down the track at forty miles per hour, for God's sake,' said Ed, putting his foot down.

As we all know, when you enter the front door of a local government office, it's a bit like going through the wardrobe into Narnia. It's a different world. It's not that local government corresponds to the clichés about it – the offices of the NRP were modern, airy and efficient – it's just different. There was an air of intelligent public service, and a big copy of Chief Seattle's famous speech, explaining that 'money can't be eaten', as we filed into NRP director Bob Miller's office. The clock on the wall was set twenty-five minutes fast.

Bob Miller had become something of a legend in the world of urban regeneration. The NRP is funnelling $400 million over twenty years into the run-down neighbourhoods of Minneapolis, but not in the normal arrogant way of architects and city officials. The decisions about where to spend the money are taken at meetings by the people who live there – whether it is about housing, community schools, traffic calming, crime-reduction or just a good lick of paint. Anything up to 5,000 people go to local NRP meetings every month, and everything is devoted to the key objective – to create a sense of place. Bob himself sat through the presentations by Ed and me with his eyes half shut, as if napping like a Mississippi alligator. The other officials took notes and looked intense, while Ed explained the different kinds of local money which seemed to be emerging and I gossiped about Britain and Ithaca and time dollars.

Hennepin County's Commonweal design team was a 'great

team and I really mean that', said their leader Jim Westcott, who sported baseball designs on his tie. The County had decided to back Commonweal in January, though their knowledge of other local money projects seemed sketchy. The trouble was that they had very efficiently sent out detailed questionnaires and letters to local money projects all over America, and had received no replies. This has disconcerted them somewhat, just as it had disconcerted me when I found the same thing. The problem is, if Americans in general are not very good at replying to letters, faxes and e-mails, anyone involved in conjuring money out of thin air is absolutely appalling at it. You have to ring them up.

We looked at some of the critical problems they would have to face. Would their involvement mean that community groups would leave all the work to the County? Would top businesses accept the Commonweal card, or just the second-rate ones? 'Yes, that's what one of our councilmen asked at the meeting,' said Jim. 'What if the only people who accept this stuff turns out to be Fuzzy's Furniture?' I assumed this was a local cliché for down-market shops, and imagined the equivalent of Fuzzy's Furniture where I lived in London, with those horrible yellow nineteen-fifties settees hauled out on to the pavement.

The trouble is, when you start asking what-if questions about local money, you never stop.

IV

That evening Ed decided that I should be introduced to American culture face-to-face, and he invited me to the ubiquitous ballgame. 'I'm taking this Boyle guy to the Saints game tonight,' I overheard him saying loudly into the phone in the next-door office. As we hurtled along in his rusty jeep, he explained how big baseball – like big football – has become a depressing and expensive business. I had already passed by the enormous Hubert H. Humphrey Stadium in Minneapolis. The St Paul Saints were re-inventing what American baseball entertainment was all about, he told me.

Baseball is one of the great American rituals. They always sell exactly the same junk food, the spectators take along headsets and even televisions to listen to the commentary and watch the play-backs – and they always play 'Take Me Out to the Ball-Game' at the start. It is a tremendously nostalgic evocation of everyone's lost boyhood. But the success of the Saints was partly down to its zany owners, one of whom was comedian Bill Murray, star of *Ghostbusters* and *Groundhog Day*, which I had seen a couple of years ago on a delightful wintry evening in Chelsea; I have been trying to pack too much into my life ever since.

And so it was that I joined 6,300 other people, of various shapes, sizes and ages, to see my first-ever baseball game. The rest of the crowd queued beside the brass band playing 'When the Saints go Marching In', under a big sign which said: 'THE FUN IS HERE'. We 'tail-gated' with two of Ed's mates from his anti-Vietnam War days – which means sitting on the end of the car and eating. As we tucked into beer and chicken, he explained what local currencies were – how the imaginary currencies in England chose bizarre names. 'They're kinda fun,' he said. By the time the crowd inside was standing up for the Star-spangled Banner, we were still drinking beer in the scalding hot evening outside. 'Don't believe a word Ed tells you about baseball,' said one of his friends. 'We'll put you right after the game.'

By the time we got inside, the game was already into its second innings – of nine – and the Sioux City Explorers were ahead by two runs. The spectators were evidently enjoying themselves: people seemed to be smiling more than they do in the UK, perhaps something to do with the endless supply of beer, chips, hot dogs and popcorn. For all the talk of violence in America, there is nothing like European-style football hooliganism at an American baseball game. Maybe their stomachs are too full.

Freight trains rumbled by the end of the stadium, beside the small hole in a wooden frame marked $100,000. A local furniture company – not Fuzzy's – promised to pay that amount to any player who hit the ball through the hole. There was a sofa on a grandstand and a hot tub, both of which were rentable to watch the game – though currently empty. You could have your hair cut in aid of a local hospital while watching. You could even have a massage from a local nun.

Sister Rosalind Gefre now has a chain of massage centres in St Paul, offering top of the list a 'Full Body Swedish Massage'. As she says in her leaflets – twice in fact: 'God created our body to function in health to achieve the fullness of life.' Her acolytes were collecting bookings, wearing blue sweatshirts with the slogan: 'Sister Rosalind, the best massage in town bar NUN'. I booked myself in. As it said in my programme, 'baseball is a game of todays, not tomorrow'.

Suddenly it was the end of the second inning and the crowd was chanting 'We want Bill!' The team mascot, a pig wearing a purple tutu, ran on to the pitch and two men dressed with flesh-coloured padding to make them look like sumo wrestlers struggled beside it, looking a little like some of the vastly fat Minneapolitans in the crowd.

While I was taking all this in, Ed was explaining to a passing face-painter – another part of the in-game entertainment – that I was from England and I had never been to a ball-game before. She scribbled furiously over my face in black and silver. I stood up for the crowd behind me who gasped and cheered. I was pleased with this unexpected reaction, and a little surprised the way people looked me in the face and said, 'Wow!'

Another innings was beginning with a home run from a lanky player trying to regain his high-paying position in the major league after a series of difficulties. What a good thing I'd seen *Field of Dreams*. The whole event would otherwise have been completely incomprehensible, both in its rules and its language. 'This is an announcement for the person with car registration number ZV5 JVX,' announced the loudspeaker as I wandered downstairs. 'You have been awarded the title of dirtiest car in the car park by Ozzy the Octopus, which entitles you to a free car wash from Ozzy's Car Wash.'

I queued up for what is known in the US as the bathroom, and glancing at my reflection in the mirror, realized why people were looking at me so strangely. The face-painter had taken my first visit to a baseball game seriously, and written 'VIRGIN' in big letters across my forehead.

And then, as I climbed the steps back to the game, I heard the loudspeaker announcing: 'We have in the audience David Boyle, from London, England, who is watching his first-ever ball-game. So give him a cheer.' A half-hearted cheer went up. Ed had nobbled the announcer. A few days later, I was introduced to the owner of a bed-and-breakfast boat on the river, and he said: 'Actually, I had heard about you already. I was at the Saints game on Tuesday.' There was something about St Paul: you run into people there.

The game was hotting up into the fifth innings, and it was time for my massage. I placed myself in the hands of Sister Rosalind, who turned out to be a tiny middle-aged lady, wearing a red dress and a gold cross. She looked completely out of place, and pummelled me like a boxer for ten minutes while the game went on below us. As she dug her knuckles into my backbone, I suddenly started worrying about what to do when she had finished. Were you supposed to tip nuns? Or were they the only kind of Americans you weren't supposed to gratify with an extra 15 per cent on the bill? Even so, the worries about understanding this new money – not to mention my relationship – began to seep away under Sister Rosalind's tough but sensitive hands.

'You do wonderful work, Sister,' said the hot dog salesman as he walked past us.

'Thank you,' she said. I began to understand that she was regarded with enormous affection by the Saints' devotees.

'God bless you, Sister,' said another large thick-necked man a few minutes later.

'Thank you,' said Sister Rosalind gracefully.

I felt much better when I got up, and smiled at her gratefully, understanding a little why she thought there was spiritual value in making people feel less stressed. But the encounter wasn't quite over. To my astonishment, she said: 'I think you need a hug.'

Or did she say: 'I think *I* need a hug'? It was hard to tell, but either way, she clasped me close. It was the closest I'd ever been to a nun in my life, and I felt very moved by it, not quite understanding what it meant. But maybe it was just a simple Catholic reaction to a man with the word 'virgin' written on his forehead.

V

Suddenly everybody is issuing their own money. I don't mean the Cahns, Glovers and Hodroffs of this world, creating money out of thin air for the good of the people around them, but people like Tesco and Safeway whose interest in the world around them depends rather on the bottom line. Take air miles, for example – or frequent-flyer miles, as they are called in the US. This is a new kind of currency issued by airlines, which you can spend on an ever-burgeoning array of goods and services, and which then disappears when you've spent it and it is finally redeemed by the airline. Unlike pounds, it doesn't carry on in circulation – it just gets deleted.

Northwest Airlines has gone one further – they sell blocks of frequent-flyer miles to charities, who split them up and trade them on at a profit. At one stage they were paying for their worldwide public relations contract, not in dollars or pounds, but in air miles. They still use them to pay many of their suppliers.

The people who organize my Midland Bank credit cards recently informed me that by using them I can earn not just air miles but Choice Points – and I can spend these on anything from insurance to membership of the Royal Horticultural Association. In the UK, the Tesco loyalty card has been such a success that Sainsbury's have had to follow. In the US, there is now a range of off-the-shelf 'incentive cards' along the same lines for companies to offer their customers. Like the VIP Award Card, the GCC Purchasing Card and the TravPass, all of which are linked to Visa. Or the Exclusively Yours, linked to MasterCard. Or the SportVenture Plus Card or the Universal Gift Pass. Every month, there are more of them, and all carrying points – money really – given to regular customers which can be spent at a variety of other places. I have at least three of these affinity cards in my wallet, all of them attracting custom and therefore pounds to their issuer.

One American organization, Scrip Plus, sells charities discount vouchers for hundreds of chains around the country, which they can then use as giveaways or trade on. There might have been a time when you could think of AT&T Long Distance Certificates as some kind of voucher, but they are really money. According to the *Washington Post* these 'shadow currencies' represent 'the gradual fusion of these plans to create a new kind of consumer credits economy. It is only a matter of time before a new generation of "central bankers" emerges to co-ordinate exchange rate issues.'

In Minneapolis, the local *Star-Tribune* newspaper issues its own Gold and Silver Extra cards, though I wasn't quite sure what the difference between the gold and the silver was. Both are issued to you as a regular reader and both entitle you to 20 per cent savings at a range of restaurants and entertainment services, including one called ClubKid, the Minneapolitan up-market place to dump the family for the day. Joel Hodroff's card was intended to work along the same lines, but more so. You earn your time dollars for what you achieve in the upside-down world of the community economy, and you can spend them in the mainstream economy. His card solves two problems at once: how do you buy what you need with local DIY money, and how can business people use the spare capacity of shops, factories, restaurants or airlines.

'On January 23 1996,' wrote the local council, 'the Hennepin County Commissioners voted unanimously to work with Commonweal to help launch the first-ever dual-currency community economic development network.' Their initial grant to Commonweal would be $25,000, they explained. 'The commissioners are cautiously optimistic that your novel approach to business-government-community partnership can put currently under-utilized economic resources into the hands of residents willing and able to perform needed community services,' they told Joel.

The new currency was to be called Commonweal Service Dollars (C$Ds).

'There's a twin puzzle in our economy where economic abundance exists side by side with human need,' wrote *Business Ethics* publisher Marjorie Kelly in the *Star-Tribune*, introducing Commonweal to unsuspecting local inhabitants. 'But the two can't come together for a simple and seemingly insurmountable reason: lack of money. Restaurants stand empty half the day while people go hungry. Movie theatres play to a handful of patrons while teenage gangs roam the streets.'

As she explained, people would be able to use their local currency earnings for part of their restaurant bill – as long as they do so during the restaurant's quiet period. Companies could structure their deals so that their dollar costs are covered, but they otherwise back the time dollar earnings of community groups. Everybody wins. The neighbourhoods get more people earning service credits by providing local needs. The businesses attract new customers without having to run expensive sales promotions. People with time on their hands feel useful. 'Participation will be totally voluntary,' said Joel in typically stark style. 'But my guess is people will flood off welfare to earn ten service dollars per hour.'

Joel came from a family of Jewish undertakers, but decided not to join the family business. Instead he devoted time to radical causes and later to self-help activities. The Commonweal idea struck him in 1991, about the time Paul Glover was doodling Ithaca Hours and when Diana McCourt and Jane Wilson were first discussing Womanshare over breakfast in New York.

In the next couple of years he refined the idea, slowly taking out the radical language. 'I used to call it "holistic political economy", but that was a little far-fetched for people,' he said. After years of testing the idea on audiences, it had changed from being a wild exercise in social engineering with important implications for business to something the other way round: a clearly-defined business project with sweeping economic and social implications. But it was an uphill effort. Joel and his friends launched a company called Commonweal in 1993, but they didn't have the business experience to make it work, ran out of money and closed the offices.

Joel was persistent and endlessly enthusiastic. A year later, he had re-organized the company, attracted business people on to the board, brought in some high-profile endorsers and was back. You can do this kind of thing in the USA: have a new idea in London, and the chances are that nobody will talk to you at parties and you have to wait for the Japanese to do it instead. But in Minneapolis, Joel was able to win the support of the influential founder of the Hubert H. Humphrey Institute for Public Affairs at the University of Minnesota, Harlan Cleveland, who joined the board. Even John Wheeler, vice-president of the Mall of America, was backing what he called this 'exciting concept'.

Cleveland wrote about the 'twin puzzle' which Commonweal was designed to solve: 'One of these is that no people's basic human needs, let alone wants, are being met by the accepted economic arrangements, doctrines and institutions. The other puzzle is that no society uses fully even its recognized existing resources (its labour force, its land-water-energy-materials endowment . . . Neither is soluble without also solving the other). The government can print more dollars only at the risk of devaluing the dollar itself . . . But what the US government cannot do (because it can't by fiat produce the additional real goods and services that would enable the supply of money to grow without reducing its value) citizens *can* do – acting through service organizations wishing to meet human needs and through business wishing to use their capacities more fully.'

It also means that businesses which accept C$Ds and use Joel's network and the people who give them their business are underpinning all that community and voluntary work which keeps society together. 'The new model is as convenient as the plastic cards we already use in many of our transactions,' wrote Joel. 'What changes is that two currencies are used instead of one, and competition is balanced with more co-operation . . . The Network is designed for people willing to go a bit out of their way to patronize businesses and organizations that are making a difference in the quality of community life.'

'Last year was a tough year,' said Joel, talking about 1995. 'I thought it was going to be the year of the breakthrough. It turned out to be the year of debate.' He found himself at church on Independence Day, giving a fifteen-minute address on real independence and money. 'I thought: this isn't going to fly. Then I got a standing ovation and sold $600 worth of pamphlets.' In the audience was a representative of the Carlson Company, which manages frequent-flyer programmes in Minneapolis, and a Hennepin assistant county administrator – so Commonweal's attention was focused back on the practicalities of the card.

In the summer of 1995, Joel discovered that there was already such a thing as a dual-track credit card. It was organized by nearby Ramsey County, whose electronic benefit system provides a card which replaces food stamps and welfare cheques, so that people on income support can use it to buy food at checkouts.

People can phone up and find out how much money they've got on it or even withdraw cash from an automatic wall terminal.

The technology was adapted and the patent for Joel's own dual-track card came through that December. It is called the Commonweal HeroCard. Not only does it carry two currencies at once, and can pay them both in one transaction, it also deducts transaction fees like a credit card – Commonweal is intended to make a profit. The card automatically takes 5 per cent of the retail price, taking twenty cents per dollar of this transaction fee to pay for the operations, ten cents each to the local community association which issued the card and to the sponsor – somebody like Oxfam – and sixty cents to Commonweal and their various banks and partners.

Joel used the example of the massive funfair in the centre of the Mall of America, Camp Snoopy. 'Because Camp Snoopy costs exactly as much to run on Wednesdays when 500 kids are there as it does on Friday, Saturday and Sunday when 5,000 are riding, they would offer a $20 ride coupon for $10 cash and 10 C$DS. Snoopy gets $9, the system gets $1 cash to cover the transaction fee, and the community service sponsoring organization gets part of that. So every part of the community benefits: community organizations become self-funding – they don't need car washes or raffles – businesses get cash and the community gets the much-needed service.'

That's what you call win-win-win, and it's true. There is so much that needs doing if we could find the money. 'And I guarantee it isn't going to come from taxes,' he said. Joel listed some of these things on National Public Radio: 'Infrastructure repair, child-care, senior-care, better student–teacher ratios in our schools, housing, environmental clean-up. Now there's nothing on that list of which there is any foreign competition, for which we lack the skills or adequate technologies. We have work to do, we have plenty of people with skills, we have adequate energy and raw materials, and the only thing that's getting in the way and preventing that work from being completed is a lack of money. We think that's absurd, because money was created to promote economic activity, not to inhibit it. We have outgrown the old scarce commodity money and it is time to introduce something new.'

VI

What lies behind all this is a very powerful 'megatrend'. As the futurist Alvin Toffler puts it, money is a kind of pure information. Traditionally there are two very important functions which money has to fulfil. It is a store of value – a way of keeping your wealth without having to turn it into things or furniture or alcohol straight away. But it is also a 'medium of exchange', so that you can know you are making an exact exchange for what you want to buy. You don't have to barter for something the other person happens to own.

So without money, you would have to find another way to keep your wealth – buying houses or paintings or vintage wine. And instead of handing over a pile of change when you want to buy something, you would have to haggle until you both agree on an exact combination of donkeys, corn or Mars bars to make the purchase.

That's money – part symbol of real wealth, part information about value, and both inextricably intertwined. But there was a mythical time when the two functions were separate, when money was just shells you might find on the beach. They were infinitely available so not valuable in themselves, but they did mean you could use them as counters to price the things you wanted to sell exactly and get an exact swap. Now, since the advent of computers, this mythical time seems to be coming back, and these two different functions of money seem to be separating. It is not money which changes hands now, it is information about value – the computer blips of information which pour across the satellite channels, or get transferred every time you use a credit card, or shift money out of your account.

Pundits point to the emergence of cyber-banking or DigiCash or the blips of information which make up Internet money. Mastercard's Mondex and the various other forms of electronic money being launched around the world are money in its purest form as information; so are the blips which slush around the computer screens of Wall Street and the City of London. But what does it mean if money is already, as Howard Rheingold puts it, 'an electronic abstraction'? Nobody has quite got their minds round this question yet, but you can think of one or two important things about it.

The main point is that – unlike old-fashioned pounds or dollars – information is not scarce. The problem with information is often having too much of it, and you have to plough through vast tracts of it to find what is useful, like searching through the phone book for a number when you have the address but can't remember the name. The only limit is our own capacity to organize and understand it. Information is freely available; wisdom is scarce. It leaks, it gets shared – and when you lose a bit of it, you don't actually lose it: it just means that somebody else has it as well. 'If I give you a fact or tell you a story, it's like a good kiss,' says Harlan Cleveland. 'Sharing the thrill enhances it.'

It's the same with information. Joel Hodroff was using the idea that money can be infinite to change our perception of it. 'We have a theory of scarce resources,' he said. 'It just seems logical to people – almost as if the earth was flat – that money should be scarce because resources are scarce. But we also inherited our money from what was a scarce resource – scarce gold coins, scarce precious jewels. And even though for a while our paper currency was backed by gold, the gold fell away over thirty years ago, but we didn't give up the notion of scarce money. On the other hand, money has to be scarce in our economic system. You could never lend it for interest or invest it for dividends if it wasn't scarce.'

So we change the system – or maybe just recognize how it is changing already. Our money could simply be a form of information; our wealth is our people and their skills, our technologies and so on. Put the two together, and you produce what you need.

At this point, Joel had a kind of revelation. He ran across a remark by the inventor of LETS, the Canadian Michael Linton, about money's measuring job, asking why we run out of money – which measures economic activity – when we never run out of other kinds of measurements? 'On the one hand our money is a unit of measure that promotes co-operation – like inches, gallons or pounds that measure the value of goods and services for exchange in the marketplace,' Joel told me. 'You never heard anybody say "I can't find enough pounds to weigh this fish". But unlike inches, gallons or pounds, they do say "I can't find enough money to do this or that".'

It's a strange and apparently abstract thought, and was launched on the world originally by the philosopher Alan Watts in *Playboy* magazine in 1968: 'The reality of money is the same as the reality of centimetres, grammes, hours or lines of longitude,' he said. 'Money is a way of measuring wealth, but is not wealth in itself.'

So if we separate the two functions of money, thought Joel, we can have a parallel currency which is not scarce, and use that to unlock all that over-production. 'The scarce nature of money has gotten in the way of the distribution of needed goods and services,' he said on National Public Radio. 'And that's why, rather than a money which is scarce like gold and silver, we need a money without that commodity nature, a money which is just a unit of measurement and exchange to get the wheels turning again.'

Or, as Michael Linton said, we need to remind ourselves that 'money is an information system we use to deploy human effort'. And if it is an information system we can change its rules according to where the human effort is most 'valuable'.

There is another implication of currency being purely information. It can be disposable. You create computer blips when you earn them and you destroy them when you spend or consume them. Like air miles, they don't sit around in the bank account earning interest. They are just information about transactions, so how could they?

In our two meetings so far, Joel's conversation had been a bit like Patrick Moore on speed. He powered ahead so fast that I couldn't write down what he was saying. I gave up even trying to take notes. I would have to interview him on tape, and made an appointment to meet him in his home in the south of Minneapolis, but I had reckoned without the local taxis. My taxi driver seemed to have little idea where his address was, but – even worse – he was offended by my refusal to advise him on the best route.

'Most of my passengers try to be a bit helpful,' he said.

'But I've never been here before in my life,' I said in an exasperated voice.

'You're kidding me, you're kidding me.'

'I'm not kidding you. I'm from England.'

The driver thought this was a great joke. 'Nah,' he said. 'If we get lost, it's down to you.'

We got terrifyingly lost and so I arrived at Joel's house twenty-five minutes late. 'I'm ruining myself here,' said the taxi driver as I refused to pay the sum on the meter, which would have made a reasonable down-payment on a small house. Joel was looking much more relaxed out of his massive suit. 'I tell you what,' he said. 'We can do the interview later. How about we take Misha for a walk round the lake first, and we can get to know each other.'

We walked round one of the city's enormous and beautiful lakes with Misha the Siberian husky. I began to understand why the car licence plates in Minnesota carry the slogan 'LAND of 10,000 LAKES': it really is the most exciting thing about the state. People were fishing, jogging and swimming or just wandering along eating popcorn. It was an idyllic urban scene and it was clean. London can learn from Minneapolis.

Joel was enthusiastic company. His fascination with new kinds of money grew out of his radicalism. In the Black Forest restaurant he had talked like an old capitalist – but thirty years ago it had been a different story. He had been radicalized by the Vietnam War after he travelled up to Washington for an anti-war rally, with his Reserve Officer Training Corps uniform stashed away in an airport locker. He was an enthusiastic convert, gorged himself on the writings of Trotsky and became a full-time activist. But, like so many others, he became disillusioned with the conventional left and turned inside – to spirituality and self-help – aware that many of his comrades were as confused inside as the world was outside. And they often muddle the two up.

'Leftists are just not aware of what is happening,' he said, as we picked our way along the lake shore towards the white-painted hut which rented boats and sold popcorn. I felt the same. For years I spent my Saturday mornings in intense committee meetings, discussing how everybody could make do with less – then spent my Saturday afternoons with girlfriends discussing how we could have very expensive foreign holidays. The trouble is, once you are aware of that contradiction – and you have to be aware of it or you become obsessive – just making a decision one way or the other doesn't help. People who do that end up projecting their own fears about themselves on to the world, and then wonder why nothing changes. I must have spent years' worth of Saturday mornings in dull committee meetings trying to change the world, and is the world a better place as a result? I might as well have gone out joy-riding.

Joel told me that three crucial books had influenced him to have a second look at money. The first of these was Robert Heinlein's *Stranger in a Strange Land* – which anyone who has read the literature of the American communes movement in the 1960s and 1970s will find endlessly cited. It is a story about a visitor from another planet, where people are brought up to love and respect each other, which – for the alien visitor – meant that their holiday on unenlightened Earth was a bit disillusioning. Its key message is that people are what the system makes them, and it sent hundreds of hippies out making love not war and founding their own communities – where, unfortunately, they usually faced a similar disappointment.

Joel's other two books were Hermann Hesse's classic *Siddhartha*, about the adolescent Buddha setting out into the world, and

B. F. Skinner's *Walden Two*. *Walden Two* is another novel of the communes movement, a utopian classic written by one of the pioneering behaviourist psychologists – a follower of Pavlov. Joel stepped back from the Pavlovian bits, but otherwise spoke of it with reverence, and revealed that one chapter was all about the 'tokens' they earned in the fictional Walden Two community. These were called 'labour-credits' which were entered on a ledger and could pay for all their food and lodging in about four hours' work a day – and that's at the productivity levels of the 1940s.

Skinner is not fashionable these days, because people shy away from the implications of behaviourism. They prefer not to think too closely about whether they behave like Pavlov's dogs, and quite right too if you ask me. So I was measured in my enthusiasm – and let's face it, my ignorance: I'd never read *Walden Two*. Joel promised to buy me a copy before I left. I said I'd send him a copy of William Morris's *News from Nowhere* in exchange. I mentally noted that this was the second time since I arrived in the USA that I had promised to do this, and wondered why I had become such a enthusiastic purveyor of the bombastic old socialist. Maybe because he was so English, or perhaps because in his own utopian classic, he imagines shops where people simply go in and receive what they want without any money changing hands at all.

This is, of course, exactly what we do now, though I can't imagine what a medievalist like Morris would have made of the modern credit card. These were in fact invented during his lifetime in another utopian romance, *Looking Backward*, by the American writer Edward Bellamy – exactly sixty-two years before Diners Club issued the first modern card in 1950.

Having read these three books, Joel had begun to think about how much money depends on our belief in it, and how it was failing to do its job properly. Fine, money can build the great gleaming skyscraper offices of the Twin Cities, and the network of motorways which links the two. But it fails to deal with poverty and alienation, and it fails to distribute the benefits of production very well – especially if it fails to raise the standard of living and shorten working hours with every twist of new technology. If we had a new kind of money which was just simple information, suddenly the possibilities would be infinite.

'But if information is the basis of the new economy, what might be the basis of the next one?' asked Joel, as we departed from the lake shore. I was unsure about this. But I said what I believe – that it will be based on something inside us, something emotional, spiritual even.

'Bingo!' said Joel. It was a bit like being with Archimedes.

I would have liked to have pursued this, but we were back at Joel's flat and ready for the waiting tape-recorder. It was early evening and sticky, even under the fan above his big wooden floor. Misha dashed to her usual cool spot under the table. 'I tell you what,' said Joel. 'Why don't we do the interview later and spend twenty minutes meditating together?'

I was unsure about this too. I do meditate when I can, because I find it puts me in a better mood, but I prefer not to have to chant things in public. But I agreed and shut my eyes for twenty minutes, and managed to let irritation with the taxi driver float away.

'I tell you what,' said Joel when we had finished. 'Why don't we forget about the interview and go and see *Mission: Impossible*?'

'Oh . . . OK,' I said, and I spent the evening with him and his new wife Kate, watching the bizarre antics of Tom Cruise in the Channel Tunnel. I carried out a brief, exhausted kind of interview as he drove me back to St Paul while Misha lay spread out over Kate's lap and the strange flashing American urban landscape zipped past in bright red and green.

'It took billions of years just to form a planet and hundreds of millions to shape up a human being,' said Joel as we drove along, quoting from a British book called *A White Hole in Time* by Peter Russell. 'From then on the whole agricultural era was three thousand to five thousand years. The whole industrial era was three hundred to five hundred years. The computer information age is reaching a peak in a mere thirty to fifty years. It doesn't really take a rocket scientist to realize that a breakthrough in sustainable economics, win-win, beyond the left-right stalemate, could roll out into the world extremely quickly.

'Everything is in place. We have businesses with excess capacity, we have people with time. We have unmet community needs. We have adequate raw materials and energy – all that is missing is money. And since money is a tool of communication and co-operation, and in the information age there are lots of alternative tools of communication and co-operation, we just have to pick one and get started.

'At the height of the Depression, you had growing poverty and hopelessness, labour and management at each other's throats, politicians fighting left and right – but then we decided it was more important to co-operate and defeat the Nazis. In a matter of months we built up to full employment, everyone was co-operating, the so-called unskilled members of society found there was suddenly nothing wrong with their skills. That was fifty years ago – there were no computers, no telecommunications systems, no transactions systems. Think how quickly we could co-operate the world over using these additional tools.'

VII

The next morning, I thought I ought to visit the Mall of America. It wasn't just the linchpin of Commonweal's economic acceptability, it was the biggest shopping mall in the USA – though the biggest in North America is actually in Edmonton in Canada. This was the way conventional money was going. 'Watch out!' warned my guidebook. 'Mind-boggling consumerism can be exhausting, even when it's fun.'

The Mall of America is a terrifying square mile of restaurants and shops, bus stations, and palaces of entertainment, as big as the old City of London with the Camp Snoopy theme park in the middle. 'Kids go to the malls to find community now that families are breaking apart,' Joel had told me.

So I took the bus from the town centre, feeding my $1.75 carefully into the slot next to the driver, shooting past the suburbs and the signs for airport pet hospital, before we drew up under a massive red-brick wall. It was a vast blank structure, a cross between a railway station and the new British Library, surrounded by a great Saharan parking lot. Empty, as it happens, except for one rusty heap with its bonnet propped open, because this was Wednesday morning, the quietest moment of the week. It was those empty Wednesdays, when people stay at home but the bills still have to be paid, which nudged the Mall into discussions with Commonweal.

Of course the Mall of America is not just for shopping. It is a theme park, leisure centre and tourist attraction, all under one roof – which is important if you happen to be caught in a Minnesota winter. There are shopping package tours all the way from Japan, and their coaches herd into the same fume-befuddling undercroft as mine did.

Inside there was even more. Within the quadrangle of temperature-controlled shops, there was the spectacular aquarium, built along the lines laid down by the late New Zealand pioneer Kelly Tarlton. There was a large dinosaur made of Lego. And special events – I found I had just missed Dr John Gray, the celebrated author of the self-help book with the annoying title *Men are from Mars, Women are from Venus*, speaking at the Mall's 'Celebrate Marriage Day'. I breathed a small sigh of relief, gave the aquarium a miss – the queue was already a hundred yards long even on a Wednesday – and started searching for a pair of white socks. I was finally fed up with people assuming I was British when they saw I was wearing a grey pair below my shorts.

The Mall was a perfect example of the phenomenon of modern shopping. The range was astonishing, the design eye-boggling, but actually there wasn't much variety. But since I was searching for new kinds of money, I was excited to find that Camp Snoopy had its own kind of corporate currency. This was called points. You could buy tickets of eighteen points – the so-called Woodstock ticket ($10) – and tickets of anything up to 110 points ($50). And while you probably can't trade points on Wall Street quite yet, they do have an exchange rate – about sixty cents a point – which meant that the log ride with the irritating recording of Canadian loggers would cost $3.60. These things add up frighteningly if you are taking the whole family out Snoopy 'camping'.

Although Camp Snoopy looked like global tat, it was actually a kind of local flavour, because Charles M. Schultz, who dreamed up Charlie Brown and all the other Peanuts, came from round here. In another sense of course, it wasn't: Scott Fitzgerald came from round here too, but they didn't make a theme park about him.

VIII

Skinner's utopian community in *Walden Two* used a kind of money called 'labour-credits', but – rather like reserved English people from a certain class – the people who lived there preferred not to talk about it. Skinner describes it like this: ' "You know of course," Frazier said with a frown, "that his is by far the least interesting side of Walden Two." He seemed to have been seized with a sudden fear that we were bored. "And the least important too – absolutely the least important. How'd we get started on it, anyway?" '

If you ask me, Frazier was protesting a little too much. You can almost feel the sweat breaking out on his palms. But there is another sense in which he is right, because if the labour-credits work as smoothly as they do in *Walden Two* – providing people with what they need – then money does become considerably less important.

It's a bit like plumbing. You don't think about it most of the time, but when it goes wrong it suddenly takes on a terrifyingly obsessive importance. What we have to do is find some automatic way of creating the wealth we need, so that it goes back to the recesses of the mind like our plumbing system. And that is what Joel Hodroff thought he had hit on. Ed Lambert believed that something like this happens in places like Emilia-Romagna in Italy or Ithaca in New York State, where everyone joins the local band, football club, darts team, hospital radio show, girl guides and so on. It's like chaos theory: the more complex the inter-relationships, the more ideas pop up. 'Possibilities emerge from the densities of relationships,' he wrote. 'Local money does the same thing. It brings people away from the television and off the couch and involved in each other.'

'Economists playing the complexity game say that the unit of vitality of life seems to be a system which can adapt and is complex,' he told me later. 'It is important to have lots of places where things start without necessarily knowing where they are going to go – you create a pattern of interaction which is as dense as you can encourage it to be. And out of the densities of those interactions, some of them will gel and some of them will not. Patterns that gel create a potentiality, new structures, new platforms and on and on it goes. It seems to be a way to describe how living systems adapt, and as it applies to economics, it seems to be more than the static assumptions that the current model is based upon.

'In that context,' he said, using the jargon of chaos theory, 'a new currency is a complex adaptive system. At least in this country, we tell people to take responsibility for family and community. We have segmented ourselves, lost the extended family notion, fragmented the community – and those aspects of community are very important to retain the kind of life that we have. That's really what's at stake here, and local currency seems to be doing something about that.' We need what Ed called 'reinforcers' and 'enablers' for good intentions – like time dollars. We need the kind of money which builds up this real 'wealth' on which we all depend.

'What is money really?' I asked. I couldn't resist it.

'Well, that kind of releases a guy into speculation,' said Ed, warming to his theme. 'I think of money simply as an acknowledgement, that others recognize as such, even though they don't know what has been acknowledged and why – acknowledgement of a gift of a product or hours of work. And it's a powerful acknowledgement which can be given to others, and they will acknowledge you. It's simply an acknowledgement made manifest. It's based on trust and hope.'

It's information – information about what we value, and Commonweal makes this apparent. Commonweal launched its first pilot project in the Lyndale neighbourhood of Minneapolis in spring 1997, but it remains in its early stages. There had been worries about how it would work in practice, like any new idea. Time dollars is money in an upside-down world, after all; real money is not. Can the two meet without strain, or will the businesses of Minneapolis complain that they are giving away their spare stock to old ladies who have earned their money making supportive phone calls? Edgar Cahn warned about the same thing, though he is a public backer of Commonweal. But then, so am I.

Joel occasionally talks about C$Ds as being 'potentially better than dollars'. I don't think we're there yet: for the foreseeable future we need to be able to price some things which are scarce – like oil or penthouse apartments next to Hyde Park. We might miss these distinctions if money suddenly became infinite. But as part of a world with lots of new kinds of money, it could work.

Commonweal remains on the verge of a big launch. 'Watch the newspapers, you guys. This could pop at any time,' said Joel enthusiastically to a group of businesspeople in San Francisco Bay. 'The economic model we're working on is a little like the first airplane: people say, "God, what a great idea! Keep me posted." But when the first one flies overhead, the whole vision will shift radically.'

When I got back to London, I received a round-robin letter from Joel and Kate, and their first newsletter – called *HeroCard*, unsurprisingly – for the pilot project in Lyndale. The first 1,000 volunteers and twenty-five merchants had been planned for. It also explained the good news that Joel had persuaded the benefit authorities to zero-rate C$Ds earnings. 'The Minnesota Department of Human Services has ruled that earning C$Ds will not count against a person's eligibility for food stamps or welfare benefits and may count towards the work requirements of current welfare reform legislation,' they said.

Joel's newsletter also explained that C$Ds could rent you a tent at AARCEE Party & Tent Rental, give you free membership of the Tool Rental Library and give you 30 per cent or so off at Camp Snoopy. Even the local medical centre was taking C$Ds in part-payment for treatment. They even sent me my own card. It was a definite start. 'Is there a way to "just say no" to the rat race?' asked Joel in the letter. 'Gandhi once said, "We must BE the changes we wish to see in the world." I believe this is sage advice.'

Chapter 7

Berkshires: money as vegetables

'It may be legal, but – geez – take one over to a colour-copier
and see what happens.'
Oliver Ireland, Federal Reserve.

I

When you are tired of diners, you are tired of life, Dr Johnson
might have said about American life – and the Deli diner in Great
Barrington, Massachusetts, is no exception. There it was, between
the Berkshire Community College and Popeye Community Store
– they like the word community round here – just like any other
diner in any other New England town, except that it was painted
a dull blue and purple. I stood outside it hoping that I would feel
some awe at the place which played such a historic role in local
currencies in the USA, but it looked so ordinary that I just
couldn't. It just wasn't awesome.

I was in Great Barrington to speak at a conference about new
kinds of currency, and it was in some ways a culmination of my
search, because many of the leading new alchemists were going
to be there, and I was fascinated to find out if they had anything
to say to each other. Great Barrington is also the home of the E. F.
Schumacher Society, the conference organizers, in the Berkshires
region of western Massachusetts. The landscape was a little like
Scotland, except greener. Endless hilly acres of green seemed to
stretch in all directions. Small polite white-washed towns nestled
in among them. And of course the pronunciation was difficult:
this isn't the English 'Barkshire': this is 'Burkshire'. Nonetheless,
a local permaculture designer called David very kindly put me
up on his floor, cooked me a meal of tofu and packed me into
his truck to look at Great Barrington. We kerb-crawled along the
wide main street of antique shops, white wooden churches with
big stars-and-stripes flags flying, and peculiar-looking Christian
Scientist bookshops.

But before we deal with the Deli, we have to take the story

back about seventeen years to 1972 and a small town across the state line in New Hampshire, and the so-called Exeter experiments. The man behind them, the writer Ralph Borsodi, had been a guru since before hippies were twinkles in their parents' eyes. His 1928 book *This Ugly Civilisation* was one of the first expressions of many of the concerns of the modern green movement. He had inspired hundreds of people to 'downshift' long before anybody ever thought of yuppies or burn-out, with his post-war book *Flight from the City*. And he was a new alchemist before the Second World War, when he helped Professor Irving Fisher with his revolutionary scrip money systems in the 1930s.

Reading it even half a century or so later, there is a refreshing fury about everything Borsodi wrote. He loved a good fight. 'The money managers of the country have, for all practical purposes, been engaged in murdering the dollar,' he wrote in his book about the Exeter experiments. And his fury really lasted, so it was at the relatively late age of eighty-five that he set off for California to start work on a new book, reflecting on the old definitions of John Ruskin, in his book *Wealth and Illth*.

Over lunch in Escondido in March 1972, he opened his copy of the *New York Times* to see that the dollar had been devalued. This was the great era of post-war inflation. IMF experts from all over the world were meeting at the Smithsonian Institution to decide what on earth to do about it. President Nixon had finally removed the last vestiges of the gold standard, inflation was running at well over 10 per cent on both sides of the Atlantic, and senior economists were claiming they did not have a solution.

Borsodi nearly burst a blood vessel. 'These are men who know all about the minutest details of what is considered economics today but not that in economics, as in everything else, ends dictate means, and that if ends are wrong, the better the means used to realize them, the worse the result,' he wrote. His only bestseller in a lifetime of writing had been called *Inflation is Coming*, and he had more than just a bee in his bonnet about inflation – he had a whole swarm. Borsodi was absolutely furious at the dishonesty of inflationary money – money which lost part of its value as you held it in your hand. He agreed completely with Jefferson that, without 'honest' money, people were the 'passive victims for the swindling tricks of bankers and mountebankers'. Inflation is 'a form of legalized embezzlement', he wrote.

So, with the *New York Times* article in his hand, he sat straight down at a typewriter and wrote what became known as the Escondido Memorandum. It set out how you might launch what he called 'an honest money system'. The new currency was to be called the 'constant', and it would stay at broadly the same value. It would show the world that such things were possible. Borsodi was so respected in New Hampshire, where he lived, that the two banks he asked to help him agreed straight away – and the first constants were issued to a conference discussing the future of the human race in nearby Conway in June 1972. The new currency was by then backed by $100,000 of his own money, on deposit in banks in Exeter, Boston and London.

The value of the new constant notes and coins wasn't linked to the value of dollars or pounds, which were anyway slowly sinking through the floor, but by a basket of thirty of the world's most-used commodities, from oil, aluminium and tin to oats, soya and cocoa. The main problems Borsodi had to solve were how to choose these commodities, how to buy them as backing – and how to store them. You clearly couldn't put $100,000 worth of oil and wheat in the bank, let alone your garage – even on the scale of American garages.

Then he had a brainwave. He would arbitrage them instead. In other words, Borsodi and his fellow-experimenters would buy shiploads of the chosen commodities while they were at sea in tankers, and sell them straight on – and make a profit while they were about it. So the backing for the value of the constant was in the hold of a number of ships, all of them on the high seas. Nobody's garage had to be disturbed.

By the end of 1972, thousands of constant money orders were circulating among the 9,000 inhabitants of Exeter. By February 1973, the University of New Hampshire Press was printing 275,000 constants in different denominations up to C100. One prestigious local school paid for its printing and supplies in constants, orders worth thousands of dollars. Exeter's local council even started accepting them as payment for parking fines.

Borsodi had set up his own non-profit organization to run the experiment, packed it full of enthusiastic volunteers and opened offices for his new company, Independent Arbitrage International. 'It rhymes with garage,' the local paper explained. He would walk to the office every morning, settle down at his desk with a large picture of his wife, and walk right back again for lunch with her. His economist friends at the local university were working out their own Dow Jones index of commodities to keep the value steady. Youthful supporters dealt with the press and paperwork.

'I drove fifty miles to buy Q-tips just to be part of the experiment,' one visitor told the local media. 'Maybe people will call it a funny money scheme,' said one local trader, 'but the question is whose money is funny – his or ours?' Even the Office of the US Comptroller of the Currency felt relaxed about it all. They came up with a statement remarkably like the Federal Reserve's remark about Ithaca Hours: 'They can circulate clamshells or pine cones if they want to, so long as people accept them. There's plenty of Canadian money circulating in northern New Hampshire.'

By then $160,000 of constants were circulating in the south of the state. The Fed will be terrified, Borsodi said. His constant experiment would reveal the truth about the dollar, demonstrating that it was being deliberately deflated. But it was not to be; Borsodi realized that if he was to expand the constant any further, it would require more than his $100,000 backing. So he wound it up, hoping that the point had been proved and that somebody younger would pick up the baton, but this wasn't to be either.

II

The experiment with 'honest' money may not have lasted long, but there were at least two influential people who sat up and took notice. One of these was the maverick planning writer Jane Jacobs, the influential author of *The Death and Life of the Great American Cities*. She urged more clutter in cities, more mess, more life, more imagination – and, recently, more money. Not money produced in the normal way – interest-bearing pounds created by banks, and backed by government debt – but money issued or backed by cities, regions or neighbourhoods, which would underpin local life. The constant lodged in her mind, and by 1984 she was using her book *Cities and the Wealth of Nations* to urge cities to launch their own currencies as a way of encouraging them to innovate rather than import.

The other new alchemist influenced by Borsodi was Bob Swann. Swann had been a wartime conscientious objector and was a carpenter by training; he has played a pivotal intellectual role since the war – founding the first socially responsible investment fund, launching the Institute for Community Economics, inventing land trusts. In 1973, just as Ralph Borsodi was winding down the constant, the pioneering alternative economist E. F. Schumacher was publishing his influential book *Small is Beautiful*. As the title was passing into the language, Schumacher asked Swann to set up an American organization to parallel the work of his Intermediate Technology Development Group in the UK. But it wasn't until 1980 – three years after Schumacher's death

– that the E. F. Schumacher Society was born. Bob has been running the organization ever since, together with Susan Witt, from a beautiful hillside outside Great Barrington. No guru or futurist passes through Massachusetts without popping in.

Driving up the hill was a bit like drawing up in a pick-up outside Shangri-la. An air of rarefied calm covered the place, a little windmill swirled – there was almost no wind – and Bob and Susan had that glow about them you might expect to find in monks or beauty consultants. The glow was even more intense inside the Schumacher Library building, which Bob had designed in the style of Frank Lloyd Wright. Inside was Schumacher's own library, collected from his London home, together with books from all over the world about new thinking in economics, and on the wall a pair of knitted socks from Lake Baikal in Siberia, the scene of one of Susan's projects.

I asked Susan if she had been in touch with Jane Jacobs, and it turned out that her conversion to local money had astonished them as well. 'She's grand,' said Susan. 'She's my current role model – very tall, smokes like a fiend and wears sneakers and is just the clearest thinker and the biggest heart.' Jane Jacobs had called unexpectedly for city currencies after she came and gave a talk for the Schumacher Society: 'I had to pick Bob Swann up off the floor, because we had been knocking on shut doors for so long. Afterwards driving her back, we said, "Jane – how did you come up with that?" She said it was logical, but she didn't know what to do with the idea. But she realized that if you want to develop diversified regions, there had to be a diversified local currency.' Jane Jacobs was signed up as a member and opened a SHARE account, which was the Schumacher Society's main money-conjuring project at the time.

The SHARE programme emerged out of a conference about regional economics organized by Bob and Susan back in 1982 as a way of helping ordinary entrepreneurs to get bank loans. Loans are, after all, easy to arrange if you are Robert Maxwell or Euro-tunnel, but if you are a struggling small business selling pans or socks or potatoes, you might be charged interest of anything up to 18 per cent. So how, in these difficult circumstances, could they help make money available to rural businesses? Bob Swann's solution turned out to be the first stage in a step-by-step project towards a permanent new kind of money. It was called the Self-Help Association for a Regional Economy, or SHARE.

Members of the programme put savings into the First National Bank of the Berkshires, called SHARE accounts, and these were used as backing for loans which the bank would never otherwise have risked. It took months of negotiations, but finally the bank agreed to lend money at 4 per cent interest, as long as the SHARE members took the risk. So the members decided who to lend to, and the banks organized the loan. 'We were helping the bank do what they really wanted, which was to make small loans,' said Bob. 'And it was seen to work. It got a good press. Every time we made a loan, there was a story in the newspapers.'

The loans were all for less than $3,000 and were aimed at building up a good track record for the borrowers. Like Bonnie Nordoff, who wanted to start a knitting business, but had a bad credit rating. Her first SHARE loan bought a knitting machine to make sweaters; her second bought another: they were paid back – all the SHARE loans were repaid in full. By the time she needed another loan to set up the business to take on staff, she was a good risk for the conventional banks. SHARE members were given a newsletter with the heading 'What your money is doing tonight'. 'It isn't impossible to involve the existing system,' said Bob. 'Bankers are not that bad. They just don't understand what they are doing.'

The global effects of a project like this are pretty small – though think what would happen if every bank in the UK did something similar – but there was also the ulterior purpose of involving local banks in something innovative. Bob hoped then that the managers wouldn't fall over with shock when he suggested a local currency.

The first hint of a new kind of local money popped up sooner than anyone expected, and this is where the Deli comes in. It was 1989, George Bush had just won the presidency with his 'watch my lips: no new taxes' gesture, and his defeated Democrat opponent Michael Dukakis was skulking in misery after having stepped down as Governor of Massachusetts. The Great Barrington Deli had celebrated this event with a special sandwich called Ex-Governor Dukakis made out of cold turkey.

The Deli was an expanding business, it needed more space and – on top of that – owner Frank Tortoriello's wife was ill. He needed $4,500 to move to bigger premises across Main Street, but the banks had turned him down for a loan. His last hope was with Bob Swann, Susan Witt and the extended group of SHARE members. 'I guess the only solution is to print our own money,' Frank said to Susan in despair.

'Yes,' she said. 'Why don't you?' The Deli did, after all, have a large extended group of its own in its customers. She knew that a long-defunct Oregon restaurant called Zoo-Zoo had managed to raise $10,000 like that about a decade before.

And so it was. In October 1989, just as the Berlin Wall was beginning to crumble over in Europe, Frank began issuing his own money. They were called deli dollars. The notes were sold for $8, and could be redeemed at phased periods over the year ahead for $10 of food. They were designed by local artist Martha Shaw, and included caricatures of Frank and all his waitresses. Within thirty days he had sold the lot, and raised $5,000.

'We suggested he did $10 for $10,' said Susan. 'But he said "That's too good a deal for me", and he did $10 for $8 because he's basically a fair person. The role of SHARE shouldn't be underestimated because, as a non-profit organization, we could get articles in the local newspapers about it. We were able to say that Frank is doing this, but other businesses could do it too.' In other words, Frank's customers were backing his loan – enthusiastically, because they felt they were helping him beat the system – and he was paying them back in sandwiches.

Then something alchemical began to happen. The deli dollars started acting like money. Parents passed them on to their student children, to make sure they were eating properly. Local employers passed them on as Christmas presents for their workers. People knew the local Congregationalist minister ate at the Deli, and soon notes started turning up in his collecting box after Sunday service. The front page of the business magazine *Entrepreneur* carried a cover picture of the noticeboard in the Deli: '3 coleslaw 75c,' it said. 'Ask about deli dollars at the counter.'

TV crews arrived to track down the banks who had refused Frank's loan, and the bankers found themselves explaining the innovation – and admitting that they had been circulating deli dollars themselves. 'He can't make loan payments with corned beef sandwiches, but he can pay me back that way,' said one of them.

By then the next stage was already beginning to emerge. One of the Deli's customers, Jennifer Tawczynski, suggested to her parents that the deli dollars idea might get over the perennial problem for farmers of bad cashflow in the winter. They have to invest in seeds, equipment and effort through the winter months – but the proceeds don't appear until after the harvest has been sold in the summer. So Dan and Martha Tawczynski of nearby Taft Farm began talking to SHARE about their own money, and they were soon joined by another farming couple, Don and Ruth Ziegler, whose Corn Crib farm shop in the nearby village of Sheffield had just been gutted in a disastrous fire. 'Some of their customers came to us and said can we do a Corn Crib note?' said Susan Witt. 'We thought: why not do a joint note? So Martha developed a currency with a cabbage on the front instead of a picture of George Washington. It would be a farm preserve note instead of a federal reserve note.'

'In farms we trust,' said the farm preserve note. 'Redeemable for plants and produce up to a value of ten dollars.' The first one was bought on 21 December 1989, by – a strange coincidence this – somebody called August Schumacher Jr. No relation. He was closely followed by the Commissioner of Agriculture for the Commonwealth of Massachusetts. Each farmer sold up to $5,000 in the first year. By 1991 it was $6,000. 'The idea of money is this: if you agree this paper is worth ten bucks, and I agree this paper is worth $10, then it *is* worth $10,' one of the farmers told a National Public Radio interviewer. And a few hundred miles away, lying in his bed in Ithaca doodling cartoons of Ithaca money, Paul Glover heard and leapt up with the idea of Ithaca Hours.

'In the final year, out of almost $8,000 of farm notes issued, the Corn Crib ended up with about $70 more than their share,' Susan told me. 'I was hoping the Taft folks would figure out a way of dealing with it that didn't involve dollars. In the end, I think, they asked for a winter's worth of potatoes. Nobody ever considered trading dollars.'

The Federal Reserve was suddenly less keen. 'It may be legal,' their lawyer Oliver Ireland told the media. 'But geez! Take one over to a colour copier and see what happens.'

III

What was it about the miserable early 1990s? Governor Dukakis wasn't the only victim of the prevailing climate. I was out of a job back in London, most of Europe was suffering and in Massachusetts the first three months of 1991 saw record business failures. Banks became increasingly shy of small loans, or dealing with small businesses at all. The people of Great Barrington certainly weren't immune, and soon the local Japanese restaurant Kintaro started issuing its own scrip. So did the local Monterey General Store. 'For the past few winters I have always gotten a loan to tide me over,' said its manager Maynard Forbes. 'This time is wasn't so easy. The store has been around for 211 years and I just want to be sure it stays. So we issued some scrip.'

Washington Post reporter Michael Specter arrived in town, looking for a story about New England town meetings, wandered into the offices of S H A R E and found himself writing about the ability of locals to conjure money instead. It was an idea 'born of a strange blend of financial desperation, civic activism and Yankee ingenuity', he said.

'Have you read Jane Jacobs' *Cities and the Wealth of Nations*?' Susan asked him, and by a bizarre coincidence he had a copy in his briefcase.

'As soon as it was in the *Washington Post*, we had international coverage within the next few weeks,' Susan told me. 'And the local merchant community was very excited about that. They saw how the topic was legitimized by the international press.'

Great Barrington was suddenly receiving unprecedented attention from around the world. 'I had to call up people at the bank,' said Susan, 'and ask if they were willing to be interviewed live on Japanese TV about why they turned down the Deli for a loan, but then went in and bought deli dollars. It was pretty exciting for the town.'

So what next? They could extend the idea again. Great Barrington has a burgeoning holiday population of 21,000 in the summer. In the winter – like many aspects of life – it shrinks. Just like the farmers, the local traders and restaurateurs earn their money in the summer, but they still have to stay open through the winter. So urged on by Susan and Bob, the traders launched a three-year scheme where they behaved like Tesco and Sainsbury's and issued their own 'loyalty money'. 'It wasn't the kind of local currency that we were dreaming of,' Susan told me. 'But the names they were thinking of were inappropriate, so we said – if they would move towards doing a permanent scrip – we would turn over the "Share" name.'

For a six-week period early in 1992, anyone who spent $10 in a local store was issued with one 'berkshare'. Then during September 6–9, when the traders were flush with summer earnings, they could spend them for up to a quarter of any purchase price. In the first year, 78,000 berkshares were issued – representing $780,000 in trade – and 28,000 ended up back in the shops in September.

'It was an incredibly good return for a giveaway,' said Susan. 'I heard about people calling each other up, saying "I'm out of town at the moment, but my berkshares are on the windowsill by the kitchen sink – don't waste them!" One couple who came as tourists and earned twenty berkshares came back in September, took another motel room, and went to all the same restaurants, just to spend them.'

Still, as she said, it wasn't really the local money they wanted. The berkshare ran for three years, and then drew breath as Susan and Bob began working out how they could turn it into a permanent farm preserve note, offering a 10 per cent discount. It would circulate locally, and – like Ithaca Hours – would boost local business but slip through the fingers of the big multinationals, the Wal-Marts and McDonald's. Their new berkshare has yet to see the light of day, but one of the key problems has been solved: how the five Great Barrington banks would deal with different berkshare accounts. The bankers themselves provided the solution: 'We can just walk down the street to one another's banks and make the exchange, the way we used to do with cheques,' one said.

Bob Swann was delighted: 'It gave these individual bankers, who are caught up in a highly centralized and fast-paced system, great pleasure to imagine recapturing in a small way the early days of banking, when transactions had a warmer, more community-spirited tone.'

Otherwise it will be a permanent 10 per cent discount note, like the farm preserve notes or deli dollars, backed in the same way as they are – by local productivity – and issued in the same way as loans. 'If we can issue loans with a local scrip we could issue it at as low as 3 per cent interest,' Susan told me. 'And that means businesses dealing with appropriate technology, or which are marginally viable at the moment, would again be viable. They would be competing with multinational companies, but the only ones which would want loans in local scrip would be local – people working with renewable energy for example.'

Local money could create a more enlightened world, where many of the things we heard were not possible in the cold world of profit, suddenly become possible. It is not surprising that Susan started adult life studying the Grail legends, about the transformation of the wasteland: local currencies may be able to do that too. But for Bob Swann and Susan Witt, any old local currency just isn't good enough. It has to be under local democratic control, and it must be 'real'. Like the constant, it must be linked to some reliable standard of value – rather than the vagaries of Wall Street or the City of London. Both are followers in this respect of the visionary Rudolph Steiner, who complained that money had distanced us from our economic relationships. Real money must be based on something in nature, he said, so that when you pass it on to somebody, you really feel what it all means.

In Massachusetts, that real product which underpins money might be firewood – which is why the Schumacher Society designed their new berkshare as a 'wood note', beautiful in red and gold, with leaves and birds: oak for 1 berkshare, maple for

5, ash for 10 and hickory for 20. 'I berkshare = 1/100 standard cord of wood (128 cu.ft)', it says on the back.

'Here in New England, if you don't burn wood, your neighbour does – so you have the value of wood in your bones,' Susan told me. 'So our initial idea was to issue a cordwood note, instead of being valued in US dollars – because it was a value that was regionally understood. Then you can always pay back the money in cordwood.' When the poet Wendell Berry discussed the idea with them, he said: 'Oh I get it. In Kentucky, it would be a chickens.'

'Everybody raises chickens there,' said Susan. 'In Arkansas, people would have their currency based on a mixed basket of goods including corn oil, because those things are grown and understood there. The idea is to put reality back into our economic system. We now have an economic system which is so abstracted that money begets money – and we talk about investing at 7 per cent! What on earth does that mean? My involvement in all this is to put a more human face into our economic dealings – so that we can have a story abut the things we use in our daily life. Because if we do, our life has been enriched. If you can say that your table has been made by a carpenter and you can talk about his children, then that table is more valuable . . .'

'What about time dollars?' I asked.

'I'm not very interested in them,' she said. 'They are a good organizing tool but they are basically a social service tool, not very valuable. I don't underestimate that, but Edgar Cahn has not included the economic issues which are fundamentally important.'

'What about manifesting own wealth?'

'Pfffffff !'

'You don't like new age gurus then?'

'I want something practical. Like land, food or shelter. We have the capability of transforming the material we now have within ourselves. It's alchemical. But we do it through our dealings with each other. Economics is a record of our dealings with each other, but we have to have an accurate recording tool – the present economic system is not accurate.'

If you believe this, then accurate money – 'real' money – can be like finding the Holy Grail. It can put us back into the right kind of relationship with each other, and transform the wasteland into something a little more homely.

When I got back to London, I tracked down a copy of Jane Jacobs' rare but crucial book in the University of London library, and read her argument that every city should have its own currency. The fluctuating value of currencies would then give cities real feedback about the attractiveness of their goods, she says, making them cheaper to export in the difficult times, and encouraging them to substitute local innovation for expensive imports.

That's how cities traditionally became rich, she argues. 'Today we take it for granted that the elimination of multitudinous currencies in favour of fewer national or imperial currencies represents economic progress and promotes stability of economic life,' wrote Jane Jacobs. 'But this common belief is at least worth questioning in view of the functions that currencies serve as economic feedback controls.' The trouble is these individual economic messages get confused if they all share the same kind of money, she wrote:

> Imagine a group of people who are all properly equipped with diaphragms and lungs, but share only one single brainstem breathing centre. In this goofy arrangement, through breathing they would receive consolidated feedback on the carbon dioxide level of the whole group, without discriminating among the individuals producing it . . . But suppose some of these people were sleeping, while others were playing tennis . . . Worse yet, suppose some were swimming and diving, and for some reason, such as the breaking of the surf, had no control over the timing of these submersions . . . In such an arrangement, feedback control would be working perfectly on its own terms, but the results would be devastating.

Hong Kong and Singapore have their own currencies, says Jane Jacobs: Detroit doesn't. A previous visitor to the library had written in pencil across the bottom of the page: 'So much for the European single currency'.

IV

'Cash is dirty, cash is heavy, cash is quaint, cash is expensive, cash is dying,' said the cover of the *New York Times* in 1996. The long article inside by science writer James Gleik revealed the extent of the corporate money revolution: old-fashioned cash is increasingly the preserve of criminals, he wrote. Deep down, people believe that cash is unclean. I have a friend who throws all her small change into the rubbish bin when she gets home every night. New Jersey Turnpike toll collectors used to use rubber gloves, and were punished by their managers, who thought it gave the wrong impression about money.

After all, we don't know where coins have been. Actually we do, but prefer not to think about the sticky hands of children and tramps, the insides of condom machines, the pavement, or – worse – my pocket, next to my handkerchief. They are also heavy. Belgian authorities planning for the European single currency estimate that it will take eighty lorries a day for three months to shift all their coins currently in circulation to make way for the euro.

These are among the reasons why coins seem to be slowly dying out. In the UK, only 4 per cent of GNP is now dealt with in cash, down 4 per cent in the past quarter of a century, but three quarters of payments above £1 in the UK are still in cash, and it still costs £250 million to count it, transport it and guard it. There are a number of radical cost-cutters in the British Treasury and outside who would like to do away with that bill completely. 'The cost of this addiction to cash is huge,' wrote one disapproving Japanese professor.

Forgery is also worrying the authorities. In April 1995, police seized £18 million in forged bank notes from a lock-up garage in London's East End – including £6 million in forged foreign notes. That is three times the total of all seized forgeries in 1992. Detecting them is increasingly difficult, and if you put £5 notes through the washing machine, they can sometimes show up fluorescent on the forgery detectors. Every year, British bankers pounce on £80,000 in perfectly good notes and confiscate them, and they end up with the other six tons of old bank notes which are turned into fertilizer every day in the UK.

How do we move away from old-fashioned cash? Credit cards showed the way, and there are now as many as 5,000 card issuers in the USA – all of them now issuing money every time somebody swipes a card through a machine. The Visa organization alone is responsible for issuing over £400 billion around the world every year. Because, just as money is turning into information, so information is turning into money – like the InfoHaus on the Internet, which *Wired* magazine described as an 'electronic bazaar of dollar-denominated digital dreck, where almost everything costs less than $10'.

InfoHaus was one of the first places experimenting with Internet money. And there is nothing very strange about that concept, except that you can charge people in the tiniest fractions of denominations, which in 'netspeak' is known as a 'nanobuck'. Traders bundle up thousands of nanobuck transactions into one, so that they are worth trading on the Internet. It really was only a matter of time before somebody invented a new Internet currency, and among those who have done so are Digital Equipment Corp, who are developing a currency called scrip.

The wonderful thing about computers is that having piles of conflicting currencies doesn't really matter. They can easily be converted on the World Wide Web by online 'brokers', just as in the City of London. Again, the very tiny amounts involved can be bundled up electronically into an exchange worth the time of human beings to carry out. You can already see some of the infrastructure appearing. DigiCash, issued exclusively as I write by the Mark Twain Bank in St Louis, Missouri, gave one hundred cyberbucks away free to anybody who asked as a way of getting them interested in Internet trading. A new website immediately sprang up called Cyberexchange, offering to trade cyberbucks for 'real' money.

The best-known computer money is Mondex, perhaps less interesting as far as 'alchemy' is concerned because Mondex just uses a computerized version of pounds and dollars – though you can download five different currencies at once on to your Mondex card. Mondex was the brainchild of two NatWest computer wizards, Tim Jones and Graham Higgins, who came up with the idea of putting the money directly on to a card in March 1990, which meant they could avoid a central computer. That has an obvious disadvantage for anyone as forgetful as me, because if you lose the card, you lose all the money on it. On the other hand, says Mondex – eager to put both points of view – you *can* lock the cards. And that might make whoever finds it more keen to send it back to you in the post, apparently.

Mondex was an ambitious and heavily-funded joint venture between NatWest, Midland Bank and British Telecom, the latter involved because you can download the money by phone. MasterCard joined during 1996, paying what was said to be £100 million for the privilege, and abandoning its own computer money idea. They had previously been doing a joint experiment with Visa in New York's Upper West Side, to see how people coped with competing computer currency cards. Mondex was launched in Swindon in 1995, when newspaper vendor Don Stanley accepted the first Mondex trade, surrounded by the world's press. 'It's cash, Swindon,' said the promotional posters. 'But not as you know it . . .'

At the end of three months there were 8,000 cards in circulation, and Mondex payments were accepted by 700 retailers, including pubs, buses and car parks. Mondex has since popped up in other places where there was some reason why its managers thought it might be welcome. Canada, for example, because it has the highest penetration of telephones in the world. Hong Kong because of their over-reliance on cash: because the ferries, railways and buses require exact change, and people lug piles of coins around with them, which they then offload at petrol stations. Mondex's rival Visacash was launched at the 1996 Olympics and the French postal company La Poste has also been working on its own 'electronic purse' since 1986. Citibank and Chase Manhattan launched their own smartcard money system – in the Upper West Side again – in October 1997. Holland is powering ahead: every other Dutch person now has a smartcard and uses it in parking meters and vending machines, and soon for buses and library fines. Even the Zambian Meridiencard can store credit simultaneously in ten different currencies.

Do any of these innovations put the power to create money into the hands of people like you and me? No, they don't. Do they change the relationships between bankers and customers, between rich and poor? No. Are they pandering to a ginger group of free marketeers who are planning to turn money upside-down? Possibly.

These are pioneers who carry around copies of an influential 1975 article by the great economist who inspired Margaret Thatcher, Friedrich Hayek. The article was called 'The Denationalizaton of Money' and it said that companies would inevitably challenge governments for the right to produce it. 'Money does not have to be created legal tender by governments,' he wrote. 'Like law, language and morals, it can emerge spontaneously.'

He seems to have been right. The thinker Edward de Bono, author of *The Uses of Lateral Thinking*, has imagined the possibility of IBM Dollars. Freelance journalists are sometimes said to use an imaginary currency called busbys – one hundred busbys are a hundred minutes of British Telecom long-distance calls – though I can't say I ever have. Tesco's Clubcard, basically Tesco money, attracted six million users in nine months. And then, of course, there are Disney Dollars in Disney World in Florida, and even McScrip – available first in a McDonald's 'restaurant' in Cornelia, Georgia.

'To make such a scheme work, IBM would have to learn to manage the supply of money to ensure that – with too many vouchers chasing too few goods – inflation does not destroy the value of their creations,' said *Wired* magazine. 'But companies should be able to manage that at least as easily as governments do, particularly as they don't have voters to deal with.' Microsoft's Bill Gates went even further: 'Banks are dinosaurs,' he said. 'We can bypass them.'

This is a small glimpse of a not-too-distant future, where we juggle different kinds of corporate money, saving Microsoft money because it's a good investment, trying to avoid Fuzzy's Furniture money altogether, and spending Marks & Spencer money – because it is widely accepted. We would hang on to the currencies which keep their value and trade others online, just like a Russian who uses roubles and hangs on to dollars. It depends on the same old division which Joel Hodroff was talking about, between money as information and money as a store of value.

One US free-market think-tank, the Cato Institute, is so enthusiastic about this computerized multi-currency future that it holds an annual conference about it. Bankers, free-market academics and libertarians all spend the days rubbing their hands with glee at some of the implications. Because, for all those Americans who cheered during the film *Independence Day* when the White House exploded, competing currencies means a possible end to US government fiscal control. The technology means that all our earnings could be entirely private which means – for example – that only people who want to pay income tax will do so. Internet sales now amount to $7 billion a year around the world, and sales tax is already extremely hard for governments to collect. This is a brave new world for politicians who daren't tax, but it is probably inevitable. Without reliable taxation, electronic money threatens the existence of the nation state – but before that it threatens the existence of old-fashioned cash.

One consultant at the Cato conference in 1996 defined coins entirely in Wall Street terms: 'Technically currency is simply a small denomination, non-interest-bearing bond of no fixed maturity,' he said. But just in case they succeed in getting rid of cash altogether, there are one or two issues we ought to think about first. Like the impact on the poor in a world with no bundles of notes, the merging of the black economy and the mainstream, and the end of small change. Beggars will find it particularly difficult if they don't happen to have a currency card reader handy.

In fact, coins and notes may be the last vestiges of concrete, touchable, pocketable money. The rest is entirely imaginary. 'In a few generations, a significant fraction of the world's economy might well have no material existence whatsoever,' Bill Frezza of Wireless Computing Associates told the Cato Institute in 1996.

We in the UK prefer to avoid issues like this entirely, and concentrate on heady areas of disagreement – like whether the new euro currency includes a picture of the Queen. Instead we probably ought to be worrying about the vast computer networks of cyber-money, which will be able to track everything we buy and sell, building up marketable data about our personal transport habits, health problems, lovers, holidays, cinema preferences and much else besides.

We may as well face up to part of the revolution, says the Australian money thinker Shann Turnbull. 'Central banking will become redundant in the next three to five years because of digital money,' he said, and he should know, because he has seen the new world of money from both sides of the tracks – as a close associate of Bob Swann's and as advisor to the Australian corporate raider Robert Holmes à Court.

There are five kinds of money, he told me when I met him at the conference in the Berkshires:

- Government money, like pounds and dollars. This is also 'funny money', says Shann, because it isn't related to reality in any way.
- Social money like time dollars, which you can give away in return for social favours.
- Labour money, based on people's work, like Ithaca Hours or LETS.
- Local currencies for financing production, like farm preserve notes, or ecological service money like energy dollars, which would allow you to pre-buy electricity from wind farms.
- Corporate money, like phone units, IBM money, air miles, McScrip or any of the others, many of them made possible by the digital revolution.

As far as Shann Turnbull is concerned, money should be defined in terms of something real. When it isn't – and usually it isn't these days – you get money monoculture and, because there are no proper feedback mechanisms about the effect on raw materials or the planet, you risk ecological ruin. If you agree with him, then the good old days of money were those of Joseph and his multicoloured coat. It was Joseph, after all, who persuaded Pharaoh to put the grain from the seven years of plenty into a barn. When he did so, he also launched 'real' money linked to the value of something real.

'The ancient Egyptians used grain as a currency,' wrote Shann Turnbull. 'Surplus grain was placed in storage houses with the depositor obtaining a receipt in the form of scratches on shards of pottery. The shards acted as a currency. However it had a negative interest rate as a storage fee had to be paid. The cost was inconsequential to the cost of not having grain to sustain life during a famine. The storage house acted as a savings bank and the shards of pottery as deposit notes.'

Ancient Egyptian money was based on their life-support system during famine, and on the value of deposited grain – which lost value the longer it was held in the bank. That's why new alchemists like Bob Swann are so keen to base their money on something productive: because 'money' originally was a natural substance which rotted if it wasn't used.

Bob and Shann Turnbull have also been raising the idea of local currencies based on the value of renewable energy. The great thing about renewable energy is that you can't transport it or store it very well, and it is worth pretty much the same all over the world. I'm looking forward to this myself, especially if it means paying for a packet of crisps with computerized amps and joules.

V

Williams College, in Williamstown right in the heart of the Berkshires, is calm in midsummer. It has tall whitewashed churches, respectable matrons, careful Volvos, beautifully manicured grass and kerbs which look as though somebody has cleaned them with a toothbrush. It was a delightful place to come to a conference, surrounded on all sides by lush wooded hillsides. A blue moon – the second full moon in a month – was appearing over the horizon, the trees were swaying gently in the wind, and the Norman Rockwell Museum, packed with homely childhood views of wholesome American life, was waiting just up the road.

But if I had been a student cooped up there for three years, I might have gone quietly round the twist. We could only find one bar in the vicinity and that was in an expensive hotel, graced with a swing band of elderly men – including a wizened bass player who could imitate Louis Armstrong – and large middle-aged couples doing the cha-cha slowly round the floor.

Gathering in the big hall of Williams College for the First US Decentrist Conference were many of the key gurus and pioneers of new kinds of money in the USA. I was a little disconcerted to find that, not only was I doing a 'workshop' on new money in Britain, but I was being billed as one of eight world experts on the idea for the big Saturday night high spot.

But the US decentralists turned out to be a gentle group of people, who believed firmly in local democracy. They were different in style from their British equivalent – who happily argue through the night about how to break up town halls into smaller units and whether it is wrong to eat at McDonald's even if you are starving. The American decentralists were in some ways more naïve, in others more down to earth. They preferred to talk quietly under trees about the power of Washington, local economic development and how to tackle Wal-Mart. The extreme decentralists in the militia had luckily stayed away. So had the people who actually believe the New Hampshire licence plates which say 'Live Free or Die'. The others were all thinkers or enthusiasts – people who wanted to design eco-communities, remap Canada, launch innovative local vegetable schemes or start local currencies in their neighbourhood. To everyone their own currency; be your own Royal Mint.

The gurus were there too. Bob Swann and Susan Witt, pulling the conference together from behind the scenes. Shann Turnbull, over from Sydney in his half-moon spectacles and shirtsleeves, laughing loudly and poking people in the stomach if they didn't agree with him. Washington law professor Lewis Solomon, whose ground-breaking book on the legality of new kinds of money unfortunately cost $55. 'Keep trying. Never despair,' he told us all later. 'It is a long road but we have a glorious goal in mind.'

There were Jane Wilson and Diana McCourt from Womanshare, in big blousy dresses, and the bronzed, quiet, T-shirted figure of Tom Greco, author of *Healthy Money for Healthy Communities*, campaigning from Arizona for money to be 'real'. And there was Gerald da Costa from Washington, a studious-looking revolutionary who was about to launch a new kind of money for the black community called AfriCa$h. He was distributing a wildly complex questionnaire, including the complicated question: 'MONEY as meaning My Own Natural Energy Yield is an accurate or excellent description of the essence of what the function of money is supposed to accomplish as a tool of human invention – strongly disagree – disagree – agree – strongly agree.'

And there was Professor Edgar Cahn, looking a little out of place – the lawyer among these grassroots activists, a few of whom seemed to veer awkwardly between anarchism and paranoia. I was pleased to see him again, and discovered later that he had not actually been invited to the conference, but had phoned the organizers and insisted on doing a presentation about time dollars. 'You have to send us a proposal,' they told him. 'I'll send two!' he said.

As I arrived, the keynote speakers were already on the rostrum in the big echoing Williams College hall. Rows of intense local activists and bearded gurus – men and women – listened with rapt concentration, taking copious notes. It was a measure of how broad-based the American decentralist movement is that the first two speakers were the anarchist and Luddite author Kirkpatrick Sale – advising people to smash their computers – and a former speech-writer for Ronald Reagan. 'The leviathan state is the death of the human spirit,' said John McLaughry, who regularly put this stuff into Reagan's speeches. 'We are on the side of history, and although it may not always be apparent, we are winning.' It transpired that Ronald Reagan's famous words in 1975 – 'I am calling for an end to giantism and a return to the human scale' – had actually been written by him.

I became restless at this point, as I tend to after the first fifteen minutes of a political meeting, and wandered out to search for a telephone. As I walked back across the tree-lined lawn, I caught sight of an exhausted, sweaty-looking figure with a jutting beard and rucksack and what turned out to be a T-shirt with the slogan 'Ithaca Festival '95'. It was the missing hero of the hour – Paul Glover from Ithaca – arriving in his habitual way: on foot, his baggage full of hour note samples. Refusing as usual to travel by car, he had caught the bus across the state line to Bennington, and walked the final fourteen miles.

'Where can I get a shower?' he said.

It was a good thing he came. Everybody wanted to hear about Ithaca Hours, and as they arrived for the conference, they were handed a fulsome photocopied article in the *Wall Street Journal* about Ithaca. The mainstream financial world seemed to be taking notice at last. And on every table and under a number of trees, the younger enthusiasts were discussing their plans to set up new hours-style currencies. I met a tall, moustachioed young man from Tennessee, who gave me a labour certificate from the Woodland Community in Roses Creek, Tennessee. A girl in a check shirt was planning another hours system in Brooklyn called 'Brooklyn greenbacks'. A natural pest control officer was organizing Dillo hours in Austin, Texas. And a woman in a white turban, described by the programme as Guru Nam Khalsa, was outlining her local currency, known as Valley Hours. Almost everybody seemed to have a local currency scheme up their sleeve. Even me: I was supposed to be running a 'workshop' about LETS schemes in Britain, and was feeling a little embarrassed that I was a mere observer, and not a walking amateur central banker myself.

The next morning, I tracked some of them down. The first was

Tom Greco, who gave up his academic career in 1989 for a free-lance attempt to track down the causes of world poverty. I found him eating his breakfast and urging that money has to be 'real'. Sooner or later, however many new kinds of money we all launch, there has to be a worldwide standard of value, he said.

'So can you paint a picture of the world in twenty or thirty years' time?' I asked hopefully: I was feeling cynically journalistic again. 'Or would it take longer?'

'No, I think twenty years will be enough time.' Greco looked unenthusiastic about this. 'I think in twenty years' time, we will have what I describe. There will be a standard index of account, or maybe more than one. And the market will decide which one or which ones would be most suitable. I think it will come down to just one. At the beginning of the micro-computer age there were dozens of different computers and they couldn't relate to each other, but in time it came down to a standard, and I think they are heading towards compatibility so that we have one micro-computer standard. I think it will be the same with a global unit of account.'

'Do you see local currencies as a stopgap then?'

'Oh I don't know, they might have a sustained life. The thing about a local currency is, number one: it can be created as needed in whatever quantity. Number two, it is interest-free. And number three, it circulates within a limited area, supporting the local economy and helping it to be self-sufficient.'

Greco was planning his own local currency in Tucson called the yesXchange. It will work like this: one of the business or non-profit members takes on a youth worker, and pays them in scrip. This can be used to buy things from any of the other employers in the system, before it gets passed back to the yesX-change for redemption.

'So what is money at the moment?' I asked him, getting down to brass tacks.

He gave a little laugh at the enormity of the question. 'Well, the major error is that bankers and economists are still treating money as if it was a commodity, and this makes the supply limited. And they operate in favour of the few, which means that the rest of us have to gather what we can. Much of the money in circulation is issued on the basis of unrepayable government debt, whereas it should be issued on the basis of real value. The Federal Reserve buys government bonds, and pays for the bonds with a cheque drawn against no money, creating new money to pay for the bond. The trouble is that there isn't enough money in circulation to pay the interest on their loans. The government has become the borrower of last resort, rather than the lender.'

There is something a little puritanical about this horror of debt. The vast US budget deficit hangs like a Sword of Damocles over American life, but the sheer power of capital and the belief in the US government's ability to pay its way keeps the torrent frothing. But then debt, as we know, is what creates money in the first place. 'A national debt, if it is not excessive, will be to us a national blessing,' said Alexander Hamilton, the first US Treasury Secretary, and the American way of money has depended on debt ever since. It may not satisfy all our needs for love, simplicity, comfort, safety, God, trees and all the other aspects of life which make up wealth, but there is no doubt about it – old-fashioned money has a tremendous power and efficiency behind it. Debt works. It just doesn't work for everything.

The other guru I tracked down was David Burman. Burman is one of the organizers of one of the most successful LETS money schemes in the world, in Toronto – begun when LETS inventor Michael Linton suddenly invited himself to stay. Toronto LETS took off in 1991 when the *Toronto Star* ran a series of articles called 'recession busters', and suddenly they had 700 members, all using a currency they called 'green dollars'. And the great thing about green dollars was that they seemed to help some of the people excluded from old-fashioned Canadian dollars.

'Some join to meet people, some because they feel marginalized,' he told me. 'We have a courier system run by mental health survivors, paid for in green dollars. Some people join because of their inability to cope with pressures of business life – although they are extremely capable, highly motivated people, yet they need the support of LETS to get jobs and develop their skills. It works on many levels.'

The aim was to get the Toronto city authorities to accept part of their local taxes in green dollars. But in the meantime they were researching how local currencies can help promote health, build people's coping skills, increase their self-esteem – like the time dollars project in Brooklyn. 'The ultimate goal is to make green dollars work for 10 per cent of people's real economic lives,' he told me. 'Whereas now, the best evidence is that it is 1 or 2 per cent of the participants' lives. After that, I can see LETS becoming a global currency based on the needs of communities and individuals rather than transnational corporations. National currencies are very bad at distributing wealth, whereas LETS systems are good at it, because they are small and efficient. So rather than LETS systems growing huge, tiny neighbourhood systems should be networked together to become a global currency which is far more efficient – allow people the freedom to do what they love to do, and maybe do away with money altogether.'

Toronto LETS has run into inter-personal difficulties since then, but what is it about North America that people allow themselves to dream dreams like this? The limit of the ambitions of so many people in Europe is that the state should run hospitals more efficiently. In America, radicals of right and left dream of going off into the great open spaces and doing it better themselves, which is why the communes movement on the left and the shadowy militia groups on the right are both interested in producing their own money.

Needless to say, the hippies and the militiamen have little to talk about, but there were representatives of one of the most successful US communes at the conference, Twin Oaks in Virginia. One had changed his name, rather disconcertingly, to Nexus. Another told how a truck of tough-looking militiamen drew up next to him at the traffic lights one day, complete with oafish armbands, rifles and xenophobic stickers. They looked down at the hippy types next to them, who were obviously from the local commune. 'We've got you on our list,' said one of the militiamen menacingly. The hippies quaked.

'Yeah,' he went on. 'When the government attacks, we're gonna protect you. We don't like what you do, but you've got a right to do it.'

VI

Everyone interested in new kinds of money gathered on the fourth floor of the university buildings, from where you could see wood-covered hills undulating in every direction, and the drizzle. The room was packed solid, mainly because of the presentations by the two star turns, Paul Glover and Edgar Cahn. On the face of it, the two men represented entirely different methods of conjuring money out of thin air. Edgar Cahn had invented 'social money' – it didn't matter to him that time dollars should add up at the end. They are a way of driving a new kind of moral social economy. Hours, on the other hand, are more like 'market money' or 'labour money'. They are released into the local economy to make it sustainable, and to stop local money drifting away. In fact, the two systems seem diametrically opposed. Paul Glover needs his hours spent. Edgar Cahn – who is on record for criticizing 'labour money' for just copying dollars – doesn't care if they are simply given back to the bank.

Paul Glover went first. Intense-looking PhD students clamoured into the room, together with thin bearded men – including one in a T-shirt which said 'For whosoever shall call upon the name of YAHWEH shall be saved'. Edgar Cahn was too late for a seat, and he propped himself up by the window looking donnish.

'The genius of Paul is to love his community,' said conference organizer Susan Witt, introducing him. Glover predictably demurred from this heroic introduction, and passed round some hour samples, slouching back in his chair in a wonderfully relaxed performance. 'And please hand them back,' he said. 'I handed some out at a Rotary Club meeting recently and was very surprised when it came to the end.'

'How do you fund yourself?,' asked one more critical member of the audience. This is always a difficult question for people who launch their own money. There's a sense that, really, it ought to fund itself. Glover explained that he was a VISTA volunteer, the programme launched by President Johnson which lies behind many local money projects. The volunteers are, in fact, not volunteers but paid employees of the federal government. 'The government usually subsidizes for the worst possible purposes, so I'm not too proud to accept their money,' he said, with just the slightest hint of defence.

Cahn looked up and made a small note in his pile of paper. He was an unusual figure to find at this conference of wild theorists and anarchists. As a former aide to Bobby Kennedy, he was probably closer to government than anybody else in the room, with the possible exception of John McLaughry with his Reagan experience. There were other people at the conference working in inner cities, but not many. He was also dressed differently. He almost certainly thought differently, and the new age radicals regarded him with some suspicion. But his audience was subtly different: the man with the Yahweh T-shirt had been replaced by a girl with a T-shirt which said: 'Pooh just is'.

He rose to his feet – none of the relaxed Glover approach – and explained that the story had moved on, even since my visit to Washington. Time dollars were now being paid to peer tutors in ten Chicago schools. As many as 1,500 schoolkids in Chicago were collecting time dollars, and the computers they would be able to buy with them would be 386 and 486 models. The Washington youth court was getting through defendants at the rate of three a week. At the housing complex I had been to, the local welfare authorities were allowing people to earn time dollars to make them eligible for benefits. Time dollars were being earned in twenty blocks, and used to buy food. There was even a time dollar jobs agency there.

'The only way I know to begin to address our problems in a way that I care about is to redefine work,' he said. 'And it's not the work which the market economy values, because the work which remains to be done is caring, loving, being a citizen, being a parent, being a human being – that work will never I hope be so scarce that the market value goes high. So in the monetary system as we know it, that work will never be adequately valued, but if we are going to reward contribution, we are going to have to find a way to redefine work. Alvin Toffler asks executives how productive their workforce would be if they hadn't been toilet-trained. But toilet-training isn't productive work, is it?' asked Cahn in his ironic style. 'Writing ads for Twinkies – now that's productive work.

'I deeply respect the work of everybody here. We are all working on different pieces of the same problem,' Edgar Cahn told his rivals in the audience. 'It is very clear to me that the Ithaca system can buy things which time dollars cannot, that the LETS system has some plusses which I can't claim. This is not us versus each other, it is about us talking together about the different problems we face and how we can rebuild communities – knowing that money has a toxic effect on them.'

I began to understand that there was a politics of local currencies which I had never noticed before. There was a division, of course, between 'social' money and 'market' money – between time dollars and hours. But there was also a division even more fundamental than that – about the key problem we were all trying to solve. Edgar Cahn, who came into the debate during the 1980s during the cash-strapped Reagan and Thatcher years, seemed primarily concerned to help poorer people get access to money. Some of the other crusty old theorists had joined the debate earlier, during the inflationary 1970s – and they wanted 'real' money, money which you could rely on.

Looking at the poor old flagging dollar, they could both unite. There it was, backed by absolutely nothing except the unfathomable national deficit, but still flooding into Wall Street, giving the crumbling estates of Washington and New York a pretty wide berth. But beyond that there was a difference: did you want to create 'free money' or 'real money'? This is a division which seems to echo down US history, through the long list of bank crashes and financial scares. The idea of a run on the bank –

probably because of the frightening and near-fatal run in 1933, just as Roosevelt was being sworn in as president – still lies deep inside the national psyche.

This same division was apparent in the famous political battles a century ago, during the tenure of President Grover Cleveland – a man of fearsome financial rectitude, pledged to linking the dollar's value to gold. Opposing him with the force of rhetoric was failed presidential hopeful William Jennings Bryan – who ended his life as the prosecutor in the famous Tennessee Monkey Trial – campaigning for money to be more available. 'You shall not press down upon the brow of labour this crown of thorns. You shall not crucify mankind upon a cross of gold,' he thundered at the 1896 Democratic convention, swinging his arms into the sign of the cross to a deafening five-minute ovation. It was one of the most famous moments of US political speechifying.

Anyone who invents their own money ends up somewhere in this age-old battle, I thought as I struggled to make sense of it over my American muffins and strawberries. Edgar Cahn didn't care whether his time dollars added up in the accounts, but for Tom Greco from Tucson it mattered very much. There was money and there was anti-money. Real money and free money, but neither position works very well if you push it to extremes. If Tom Greco keeps a strict control over his money because it has to be based on something real, the danger is that it stays in such short supply that none of us can afford it. You can, if you are really ingenious, find some standard measurement for money – but not for the broader human aspects of 'value'. And if Edgar Cahn wants to make time dollars more available, he could give them out in packets in a Washington street, but then they would be worthless and there wouldn't be any point either. Anyone who invents their own money has to balance these two extremes – between deflation and inflation.

Why is it that we don't have arguments like that in London? Is it because we have no colourful tradition of bank crashes? Or because we leave such issues to our bankers, who prefer not to consult us? Or is it because we are so bored by economics that we never talk about it? We don't even argue much about the details of the European single currency, which seems like a whole new dinosaur in the emerging multi-currency age. Maybe we Britons have decided we have no power to create our own money and wealth. If so, it's time we sat up and took notice.

VII

The hour of the Saturday night plenary session was approaching. I was nervous of this, because I knew I was going to be introduced as an expert when I wasn't one. I had not the least idea what to say, but I wanted to make sure I did nothing to worsen the possible rift. A couple of hundred expectant radicals stared up from below us. It was a beautiful summer Saturday evening and, as usual on these occasions, I was astonished that people wanted to stay in discussing changing the world, rather than sitting on the grass drinking beer and watching the evening shadows lengthen.

Many of the speakers seemed to want to conjure the ghost of Henry Ford on their side. 'We have the productive capacity to take care of everyone,' said Edgar. 'Sooner or later we are going to discover what Henry Ford knew, that if we don't provide people with the income they won't be able to buy the products. We need to create a currency which confers value on the things we say we value.'

Bob Swann mentioned him too, but Tom Greco managed to leave Ford alone: 'People have a superstitious belief that money is a province of government – actually the government shouldn't be involved in money, for exactly the same reason that they shouldn't be involved in making yardsticks or scale weights.'

Then it was my turn. 'One experiment is not enough,' I said. 'One pattern is really only a small improvement on what we have already. We need to keep the movement dynamic, community-driven and exciting. If we do that, the chances are we will find that the hard-won solutions of one system might be adapted to help the others.'

Nobody clapped. Probably they were right. I felt hypocritical coming to an American conference dedicated to local power when I lived more than 4,000 miles away.

Edgar Cahn spoke immediately after I did, and I had been fascinated to find out what he would say. In the event there had been no attack on 'market currencies', no denigration of the kind of money based on productivity which the old guard were talking about. His trenchant papers about how LETS and hours simply copy the old-fashioned brutal market economies were put on one side, and instead he confessed to a change of heart. 'I came here with a point of view,' he told the earnest faces below. 'That you can't get away from materialism with currencies that just replicate market pricing. But I have now come to think we can try to have both social and market currencies side by side.'

It was a significant change. Only the day before he had been telling me about the difficulties Joel Hodroff and Commonweal would have if they tried to translate time dollars into dollars. And as I dashed down the corridor the following morning, dreaming of fried eggs, I passed Edgar Cahn and Paul Glover in rare conversation. It seemed to confirm that the two high-profile money pioneers in the USA were reaching some kind of rapprochement.

I ran into Edgar later, peering at the books for sale in his distinctive manner, and getting ready to drive back to Washington. He looked tremendously pleased: he was hoping to get four youth cases through his court every week by the autumn, he told me.

'We've agreed to try an experiment and set up a time dollar project in Ithaca which links to hours,' he said. 'Of course we still have to discuss some of the details.'

'Like what?'

'Like whether you can earn by making supportive phone calls.' Cahn had been so proud of this aspect of time dollars – that old people could earn them by doing things like computer training or sitting around playing draughts. But he realized that he and Glover were actually trying to achieve similar things. They both wanted to turn economics upside-down. It made sense for them to work together.

'Between the two of us, we receive the lion's share of publicity about local money,' said Edgar. 'So if we work together we can really do something – which is better than killing each other, which is what might usually happen.' The alliance also meant that Ithaca Hours could benefit from the Time Dollar Institute's non-profit status, and their detailed legal and practical knowledge about dealing with welfare authorities. It meant that time dollars could benefit from Ithaca's excellent links with local business. The whole project had the potential to be a driving force for local money in the USA.

I told Edgar my theory about the difference between the free money activists and the reliable money activists – and how it seemed to be a division deep in American history and politics. 'I don't see anything like that in British politics now,' I said. 'But as a Brit I recognize it as the age-old difference between cavaliers and roundheads. You're a cavalier.'

He seemed quite pleased. And who wouldn't: it's like telling someone they look as dashing as Prince Rupert of the Rhine. But afterwards, I realized I had got it the wrong way round.

Five centuries ago, the old alchemists like the mysterious Paracelsus – wandering round Europe in a coloured coat which he never washed – were the inspiration behind a Protestant revolution against the old order of authority and control. They toppled the old certainties of medicine and politics with their dreams of a 'chemical revolution' which would restore the wasteland, attacking monopolies and putting power and medical knowledge into the hands of ordinary people. The new alchemists are doing the same with money.

They are the vanguard of a money revolution which allows us all to do what only governments and bankers have been able to do so far – create money. As such, Edgar Cahn would clearly be on the roundhead side in the English Revolution, and so would all the other new alchemists in this book.

But there is still a division between them, between those who want to spread this new money around and those slightly more puritanical pioneers who want to defend its value. And don't let's disparage those on the puritanical side: if we had a reliable standard of value, which remains steady when the traders get the jitters, which doesn't go into the red every time the Tokyo stock market gets the blues – which keeps its value even if you keep your savings under a mattress for a lifetime – there would be enormous advantages for us all. Because stable money makes it easier to shift out of one kind of money and into another. It means less of the helter-skelter of currency fluctuations for their own sake, and considerably less need for a European single currency – and less fun for the speculators.

'Yet the fact is that billions of dollars are made available by bankers everywhere in the nation for this purpose daily,' wrote Ralph Borsodi a generation ago. 'Wall Street could not survive without this flow of money from all over the nation. It could not carry on without the flow of billions of dollars which, if properly laid out by bankers on genuine production loans, would transform a worried and distraught nation into a saner and more civilized one.'

So there we are. Real money and free money: they both have the ability to transform the wasteland, but they go about it differently.

Chapter 8

How to be richer

'One day I will die, and on my tombstone it will say, 'Here lies
Reginald Iolanthe Perrin. He didn't know the names of the
flowers and the trees, but he knew the rhubarb crumble sales
for Schleswig-Holstein.'
David Nobbs, *The Fall and Rise of Reginald Perrin.*

I

So I went back to England, and found it parched and yellow from
one of those regular phases of drought we have nearly every
other summer these days. Unfortunately the relationship didn't
follow me back. The possible pitfalls of living with each other in
the USA seemed so enormous to me that it drove out more
important issues, such as what I felt: it seemed foolhardy to leave
behind everybody who might employ me on the other side of
the Atlantic, while I faced the prospect of health insurance, car
insurance and all the other expenses of living in America. Money
had got in the way again. While for her, there were the irritating
vast depths of my indecision about almost everything. I hadn't
expected it to be such a debilitating shock, but the summer
seemed bleak and fierce afterwards, as I went through my regular
muddle about love. I missed her smile and little things like the
way she wrapped a bath towel round her head every morning.
The truth was that I found America disabling. There is a wildness
at the heart of it somehow, as if someone had just concreted over
Africa and you could still feel it pulsating underneath your feet.
I was unsure whether the people who lived there – with their
generosity, certainty and firm handshakes – were unaware of
this or whether they were just at ease with it. It seemed to fit
awkwardly with the enormous affluence and respectability of so
much of American life, and it disturbed me.

There is always an initial thrill about losing love, however
distressing it is – a kind of buzz of possibilities, as if you've suddenly got a choice and the freedom from worrying about some-

body else, and all those other freedoms of adult life we willingly give away in a relationship. But the thrill usually pales shortly afterwards when you remember there wasn't much choice anyway, and you find you miss worrying about someone else – and you miss them too. I also remembered that, like many of my contemporaries, I seemed to have confused the ceaseless search for money and the ceaseless search for love and had failed to pin down either of them. I never could seem to attract quite enough, as if there was a finite amount which I had to battle for.

I mention all this because it made me suspicious of my attitudes to money. People's emotions so often seem to mould what they believe: Conservatives believe they were born to rule, Liberal Democrats feel left out, and Labour supporters are more resentful than everybody else. Maybe I just wanted money to be infinite because I wanted love to be infinite. Maybe I wanted a philosopher's stone which would turn the base metal of my life – not into gold, which would be ironic given what I have been writing – but at least into dreams made reality.

And it's true: I did want that. But then again, if we really could find a way of tapping into the infinity of money – or if we could, at any rate, make it considerably more available to us ordinary mortals – perhaps it didn't matter why I wanted it. It could give us the freedom to get on with more important aspects of our lives. The trouble is, there has never been a moment in the history of humanity when scarce money has seemed as set in its ways as it is now. The money system carries us all before it with almost death-defying power. James Buchan tracked its progress to this point in his book *Frozen Desire* – the title is in itself a thrillingly apt description of the nature of money – explaining what a powerful liberator it has been through the past five centuries or so.

Money imposes a kind of equality on people which undermines aristocracy, tyranny, privilege, and even violence: it was not for nothing that the reforming Liberal Party of the nineteenth century was powered by the new industrialists against the ancient power of land. It was the inflation caused by printing money which paved the way for the French Revolution, money which forced the universal franchise, money which created the modern world with all its comforts and technologies, and now it is the power of unrestricted capital which has been undermining the stagnant corruption of governments in the Far East. It's not so much democracies that never go to war with each other, as Margaret Thatcher used to say, it is market economies. War is just too expensive.

But money is also a double-edged sword. It has given us a

more civilized, peaceful world, where we are so much less subject to the arbitrary authority of priests and lords, but it has lost us something human as well – as Jane Austen, Don Quixote or *Pretty Woman* constantly remind us. And if, as James Buchan says, America is the place where the money system rules more completely than anywhere else, there is also a kind of yearning at the heart of American life which recognizes this – and longs for homespun, small-town life where everyone returns fleetingly for Thanksgiving. It is a nostalgic kind of yearning because, says Buchan, no human values – love, beauty or hope – can survive in the age of money:

> For any beauty must be exploited, reproduced a million million times by every medium open to commercial ingenuity, till one can only cover one's eyes and stop one's ears. The sole aesthetic sensation of modernity is nausea: permanent, lethal nausea. These contradictions lie at the heart of the great sadness of our civilization: that by using money, we convert our world into it. Humanity is . . . estranged by money from its natural habitat, without any hope of appeal. We are also – and here the Romantic movement loses its self-control and, like the Don himself, becomes violent – estranged by money from one another.

And if we convert ourselves into money, we become frighteningly dependent on it when it fails – like the Irish on the potato before their disastrous famine. We can't eat money, as Chief Seattle may or may not have said. In the end it increases our insecurity and separation. Even if we keep our jobs, and increasingly we fear we won't, we may end up living out the bizarre joke in the film *Donnie Brasco*, where two mafia underlings thank each other for their respective Christmas presents which were just of wads of cash in envelopes.

Now that human values have been all but subsumed into the money system in the phenomenon of price – £5,000 for an Albanian baby, £100,000 for a human life in India or Africa, £800,000 for a four-bedroom house in St John's Wood – it is time to rediscover some of them in a post-money age. But how? Well, probably there are only two starting points: first unpick the centuries of overlap between love and money; then start using our ingenuity to create different kinds of money of our own.

II

In an ideal world, love and money would never be super-imposed, one on the other – there is all the difference in the world between the two, and no way that one can give you the other. But in spite of that, we have been muddling the relation-ship between love and money ever since the first Lydians went out with it jangling in their pockets to sell their womenfolk. Almost every chapter of this book refers to the same confusion, pointing back always to the story of King Midas, the mythical king who wanted everything he touched to turn into gold. Another story about Midas, incidentally, is that he was given the ears of an ass for choosing Pan instead of Apollo – choosing the earth against the heavens, which is what mankind does every time it puts money on too high a pedestal.

One movement which is currently unpicking the two is the American phenomenon of 'downshifting' – deciding to do what you love rather than what brings in most money. And it rests on a strange paradox. Some of the most successful places on both sides of the Atlantic are booming because of a continual influx of new, well-off people, many of whom are actually going to live there to get away from the rat-race and earn less. When people downshift in the UK, they move to Dorset or Norfolk or a range of other places. When they downshift in the USA, they move to Boulder or Seattle.

They do so because overwork is a peculiarity of both British and American cultures. In the USA, people tend to get only two weeks' holiday a year. In the UK, people work an average of forty-four hours a week, more than any other European country, and as many as 3.3 million work more than fifty hours a week. And to drive this exhausting schedule, keeping people in a frenzy of consumption, the average British teenager will have seen a terrifying 150,000 television adverts by the age of eighteen. No wonder so many of us are trying to take it a bit more easy.

'We are speeding up our lives and working harder in a futile attempt to buy the time to slow down and enjoy it,' said Paul Hawken in *The Ecology of Commerce*. It's a peculiar paradox, which seems to have something to do with the usual contradiction at the heart of money. Money is not the same as wealth, and although we all know that, there is something about the money economy which continually blinds us to it and deludes us.

Downshifters also remind us that money has nothing to do with happiness. When the former World Bank economist Herman

Daly teamed up with theologian John Cobb to create an 'Index of Sustainable Economic Welfare' to measure these things, they found that money growth and feelgood growth went up in parallel in the USA until the early 1970s, when something very different happened. Money growth carried on climbing, but 'economic welfare' began to fall. The New Economics Foundation tracked the same idea in the UK and found exactly the same phenomenon. 'If economic progress means that we become anonymous cogs in some great machine, then progress is an empty promise,' said Charles Handy. But we can't use money to measure how cog-like we have become. Who wants to be the richest anonymous cog in the world?

If you take things slower, you often end up spending less money anyway. It's almost as if we are paying extra in order to earn more. 'We now have the time and energy to cook and eat *in* five times a week instead of *out* five times a week,' wrote Polly Ghazi in her book *Get a Life*. 'Secondly, I no longer speed around in taxis because my life is so busy I don't want to waste time walking or waiting for the bus. Thirdly, my deep need for retail therapy has abated dramatically . . .'

The main problem about this is that we are all addicted to money growth. If the growth slows down, the economy plunges into recession and we all get poorer. Its growth depends on our staying addicted. The *Wall Street Journal* has already warned against damage done by downshifters. 'Our enormously productive economy,' wrote the post-war retail analyst Victor Lebow, 'demands that we make consumption our way of life, that we convert the buying and the use of goods into rituals, that we seek our spiritual satisfaction, our ego satisfaction, in consumption . . . We need things consumed, burned up, worn out, replaced and discarded at an ever increasing rate.'

We may not want to: we may realize that the things which get worn out and burned up are actually ourselves. We may rebel at having to carry on the ultimately self-defeating dance to keep the economy moving a little bit longer. But it is difficult to opt out when we all depend, apparently, on its froth. It isn't a matter of morality: it may be just simple self-preservation. We down-shifting aromatherapists, astrologers, masseurs and journalists may have difficulty earning anything at all if the economy dips.

The American guru of downshifting, Amy Dacyczyn, and her husband Jim had both been working for twenty years – she as a graphic designer, he in the navy – but had amassed savings of just $1,500. So they set about the task of not spending money with enormous imagination and enthusiasm. After seven years, they had saved $49,000 from Jim's salary and bought a farm-house in Maine. But that wasn't the end. Amy put her discoveries into a newsletter called *The Tightwad Gazette*, so that everybody else could benefit from her ideas, which include: avoid make-up when nobody is coming to visit; when you boil the kettle, pour the excess into a thermos so that you won't have to waste energy re-boiling it later; eke out your margarine with skimmed milk.

Amy wears out her cheap sneakers on a strange three-year cycle to make them last longer, and made such a success of *The Tightwad Gazette* that it now has a circulation of over 100,000 and she is rich enough to retire.

Money and role are becoming increasingly disconnected. The way you pay for your life no longer provides you with the defining role it once did. And that is the idea behind the New Road Map Foundation: they want people to put their lives back together so that money is no longer discussed separately from all the other things you want to achieve. It gives you the 'freedom to think for yourself', says Vicki Robin, co-author of *Your Money or Your Life*.

Their instructions are simple to explain, but rather more difficult to carry out. First, work out the total amount of money you have earned in your lifetime, your net worth and your liabilities. Next, work out what you earn, and take away what it costs you to work – suits, therapy, childcare, transport and so on. Then keep track of every penny you spend and compare it with the time you have really spent to earn it. You are spending life energy, you say to yourself when you go over the books every month: was it worth it? *Your Money or Your Life* claims that you can slash your spending by 15 to 20 per cent just by being aware of it. And being aware of it in this way is what they call 'an internal yard-stick for fulfilment'. You make peace with past excesses and calmly watch the money come and go, like a meditating Buddhist monk.

And then what you do – and this is the crucial bit – is invest the difference in Treasury bonds until the income from the bonds is equal to your much reduced outgoings, and suddenly you are financially independent. I tried the idea for a month or so after I came back to England, but found it impossible to remember to write down what I spent: it was too embarrassing to whip out a notebook at the time. There you are: pride and fear of appearing obsessive has prevented me from being richer.

The only trouble is that by investing in Treasury bonds, you remain dependent on a bizarrely corrupt financial system which may crumble at any moment. It's another unavoidable paradox.

In the end it comes down to whether we can find fulfilment in spite of our tyrannical spending, and tyrannical work to provide the shrinking income. 'Work is love made visible,' said Kahlil Gibran. If ours isn't, maybe we should do something about it.

III

We most of us have the Beatles singing 'Money can't buy me love' echoing in our head, and know that we could never make such a mistake ourselves. But the paradoxes of downshifting show that the overlaps between money and love are actually rather difficult to unpick. We all know the stories of love-starved rich children, but however much we laugh at other people's worshipful attitude towards money, we can still fall into the same confusion ourselves. 'The grasshopper played all summer while the ant worked and saved,' wrote Woody Allen in his book *Without Feathers*. 'When winter came the grasshopper had nothing, but the ant complained of chest pains.'

In part of our minds, we know perfectly well that money is not the same as wealth. In the other part, we organize our lives as if it was. Even if we don't actually measure our own success in terms of money – and most of us do – we are still part of an economy which measures nothing but profit. We all vote for governments which measure money, but not the other aspects of life we all want to achieve – happiness, beauty, fulfilment, health and so on. We teach our children that money is not the most important thing in life, and then behave as if it was – insuring our lives up to the hilt, urging them towards well-paid careers and bright shining mortgages, and squabbling over our possessions when we get divorced. It is a kind of schizophrenia, because we daren't quite admit how much money is playing an all-embracing religious role for us.

Just how deep this confusion can go was shown in a strange anecdote about Picasso, who made a repeated and peculiar Freudian slip about his own child. When he was living in France, he would wake in the middle of the night about twice a week, sit bolt upright and gasp: 'The money is dead. I don't hear him breathing any more . . . You know very well what I mean,' he said crossly, looking at the confusion on the face of his partner. 'I mean the child.'

But Picasso's mistake wasn't the usual modern one that love is just a subset of money, like Shylock in *The Merchant of Venice* shouting 'My daughter! O my ducats! Oh my daughter!' – he was confusing the two so that money was less important, using the language of money to talk about love. Of course, there might be a muddle about babies and money – they do tend to cost a great deal – but Picasso didn't say: 'I don't hear the expense breathing any more' or 'I don't hear the bills breathing any more'. He was muddling the French word *l'enfant* with *l'argent*, but he was mainly talking about what he valued – his wealth, his riches, his child. The more you think about the story, the more moving it becomes, because Picasso was making the muddle the other way round.

It is a kind of conceit, but it struck me that perhaps Picasso was right. Perhaps we could try putting money back in its proper place as an inferior kind of love. We might then be able to understand its behaviour better. Money would then – like information – be inexhaustible, limitless, transforming and always freshly available if you knew how to conjure it. It would be limited, not by how much the bank had lent you, but by your understanding of the love system: that love tends to come to you when you spend it yourself.

Gresham's Law – that bad money drives out good – would still apply. Bad, perverted, power-obsessive love does make it hard for the selfless variety to root itself. And in those circumstances, just as people hoard the valuable money for themselves and leave the dross in circulation, so people keep the most intimate love for themselves, and melt it down. Meanwhile the public, compromised, dulled love remains in the outside world. It is the privatization of love: it stays behind the bedroom curtains, leaving social services and the police to deal with its failures.

Money would then stand in relation to love in the same way as lust. It's useful and rather fun, but it isn't the real thing. You can calculate and measure money and lust; you can't do the same with love because it is part of the stuff of life. 'There is no wealth but life, including all its powers of love, of joy, and of admiration,' wrote John Ruskin in 1860. 'That country is the richest which nourishes the greatest number of noble and happy human beings.'

The strange thing is that, at some level, the money system understands this too. It subsumes its critics with clever marketing to bohemians. Bohemians used to live in garrets, worry about art, earn very little money and dress in dowdy clothes. In the evenings they sat in bars, fell in love with each other and then trashed the place in drunken rages. But more than a generation ago, the American critic Malcolm Cowley showed us that we are all bohemians now. Bohemians keep the tottering money system upright, by increasing the amount we spend on the bizarre, the fashionable, the shocking and the extreme.

I was thinking about this in a SoHo fashion emporium in Manhattan, painted as if it was a strange North African encampment, selling clothes which 'fuse folk traditions and design' – and look as if they would fall apart after their first encounter with a washing machine. 'We guarantee to give each person a look which is unique to them,' said the shop. The system markets to us as bohemians these days, but the money system remains in control. Even bohemianism has a price, but we still look over our shoulders, peering beyond the figures to find out why we still feel dissatisfied.

'The money changers have fled from their high seats in the temple of our civilization,' said Franklin Roosevelt in his inaugural address in March 1933. 'We may now restore that temple to the ancient truths. The measure of the restoration lies in the extent to which we apply social values more noble than mere monetary profit.' Roosevelt's rhetoric takes no account of the twist – that even if you can follow his instructions, the money system has a clever way of coming back at you when you least expect it.

Ruskin used to distinguish between the 'wealth' of life and financial wealth, which he called 'illth'. The trouble is, as the social critic David Korten says: 'So many of us have become willing accomplices to what is best described as the war of money against life.' We have to remember that money is primarily an attempt at measuring wealth – and if you are very muddled, of measuring love – it isn't necessarily wealth itself and it certainly isn't love.

IV

Which brings us to the second part of the solution – using our power to create new kinds of money which have our values embedded in them. And here President Roosevelt was less helpful: the same day that he spoke about restoring the temple, he also outlawed the depression-beating local currencies which had been springing up all over America.

But now they're back, and at the same time barter has been growing as a means of world trade. The whole idea is traditionally derided by economists, who are – as we have seen – blinded by the idea of old-fashioned money. Businesses worry that barter dealers hike the value of useless stock to get a better deal. The government worries about exactly the reverse: that dealers will understate the value of the deals to avoid paying tax.

For those reasons, and others, academics and officials find it enormously hard to get reliable figures for how much barter is going on in the world. The alternative economist Hazel Henderson estimates it may now cover as much as a quarter of world trade. In the USA, it has been growing at double-digit rates for the past five years according to the International Reciprocal Trade Association. One American economics professor, Jim Stodder from Troy in New York State, has found that bartering grows in recession and shrinks when the economy is booming. This is what economists call 'counter-cyclical', which is considered a hopeful sign: it means that not everything collapses when the economy dips. Economies which use money are less stable than the ones which don't, which is another plus for bartering. But it was Albert Einstein who really rescued the idea. 'If I had my life to live over again, I would elect to be a trader of goods,' he said. 'I think barter is a noble thing.'

He would presumably welcome the rise of local barter currencies both in America and Europe – especially the explosion of LETS currencies in the UK. They are mainly small-scale, compared to Ithaca Hours or some of the local currency success stories in Australia, but there are at least 400 local currencies now in local circulation. Getting on for a quarter of the local authorities in the UK – desperate for something inexpensive to do about poverty – are finding ways of supporting their local money. They are finding that LETS has the potential for organizing affordable childcare, building the confidence of unemployed people, rebuilding what economists are calling 'social capital' and much else besides.

LETS money can provide a kind of 'Heineken effect', helping council officers reach into sectors of the communities which it is otherwise very hard to reach. Leicester City Council has already launched Naari LETS – a system for Asian women, aimed at doing something to reduce their isolation. Stockport has launched a system as part of its social services department. Hampshire and Surrey county councils are among those using LETS as a way of integrating people with mental health problems back into the world of work. Islington Council is backing a LETS Build pilot scheme, to bring accommodation into the loop; Bristol, Gloucester and Stirling are among those linking LETS to allotments to make food available to people on low incomes. Even the European Union has been funding an ambitious local currency for businesses in west London called West London Interest-Free

Trading, modelled on the enormously successful parallel currency in Switzerland known as Wir, which after sixty years' trading has 80,000 account holders.

LETS has been around long enough to attract a great deal of fascinated coverage in the newspapers and television, and also the usual sneering from the world-weary London intelligentsia. But it is also part of a great British tradition, as you can see if you visit the new Money Gallery in the British Museum. This concentrates heavily on the products of the Midland Bank – presumably because it is sponsored by Midland's owners HSBC – but you will still find the tradition tucked away. There is a note produced in 1810 by Royds Ironworks in Leeds. There is a copper halfpenny from Coventry in 1792, inscribed 'for the public good' and carrying a picture of Lady Godiva, who famously processed naked through the streets of that city to protest against taxes. And there is one of the famous but failed Labour Certificates produced by the great co-operator Robert Owen.

The tradition is spreading to other parts of the world. The Australian parliament has passed the so-called Deahm amendment, which means that people on welfare no longer have to declare their LETS earnings. In Sweden, interest-free JAK money now has over 38,000 members and a turnover of £300 million. In Mexico City, a new currency circulates called 'tlaloc', after the local rain god. In Holland, you can now earn 3,000 local currency units a year without it affecting your tax or welfare position. In Italy, there are a hundred *Banca del Tempos*, including one in Perugia set up by the local council. In France, there are now 300 local exchange networks called *Grain de Sel* – or grains of salt – which arise spontaneously wherever local unemployment reaches 12 per cent. One Parisian group trades on the Internet, using the value of one fresh egg as their standard of currency.

The out-going president of the European Commission, Jacques Delors, urged Europe to investigate local currencies to mitigate the effects of unemployment, and other establishment voices have been raising fears about the conventional money system. 'The history of government management of money has, except for a few short happy periods, been one of incessant fraud and deception,' wrote Friedrich Hayek. 'In this respect, governments have proved far more immoral than any private agency supplying distinct kinds of money in competition possibly could have been.'

All this spells out a revolution in the way we understand money. Whether or not we accept European monetary union, there will soon be euros circulating in British shops, not to mention air miles, reward cards, loyalty bonuses, Mondex, and all the range of new corporate currencies. Don't be taken in by the single European currency: we will soon be living in a multi-currency world where DIY money and corporate currencies – probably backed by unit trusts – compete for our attention. 'The worldwide conspiracy over the issuing of money will finally have been smashed,' information technology professor Ian Angel told Channel 4 viewers in 1997.

But even these are kinds of money which are linked into the main system and subject to it. The new alchemists are, in different ways, creating money from somewhere else – and that seems to me to be far more interesting. There are many different reasons why they are doing so. Some of them are revolutionary; some of them are conservative attempts to keep life bearable in the face of enormous international change. Some of them have been trying to answer questions like these:

- How can society afford the enormous costs of looking after growing numbers of old people – especially when government budgets are being cut?
- How can communities defend their local economies, when local earnings are siphoned out of the area by big business or distant utilities?
- How can we create a more diverse and sustainable economy locally – and reduce the need for goods to be transported at heavy environmental cost?
- How can we create a reliable measure of value so that our local products and earnings stay valuable during inflation or worldwide currency instability?
- How can we rebuild communities, friendships and a sense of family so that people look after each other?

The answers to all these questions were the same – create a new kind of money – but each answer was slightly different. They all compromise on a different balance between providing people with exchangeable wealth and providing them with reliable value, between doing deals and hanging on to savings for a rainy day.

All have been trying to make communities sustainable, but again in different ways. Time dollars have been searching for social sustainability, providing 'money' to people who the conventional economy leaves behind. Womanshare has been looking for local psychological sustainability. Hours, LETS and berk-shares are aiming at ecological sustainability, via local economic sustainability. Commonweal has been trying to underpin the whole social system by tackling poverty.

All the new alchemists criticize conventional pounds and dollars as funny money, backed by the commitment of governments not to default on their budget deficits. All their currencies are backed instead by something which their creators believe is more reliable. Time dollars are backed by the sense of local neighbourhood responsibility. Womanshare money is backed by local friendship, LETS by local skills, and hours by the power of local production. Berkshares are backed by the value of local farm products and Commonweal money by the commitment of local business to direct over-capacity in their direction.

Taken together, the new alchemists have used the King Midas story to launch a revolution which could change the way we perceive money. It is a revolution in three distinct moves:

- First, realize that money is not the same as wealth or value. And take those other things we value – skills, neighbourliness, trust and local care – and find ways of turning them into exchangeable 'money'.
- Second, use that money to fuel a separate social economy which can look after people's needs and protect people's lives.
- Third, plug that money back into the main system, so that it can access the enormous productivity and over-capacity in the international economy.

We are rich already, say the new alchemists. But we can also create money from our forgotten capital, if we just believe we can.

All the indicators show that people are feeling increasingly insecure in their jobs and incomes, both in Europe and the USA. This mounting insecurity – both about our jobs and our terrifying powerlessness in the face of the twists of the international economy – is fuelling the growing debate about currencies. I went to one of these at the alternative economics summit in Colorado in 1997, and watched the inventor of LETS, Michael Linton, and the inventor of the Mexican tlaloc money, Luis Lopezllera, slugging it out with Jhym Phoenix, who launched an hours currency in Boulder, Colorado and was now helping run a currency in Idaho called Carbondale spuds. And with John Turmel, the Canadian money campaigner, who is probably the most unusual of the new alchemists. John holds the Guinness Book of Records nomination for the most unsuccessful attempts at standing for parliament (forty-four), is a professional gambler – he did time in 1994 for running an illegal gambling house – and devotes his life to popularizing the idea of local money, usually wearing a broad tie which looks as though it has been made out of playing-cards.

As the controversy over reforming the benefits system began to gather speed, I invited Edgar Cahn to the UK for a series of conferences organized by the London Health Partnership and the New Economics Foundation. For a little over a week, I shepherded him from meeting to radio studio and back again, via his small hotel behind Whiteleys in Paddington. I took him to see Stonehenge and to Westminster to meet Paddy Ashdown – 'How will all this help us with the upkeep of my local station in Yeovil?' he asked, demonstrating the traditional British pragmatism about such things. I even took him to 10 Downing Street: in fact, I wouldn't have got in without him. Paddy Ashdown backed the idea in a major speech in March 1998.

By the time Edgar arrived, the time dollar idea had developed that much further in the USA. The youth court was powering ahead, there are creative writing classes and art galleries using time dollars, the time dollar food and clothing bank was up and running – not in Arthur M. Capper, but in Benning Terrace, the housing complex with the famous graffiti: 'You are now entering a war zone'. Edgar was also trying to persuade housing officials to reduce the rent and charge part of it in time dollars. He had developed the idea of what he called 'reciprocity' – that instead of just giving away grants or benefits, society could expect something in return. By giving 'reciprocal' grants, repayable in time dollars, agencies could magnify their impact tenfold, creating a debt which could be repaid by a local community. They could also stop giving the debilitating impression to people receiving the grants and benefits that they had nothing to give that anybody could possibly want. Already the new US welfare laws require twenty hours' work before you can become eligible for benefits – and that can include doing community service or earning time dollars. By expecting something back – but broadening our current limited definition of what constitutes 'work' – we can tap the human resources which the system is now wasting.

The idea, he said, was to 'create a world where any person willing to contribute by helping another will be able to earn the purchasing power and status needed to enjoy a decent standard of living and the opportunity to learn and to grow'. Now that the computer Deep Blue had beaten human chess champion Gary Kasparov, there was no point in wasting time worrying about what human beings can be replaced doing, he said. 'We need to think about what we *can't* be replaced doing,' he told an audience of health administrators and local government mandarins.

He also distributed an article of his own about dogs, called 'Cave Canem'. 'With some notable exceptions, this species has no marketable skills,' he wrote. 'And there is no movement afoot to insist that all members be required to master marketable skills and go to work in order to obtain sustenance. No one labels the provision of sustenance as a form of dependency. No one thinks there is anything wrong with a being that survives in a potentially inhospitable world simply because it is loved and lovable, because it brings joy, brightens our day and reduces human loneliness . . . Wouldn't it be remarkable if we extended the same care for babies and children and the elderly.'

V

Discussing new age mysticism might seem out of place in a book about economics, except that it is clearly now very big business, and the book which started 'wealth consciousness' – Napoleon Hill's *Think and Grow Rich* – is still in print after sixty years. He wrote it after years of interviews with the richest men in the world, distilling their advice down to focusing clearly on your goal, meditating and visualizing it quietly every day, and never ever giving up.

I mention it here because it is another way of looking at the limits of money as psychological. It assumes that money is basically infinite, a kind of energy which comes out of our common life and which we can tap into. 'It's not a good energy or a bad energy, it's just an energy,' Robin Currie told me, after the 1993 launch of his *New Money* newsletter, which was funded by the insurance company Manulife Group simultaneously to raise consciousness about money and to sell financial packages. 'Money is a very sensitive measure of what is happening in our lives, which is one of the reasons people get so freaked out about it,' he went on. 'It is very bound up with childish emotions like fear, shame and guilt, so it takes a long time to reach any kind of equilibrium.'

Money follows the energy, in other words, rather than the other way round. Once you understand this, according to the new age guru Deepak Chopra, 'it will give you the ability to create unlimited wealth with effortless ease'. If money is life energy, then we have to keep it moving: if we stop circulating it, it will stop circulating back to us. Step back from it, let it go, make sure you are motivated by love, says Chopra – and the money energy will flow to you. But there is a warning: 'Even with the experience of all these things, we will remain unfulfilled unless we nurture the seeds of divinity inside us.'

If you are completely cynical about this kind of thing – and I'm not – you will see this as a convenient get-out. Anyone who fails to manifest the wealth they need simply wasn't nurturing their own divinity, which is a vague enough concept to catch anybody. But there is no doubt that imagination, energy and being open to new possibilities do seem to attract money faster than narrow-minded obsession. This is a teaching which takes no account of the structure of the world – we are not going to feed the starving by airlifting books by Deepak Chopra – but the new age gurus do at least recognize that money is a way of calculating and accessing the energy which people produce when they work together. Bank balances, in other words, are not the ultimate way of measuring it.

'This isn't a zero sum game,' the billionaire trader and phil-anthropist George Soros told ABC *Nightline*. 'Your gain is not necessarily someone else's loss.' I think he is right: because there is no finite amount of gold underpinning a finite amount of money in the world, there is a sense in which we can all shift energy into money – or shift other kinds of wealth.

New local currencies do seem to conjure money out of nothing, but actually it isn't quite nothing. They use people's trust in each other, their common wealth and their skills and imagination. New age gurus would say that the time dollars or the hours notes are beside the point – that they are a kind of focus for the imagination, like the bread and wine in a mass, when the real change is happening in people's belief. I don't know what to make of it. Belief clearly plays a major role in whether or not we make money. There are self-appointed gurus who prey upon the weak-minded, urging them to new levels of relaxation which can attract their wildest dreams, but which they can never achieve. And yet money does seem to work a little like this: it does find itself flowing to the people who believe in it, and not to the people who simply need it. When you look on money as a kind of energy, it does indeed seem limitless. If you look at the broader concept of 'wealth' in the same way, it obviously is.

For the old alchemists in their laboratories, it was supposed to take exactly 252 days to turn base metal into gold. But many of them were more ambitious than that, because the philosopher's stone they sought was about much more than simply gold – it was about life. The thirteenth-century pioneer Roger Bacon explained that alchemy 'teaches us how to make the noble metals and colours and many other things better and more copiously by art than they can be made by nature'. It is more important than other sciences, he went on, 'since it produces most useful products, giving not only the monies and other expenses of the state, but the wherewithal to prolong life'.

The new alchemists aren't all that different. They are taking those things we have around us and using them to enhance life, and they are demonstrating how – by working together – we can all create the equivalent of gold.

There is a traditional alternative point of view about creating money. It says that banks should be rigorously controlled, and that only governments should be allowed to carry out this sacred priestly task. But suddenly it isn't just banks doing it, but supermarkets, airlines and goodness knows who else. And now the new alchemists have launched an extension to the Protestant revolution: no longer will money creation be the exclusive preserve of the priests in the big banks. We have the power in all of us to create money.

Because of them, we can add a few more ideas to the list drawn up by Francis Bacon about how to get more money. 'The ways to enrich are many, and most of them foul', he said. Included on the list were parsimony, improving the ground ('slow'), looking for bargains as a result of the desperate financial situation of others, usury, monopolies, using your position at court and 'fishing for testaments and executorships'. Most of these are still recognizable methods used by the British establishment, and probably the American establishment too. But we can add a few more acceptable ones:

- Measure things differently so that you can see what you want more clearly. Use a broader definition of wealth in your own life. If you live rent-free in a small cottage in the Lake District, then however little money you have, you could still be 'wealthy' – and deeply envied by people living in expensive homes in Paddington.
- Create wealth Boulder- or Seattle-style by imagining it, visualizing it – or just by being more generous with it. Though to do so, you have to let go of the deadwood emotions of the past, and embrace the future with some enthusiasm, which is sometimes difficult if you are grindingly poor.
- Give joyfully and the world may then give to you. This is logically impossible, so you might as well try it.
- Relax. Compared with the amount we all worry about money, the crunch very rarely comes. The arrival of money in your life is very rarely logical either.

- Look for treasure. After all, only £343,448 of the £2.6 million stolen in the Great Train Robbery has ever turned up. But bear in mind that the real treasure is probably nearer than you think.
- Avoid shops: the real reason we go there is esteem-boosting, socializing, status-grabbing and various other things, which we could get more cheaply in other ways. And wear out what you have before buying more.

But you probably don't have to set up your own currency, because there will be people doing it for you – computerized, imaginary, backed by vegetables, time or just printed. All you have to do is help them conjure the necessary faith to make the whole community richer. *(See appendix for helpful addresses.)*

But most of all, don't get caught in our British sense of powerlessness about money. It doesn't descend from heaven; it is created by people like us. If you were a North American Indian, this used to mean collecting dentalia shells from the seabed – and so successfully that Boston traders tried to counterfeit the shells using porcelain in London. If you are the Bank of England or the Federal Reserve, it means buying Treasury bills by writing a cheque against nothing except the national debt. If you are a credit-card operator it is even simpler, you just send out cards – and Americans charge $195,000 a minute on Citibank credit cards alone. And if they can create money, so can we all.

VI

'Money has been introduced by convention as a kind of substitute for need or demand,' said Aristotle, writing three centuries before the birth of Christ. 'And this is why we call it *nomisma*, because its value is derived, not from nature, but from law, and can be altered or abolished at will.' But law does not necessarily mean governments, it means common agreement. It could be very local agreement: it could just be a few households who give value to baby-sitter tokens. By common agreement we can create new kinds of money.

But watch out, because there are going to be pitfalls, and here are a few of them:

Pitfall 1: Inflation. Inflation is when too much money is in circulation compared to the work which is going on in the economy. The result is rising prices and collapsing confidence in the currency. There are already considerably more conventional pounds and dollars out there than can possibly be justified by what is really happening in the economy, which means the prices are always rising – so we are subjected to periodic bursts of high interest rates to make sure it all stays safely in our savings accounts. What would happen if we all started using new currencies as well? You could imagine the circumstances where enthusiastic alchemists get too busy with the printing press and piles of notes end up in our bottom drawers.

But remember that money is only tracking a very limited kind of work in the economy. Currencies like time dollars and LETS are created only when the work happens, so they are unlikely to be inflationary unless they are abused. They are also tracking a much broader definition of work, currently left out of the conventional definition altogether. The UK is so prone to inflation partly because we make so little of what we need: if local currencies can help us provide what is needed locally, they will be anti-inflationary.

Bernard Lietaer, a Belgian former central banker who has been popularizing local currencies over the Internet, asks about air miles. Do they push up the price of air travel? The answer is that they don't because they are simply accessing spare capacity which ordinary money is not able to do. It's the same with local currencies: as long as there is enough available to buy with our new money, it won't be inflationary.

Pitfall 2: Backlash. The establishment are pretty happy about the money situation as it is at the moment – they've done rather well out of it, and they don't want the rules changing. In 1996, the Bank of England stepped in – for the first time in 126 years – to prosecute a county council for minting its own trade tokens. Magistrates found the Isle of Wight guilty, but gave them an absolute discharge.

There have also been ominous signs in the media that some opinion-formers are concerned about local currencies. They could regard the idea as a welcome means whereby people can stand on their own two feet without state support, but no – the *Daily Mail* still carried the headline '40,000 escape the taxman by working for each other'. A day or so before, we had the querulous *Times* headline, 'Jobless use barter schemes to overcome benefits rules'. It was rather a depressing week.

There have been other examples of official obfuscation. LETS-link Scotland, the support group north of the border, had its application for charitable status turned down because helping disadvantaged communities was not considered a charitable purpose. Then, in the autumn of 1997, the small French town of

Foix became the scene of a strange *Clochemerle*-style trial of three Britons for bartering a roof repair through their local SEL system. Possibly the fact that they were members of a feminist vegan group did not endear them to local farmers when former post-woman Sarah Two had her roof fixed in return for tofu. 'You made what?' asked the incredulous magistrate, who had never heard of it.

'This kind of behaviour upsets traditional structures and institutionalizes a parallel economy,' warned the lawyer for the local builders' federation. 'It is destructive to our entire political and social system.' He won the case, but the magistrate ruled that the fine ought to be suspended and that Sarah Two should pay a symbolic one franc damages to the local artisans' guild. Press coverage brought floods of inquiries to other SEL groups.

As the changing structure of money makes individual taxation increasingly difficult, we can expect more examples of this kind of thing from frightened politicians. But sensible officials will probably follow the Irish example in the end, simply because being involved with local money has been shown to keep welfare claimants healthier and saner – which means less public spending later on.

But if you really want to scare the bureaucrats, remind them what happened two centuries ago when Virginia, Maryland and Carolina faced money shortages and issued their own local currencies. Their innovation led directly to the American Revolution.

Pitfall 3: Muddle. New alchemists are finding new ways of breaking down the strict barriers between very different values. Love, neighbourliness, time, skills are all different kinds of wealth, and time dollars – for example – can transform them into 'money' to buy food, computers and services. Hours can take people's work and transform it back into neighbourliness.

Transforming neighbourliness into a kind of money is one thing, but it would be disastrous if we allowed the system to work the other way round, so that you could buy up our neighbourliness with dollars and pounds. The prospect of having to give old people lifts to the doctors to pay off the national debt is very unattractive, so we have to be careful. The new kinds of money can track the value of dollars and pounds, but they must stay separate – or they will fall victim to whatever happens to the international money markets. The point is to set up alternative systems of money, not to extend the scope of the current system.

And when these new kinds of money become mainstream and successful, we must always remember they are a means to an end rather than an end in themselves. I was reminded of this in New Zealand, as I went to visit a small green dollar system on an island a short ferry ride away from Auckland. I interviewed the local builder who ran the scheme, who was also building a new house for himself – curiously, in his ex-wife's garden – and took a lift back to the jetty with a local Maori fisherman. 'I think it's really bad,' he told me when I asked him what he thought of this new money idea. 'In the old days we would help each other out, I'd do something for them and they'd do something for me, and that would be fine. We didn't have all this careful measuring we have now.'

It brought me up short. I remembered that the word 'work' in the Maori language also means 'labour of love'.

In the end, money is just an approximation: it is not love. 'It is still exceedingly difficult,' said the great pioneer of economics, David Ricardo, 'to discover or even to imagine any commodity which shall be a perfect measure of value.' Or as Keynes put it, about the money system: 'We have to pretend for a while that foul is useful and fair is not'. The problem comes when we forget we were just pretending.

Pitfall 4: Cynicism. Conjuring new kinds of money – and benefiting from other people's – requires an enormous leap of faith. It requires belief. As I took an internal flight with Continental Airways, I read a book of short stories by W. B. Yeats. They included tales about a wandering Irish poet called Hanrahan the Red who could – like other travelling bohemians in days gone by – curse a person by ridiculing them in a poem or song. Satirizing somebody can make their crops dry and their money shrink.

I was thinking about this in the light of the miserably cynical articles in the British media, our narrow views of money and politics, and the narrow group of cynics who promote them. Because for all our glittering satirical success – from Gillray's cartoons to TW3, from Swift to *Spitting Image* – satire seems to have got into our bones in England like frost. Fear of the unusual or the fringe, metropolitan snobbery about anything regional, seeps out of the pages of every Sunday paper and radio discussion.

This cynicism gets in the way of finding new ways of creating money. It prevents us making those enormous open-minded leaps of faith which can conjure new kinds of money wealth into existence. You have to believe in time dollars or hours for them to exist. Faith underpins money: if you believe in it, it exists; if you don't, its value fades away like Tinkerbell. 'If the Sun and

Moon should Doubt,' wrote William Blake, 'They'd immediately Go out.'

There is a kind of innocence about local money. Yet in the face of cynicism and astonishment, the new alchemists press ahead, turning assets which the world devalues – old people's time, people's trust in each other – into real wealth. And not just heart-warming, cuddly, unbankable wealth either, but something you can eat or move around with or transform your life with. It is, as Paul Glover said about Ithaca, a 'community magic act'.

If money depends on our faith in it, then refusing to believe in anything is liable to make us poor. Poor old England, with its crops and innovations frazzled by satire.

VII

We still face enormous political and economic problems if we are going to guarantee the survival of the human race, but I am enough of a romantic to believe that now the Cold War is over, if an idea works, it will be adopted. For those without access to the main system – more and more of us – DIY currencies could be the solution we have all been waiting for, providing an approach to poverty, the missing link for rebuilding social capital, and the missing anaesthetic which keeps us alive during painful economic operations.

If it has the increasing influence which seems likely, this kind of alchemy will alter the way we all perceive the other kind of money. It will make us realize that our collective belief in any currency underpins its value. And if money depends on our collective psychology, we should be able to find ways of conjuring more of it. The new alchemists are showing us how, but they have developed something else too – something more natural than Wall Street or City of London currency. They have unveiled a kind of self-generating money.

In the natural world, when a baby sucks at its mother's breast, that act of needing produces more milk. We are moving towards a kind of money which doesn't depend on scarcity for its value, but which is generated simply by need. If this new money is rooted firmly in what is real, like berkshares or constants, it can provide us with the reliable store of wealth we need – one which doesn't disappear on the whims of a couple of Japanese currency traders. If it is rooted in people's lives, like LETS or time dollars, new money can provide us with an infinite means of exchange, conjured into existence just because somebody needs something.

This is where money came from originally, when it was just shells for counting you could pick up on the beach. Local money is not scarce: you don't have to hoard it. Money which appears because people need it is a strange and outlandish idea, and it may be the first practical glimmering in the distance of a world where money is much less important than it is now.

We may never abolish money altogether, as William Morris dreamed in *News From Nowhere*: it is too useful for that. But we could perhaps make it work so effectively that it disappears into the background of our consciousness, like good plumbing. We may still have to call out the money plumber once in a while, but for the rest of our lives we will be able to get on with something more useful.

A world where money is as available as water is a world without continual scarcity, and that is why we can learn from the American sense of abundance. 'Bizarrely, the feeling of plenty even extends to those who have little,' says Simon Hoggart, and he's right. But then, would we all have the same cavalier attitude to the limits of the earth as the Americans do? How would we deal with limited resources which we now use money to ration?

The answer is that a world without money requires people who no longer need to over-consume. It needs people who are emotionally intelligent enough to trust their ability to get what they need – people whose challenges are psychological rather than narrowly economic. When psychological limits are the stuff of a new kind of currency, then we will find old-fashioned money can slip quietly away. In the meantime, we have to struggle on with it, and that may be for some time to come.

This doesn't mean, for now, that DIY money should be expected to do everything which dollars and pounds can do. But there are many areas where dollars and pounds are simply not effective: they do not build communities, they do not respond to needs, they do not build families, they do not tackle poverty. Local money does, and for that reason, I believe it will work. And it will do so for the reasons that John Ruskin set out back in 1862 in *Unto This Last*:

What would you say to the lord of an estate who complained to you of his poverty and disabilities and, when you pointed out to him that his land was half of it overrun with weeds, and that his fences were all in ruins, and that his cattle-sheds were roofless, and his labourers lying under hedges faint for want of food, he answered to you that it would ruin him to weed his land or roof his sheds – that those were too costly operations for him to undertake, and that he knew not how to feed his labourers nor pay them? Would you not instantly answer, that instead of ruining him to weed his fields, it would save him; that his inactivity was his destruction, and that to set his labourers to work was to feed them?'

In spite of these continuing problems, there are people who think that money has been so successful that we are now at a dull, comfortable end of human endeavour, which Francis Fukuyama described as 'just the perpetual caretaking of the museum of human history'. In a strange article in the *New York Times* in 1997, columnist Russell Baker also described a mythical time in the not-too-distant future when 'all the money had been made'. 'Many committed suicide,' he said. 'The notes they left were all much alike. They had lived to make money, they said. Now that all the money had been made, there was nothing left to live for.'

But it's not going to be like that. Because – just as the social critics thought we would all settle down to post-modern contentment or hopeless dependency – a new exploration suddenly beckons. This book has tried to show that some people have set sail already.

Epilogue

A funny money world

'Money is better than poverty, if only for financial reasons.'
Woody Allen

Money exists in the mind, so we're going to have to find psychological ways of creating more of it. Or that's what I told the interviewer on London's radio station GLR when this book first came out. 'It's a dangerous thought,' I said, warming to my theme. 'You just have to cast doubt on the real existence of the money markets and they could just shrivel away. Anything could happen.'

I was quite pleased with myself as I went outside, and as I walked down to the underground station at Oxford Circus I suddenly saw the newspaper billboards for the evening paper: '£51 billion wiped off stock market', they said. This gave me a very brief over-inflated sense of my own influence. If the stock markets crashed because I cast doubt on their real existence on GLR, what would happen when I said the same on network radio?

OK, so it wasn't me. But since then, the world economy has been even more funny than usual. You know things are topsy-turvy when the internet provider Yahoo is suddenly worth more than British Airways, when Silicon Valley graduates sell their loss-making internet ventures for over a billion dollars, and when property on the American west coast is so scarce and expensive that estate agents advise you to get your children to write cute letters to the vendors, explaining why they want to live there. And even if I can't do it all by myself, scepticism about the current money system *can* have an effect. So can the growing sense that unrestricted market growth can drive out everything we really value. So can empowering people to start inventing their own currencies, especially as people realise that big currencies like the euro could impoverish our local economies – even if they are necessary to protect people from the speculators.

The inventor of communitarianism, Amitai Etzioni, recently described the plight of American truck driver Rod Grimm, delivering his loads from Los Angeles to Maine. His work keeps him on the road 340 days a year, so his wife moved into the cab with him. Their friendships were reduced to occasional encounters and their relationship with their daughter reduced to a cellphone link. Rod Grimm's efforts all add to the economic indicators of success, but you can't help wondering whether earning this kind of money is good for the long-term health of the community – let alone poor Mr Grimm.

I'm optimistic enough to believe that new kinds of money can emerge which might support a different kind of success. The first two time dollars systems have launched in Britain, in Stonehouse and Newent in Gloucestershire. The number of local councils investing in LETS currencies is rising fast and – as I write – the government looks set to allow people to earn some funny money while they're on benefits. My wallet now includes four different loyalty cards, with which I can buy anything from holidays to bouquets of flowers. I will shortly have an account in the new internet currency beenz.com. And next door to the MI6 building on the Thames at Vauxhall, an abandoned 17-storey office block has been taken over to train young people how to refurbish old computers, which they will be able to buy with time dollars.

So the glimmer of hope is a little brighter. And the next step is to think through some of the following:

Affordability: financial packages which benefit the better-off, like health insurance and mortgages, are increasingly out of reach of most of us – but bundling up time as part of the deal could make them more affordable. Especially if projects need people's time in order to succeed. In Baltimore, housing tenants are now paying part of their rent in time, because it improves life on the estate. They agreed, on condition that it was the residents – and the residents alone – who decided what to do if anyone didn't pay. And if people can reduce the price of their groceries at shops by using loyalty points from their town centre, then why don't we give people the chance to earn these points by helping other people? It would keep them shopping locally as well. The New Economics Foundation is working on a scheme just like that.

Education: education grants and loans are increasingly difficult for poorer people to afford, but you could imagine structuring the system so that people on low incomes – if they wanted to –

could pay in time. AmeriCorps now have an education grants programme that allows students to pay tuition fees or student loan payments in this way. Berea College in Kentucky has always required students to pay part of their fees in community service. Literacy programmes in the USA are beginning to accept time dollars in payment for more advanced courses. A new project in south London is planning to introduce money called 'training pounds', so that people can access training courses by helping their next-door neigbours.

Taxes and fines: it's not just Tony Blair's Third Way which is stuck between the devil of demanding people's responsibility and the deep blue sea of prosecuting them if they fail. What can authorities do if property taxes, fines, or family maintenance payments are ignored – but the people concerned simply don't have the money to pay? The expense of taking them to court often goes far beyond the outstanding amount, and sending them to prison risks turning them into hardened criminals. Asking them to pay in time provides another, less authoritarian, option. It may not help the estranged family or the tax authorities, but then they lose out anyway. In fact, if people would otherwise lose their homes, Boulder in Colorado already allows old people to pay their property taxes by volunteering their time.

Unemployment: one of the difficulties of making Workfare succeed in the USA is that the lack of social facilities and public transport in the worst unemployment blackspots make it particularly hard to get people into jobs – however little money they have. The extended families of the past are gone. Single mothers are expected to commute to work when there are no child-minders and no buses. And all the informal work which unemployed people used to do is left undone. It may be impossible to shift enough people into paid jobs unless we redefine productive work to include work that is not yet defined as such. If we need the work to be done, and there isn't any money to pay for it, then at least let's pay people to do it in time – and back those earnings with the necessities of life.

When we start asking people to pay in time, it gives a built-in advantage to people who have it – against those who have lots of money instead. And if you don't believe people's time and contribution is worth the old-fashioned money we might lose, then try living in a world where nobody gives their time and nobody makes a contribution. Life there would be like Thomas Hobbes's description of a world without law – nasty, brutish and short.

So the new money revolution *is* happening. And the evidence I found most compelling is, in a way, the least important of all. It was the news that teenagers in Los Angeles are earning time dollars helping older people and spending them having their tattoos removed.

Funny money for a funny old world.

Find out more

Books and articles

Anderson, Ruth, Griffiths, Ian and Whitfield, Ruth: *Alternative Economy Systems in Rural Scotland*, Rural Forum (see under organizations below), 1997.

Bloom, William: *Money, Heart and Mind*, Viking Books, 1995.

Borsodi, Ralph: *Inflation and the Coming Keynesian Catastrophe: The story of the Exeter experiment with constants*, E. F. Schumacher Society (see under organizations), 1989.

Boyle, David: 'The transatlantic money revolution', *New Economics*, winter 1996.

Boyle, David: *What is New Economics?*, New Economics Foundation (see below), 1993.

Brandt, Barbara: *Whole Life Economics: Revaluing daily life*, New Society Publishers (US), 1996.

Buchan, James: *Frozen Desire: An enquiry into the meaning of money*, Picador, 1997.

Cahn, Edgar and Rowe, Jonathan: *Time Dollars*, Rodale Press (US), 1992.

Chopra, Deepak: *The Seven Spiritual Laws of Success*, Bantam Press, 1996.

Dacyczyn, Ann (ed.): *The Tightwad Gazette*, Villard Books (US), 1993.

Daly, Herman E. and Cobb, John B.: *For the Common Good: Redirecting the economy towards community, the environment and a sustainable future*, Green Print 1989.

Dauncey, Guy: *After the Crash: The emergence of the rainbow economy*, Greenprint, 1996.

Dominguez, Joe and Rubin, Vicki: *Your Money or Your Life: transforming your relationship with money*, Viking (US), 1992.

Douthwaite, Richard: *Short Circuit: strengthening local economies for security in an unstable world*, Green Books, 1996.

Egeberg, Olaf: *Non-Money: That 'other money' you didn't know you had*, McGee Street Foundation (PO Box 56756, Washington D C 20040, USA), 1995.

Ekins, Paul with Hillman, Mayer and Hutchison, Robert: *Wealth Beyond Measure: An atlas of green economics*, Gaia Books, 1992.

Elgin, Duane: *Voluntary Simplicity: Toward a way of life that is outwardly simple, inwardly rich*, William Morrow & Co (US), 1981.

Ferguson, Andrew: *Creating Abundance: How to Bring Wealth and Abundance into Your Life*, Piatkus, 1992.

Ghazi, Polly and Jones, Judy: *Getting a Life: A downshifter's guide to happier, simpler living*, Hodder & Stoughton, 1996.

Grant, James: *Money of the Mind*, The Noonday Press, New York, 1992.

Greco, Thomas H.: *New Money for Healthy Communities*, Greco (PO Box 42663, Tucson, Arizona, 85733, USA), 1994.

Hill, Napoleon: *Think and Grow Rich*, Wilshire, 1937.

Kennedy, Margrit: *Inflation and Interest-Free Money*, Permakultur Institut (Ginsterweg 5, D-3074, Steyerberg, Germany), 1988.

Lang, Peter: *LETS Work: Rebuilding the local economy*, Grover Books, 1994.

Lewis, Michael: *Liar's Poker*, Hodder & Stoughton, 1989.

Mogil, Christopher and Slepian, Anne: *We Gave Away a Fortune*, New Society Publishers (US), 1993.

North, Peter, Barnes, Helen and Walker, Perry: *LETS on Low Income*, New Economics Foundation, 1996.

Robertson, James: *Future Wealth: A new economics for the 21st century*, Cassell, 1990.

Rowan, Wingham: *Guaranteed Electronic Markets: The backbone of a 21st century economy?*, Demos, 1997.

Rowe, Dorothy: *The Real Meaning of Money*, HarperCollins, 1997.

Seyfang, Gill: *The Local Exchange Trading System: Political Economy and Social Audit*, Seyfang (PO Box 319, Aylsham, Norwich NR11 6XB), 1994.

Seyfang, Gill: 'Local exchange and trading systems and sustainable development', *Environment*, Vol. 38, No. 2, 1996.

Williams, Colin C.: 'The emergence of local currencies', *Town & Country Planning*, December 1995.

Publications

Green $ Quarterly, PO Box 21140, Christchurch, New Zealand.

Monetary Reform, RR#2, Shanty Bay, Ontario L0L 2L0, Canada. (E-mail) editor@ monetary-reform.on.ca (Web) www.monetary-reform.on.ca.

More Than Money, The Impact Project, 2244 Alder Street, Eugene, Oregon 97405, USA.

New Economics, New Economics Foundation, Cinnamon House, 6–8 Cole Street, London SE1 4YH, UK. (Tel) 0171 407 7447 (E-mail) info@neweconomics.org

New Money, 92 Folly Lane, St Albans, Herts AL3 5JH, UK. (Tel/Fax) 01727 833441, (E-mail) robin@newmoney. demon.co.uk (Mainly about personal investment).

Ozlets, PO Box 1640, Armidale, New South Wales 2350, Australia.

The Tightwad Gazette, RR1 Box 3570, Leeds, Maine 04263–9710, USA (About saving money).

TRANET (Transnational Network for Appropriate Technologies), PO Box 567, Rangeley, Maine 04970, USA. (Tel) +1 207 864 2252.

Turning Point 2000, The Old Bakehouse, Cholsey, Nr Wallingford, Oxfordshire OX10 9NU, UK.

Yes! A journal of positive futures, PO Box 10818, Bainbridge Island, Washington 98110, USA (Tel) +1 206 842 0216, (E-mail) yes@futurenet.org (Web)www.futurenet.org (*See the money issue, Spring 1997*).

Local currencies

Commonweal Inc. PO Box 16299, St Louis Park, Minnesota 55416-0299, USA (Tel) +1 612-341 4265, (Fax) +1 612-729 1085 (Organizers of the Commonweal currency).

Community Information Resource Center, PO Box 42663, Tucson, Arizona 85733, USA. (E-mail) cir@azstarnet.com (Web) azstarnet.com/-circ/circhome.htm (Networking and information source).

Irish LETSlink, Lower Aiden Street, Kiltimagh, Co. Mayo, Republic of Ireland. (Tel) +353 94 81637, (Fax) +353 94 81708.

Ithaca Money, Box 5678, Ithaca, New York 14851, USA. (Tel)+1 607-272 4330, (E-mail) hours@lightlink.com (Originators of the hours currency).

Landsman Community Services Ltd, 1660 Embleton Crescent, British Columbia V9N 6N8, Canada. (Tel) +1 604 338 0213/4, (Web) www.u-net.com/gmlets (Originators of the LETS currency).

LETS Connect, 12 Leasowe Green, Lightmoor, Telford, Shropshire TF4 3QX, UK. (Tel) 01952 590687, (Fax) 01952 591771.

LETSgo, 23 New Mount Street, Manchester M4 4DE, UK. (Tel) 0161 953 4115, (Fax) 0161 953 4116 (Promoting LETS to businesses).

LETSlink UK, 2 Kent Street, Portsea, Portsmouth PO1 3BS, UK. (Tel) 01705 730639, (E-mail) 104047.2250@ compuserve.com (UK organization for promoting LETS).

LETSlink Northern Ireland, 20 Beechwood, Banbridge, Co.Down BT32 3YL, UK. (Tel) 018206 23834.

LETSlink Scotland, 31 Banavie Road, Glasgow G11 5AW, UK. (Tel 0141 339 3064.

LETS Solutions, 124 Northmoor Road, Manchester M12 5RS, UK. (Tel) 0161 224 0749, (Fax) 0161 257 3686 (Promoting LETS to businesses and voluntary organizations).

Rural Forum Scotland, Highland House, 46 St Catherine's Road, Perth, Scotland PH1 5RY, UK. (Tel) 01738 634565, (Fax) 01738 638699, (E-mail) rural@ruralforum.org.uk (Web) www.ruralforum.org.uk (Organizers of Scotland Organizational Currency System).

E. E. Schumacher Society, 140 Jug End Road, Great Barrington, Massachusetts 01230, USA. (Tel) +1 413-528 1737, (Fax) +1 413-528 4472, (E-mail) efssociety@aol.com (Organizers of Berkshare currency ideas, and publishers of electronic *Local Currency* newsletter).

Time Dollars Institute, PO Box 19405, Washington DC 20015, USA. (Tel) +1 202-686 5200, (Fax) +1 202-537 5033, (E-mail) TIMEDOLLAR@aol. com (Web) www.cfg.com/ Timedollar

Womanshare, 680 West End Avenue, New York, New York 10025, USA. (Tel) +1 212-662 9746, (E-mail) Wshare@aol.com.

New money organizations

Breakthrough Centre, Wester Marchhead, Elgin, Moray IV30 3XE, UK. (Tel) 0181 347

7484, (E-Mail) breakthr@
dircon.co.uk (Centre helping
people to downshift).

Campaign for Interest-Free
Money, Global Café, 15 Golden
Square, London W1 3HB.
(Tel) 0171 328 3701, (E-mail)
sabine@globalnet.co.uk

Ethical Investment Research
Service (EIRIS, 504 Bondway
Business Centre, 71 Bondway,
London SW8 1SQ, UK. (Tel)
0171 735 1351. (Fax) 0171
735 5323.

Impact Project, 21 Linwood
Street, Arlington,
Massachusetts 02174, USA, or
4501 Spruce Street,
Philadelphia, Pennsylvania
19139, USA (Wealth
counsellors).

Ministry of Money, 2 Professional
Drive, Suite 220, Gaithersburg,
Maryland 20879, USA (Tel) +1
301 670 9606. (Looking at
money from the perspective of
faith).

Mondex, PO Box 7531, London
NW1 0YT, UK. (Tel) 0171
284 4950, (E-mail)
mondex@int.mondex.com

New Economics Foundation,
Cinnamon House, 6–8 Cole
Street, London SE1 4YH, UK.
(Tel) 0171 407 7447 (E-mail)
info@neweconomics.org

New Road Map Foundation, PO
Box 15981, Seattle,
Washington 98115, USA (Tel)
+1 206 527 0437. (Helping
people shift to
low-consumption lifestyles).

Probono Network, 1 The Warren,
Handcross, West Sussex RH17
6DX, UK. (Tel) 01444 400403,
(E-mail)
Ranger@probono.org.uk
(Internet organization for
business and human
development).

Redefining Progress, 1 Kearny
Street 4th floor, San Francisco,
California 94108, USA. (Tel)
+1 415 781 1191. (Think tank
about indicators of economic
success).

Index